C000056144

Learning Disobedience

'Murrey and Daley take no prisoners in their sharp decolonial analysis, they are unapologetic in their decolonial critique development, and they are fired up in their envisioning of the future. *Learning Disobedience* is far from a post-development treatise; it is a work of dismantlement of that which harms humanity in the name of humanity.'

—Sabelo J. Ndlovu-Gatsheni, author of *Beyond the Coloniality of Internationalism: Reworlding the World from the Global South*

'This is the book we've all been waiting for to divest from Development Studies. It engages the abolitionist imperative as imaginable, intelligible, and doable; as a labour of love, solidarity and abundance rather than refusal or "cancel culture".'

—Olivia Umurerwa Rutazibwa, Assistant Professor in Human Rights and Politics, Department of Sociology, London School of Economics and Political Science

'Invites us to abolish development, not as simple rejection, but as a life-affirming pathway into liberation and freedom beyond coloniality. Development is violence actively producing impoverishment, epistemic dispossession and erasing peoples of the Global South's knowledges, experiences, and sensibilities. Through a plurality of African intellectual anticolonial and decolonial archives and musical soundtracks of liberation, Murrey and Daley enact a practice of epistemic disobedience that refuses colonial heteropatriarchal and racial global imaginaries of international aid and humanitarian interventions. Full of intellectual energy and radical love for the learning possibilities of autonomy, communities of struggle and marronage, this is a must-read for present struggles for dignity and pluriversal, decolonized solidarity.'

—Dr Rosalba Icaza, Professor of Global Politics, Feminisms and Decoloniality, Erasmus University of Rotterdam, Netherlands

Learning Disobedience

Decolonizing Development Studies

Amber Murrey and Patricia Daley

PLUTO PRESS

First published 2023 by Pluto Press
New Wing, Somerset House, Strand, London WC2R 1LA
and Pluto Press, Inc.
1930 Village Center Circle, 3-834, Las Vegas, NV 89134

www.plutobooks.com

Copyright © Amber Murrey and Patricia Daley 2023

The right of Amber Murrey and Patricia Daley to be identified as the authors
of this work has been asserted in accordance with the Copyright, Designs and
Patents Act 1988.

British Library Cataloguing in Publication Data
A catalogue record for this book is available from the British Library

ISBN 978 0 7453 4714 1   Paperback
ISBN 978 0 7453 4717 2   PDF
ISBN 978 0 7453 4716 5   EPUB

This book is printed on paper suitable for recycling and made from fully
managed and sustained forest sources. Logging, pulping and manufacturing
processes are expected to conform to the environmental standards of the
country of origin.

Typeset by Stanford DTP Services, Northampton, England

Simultaneously printed in the United Kingdom and United States of America

Contents

Acknowledgements

Many people, experiences and conversations helped to bring this book into being.

We would like to first thank our students who have inspired, motivated and challenged us. So many parts of this book are reflections of our encounters with critical students; our learning has always been together. Our students are international, and we have made our classrooms in many countries over the years, from Ethiopia to Egypt, the United Kingdom to the United States, and Cameroon to Tanzania. We are thankful to four Oxford students in particular, Caitlin O'Shea, Elisabed Gedevanishvili, Oluwaseun Matiluko and Paulina Maziarska, who worked with us to research and explore the potentials of social media as a platform for the exchange of ideas around decolonizing, queering and abolishing international development. Everywhere in the world, our students have pushed us to better articulate our ideas, remain dedicated to our political orientations and be responsive to new forms of activism and action. Transformation of the university is impossible without pressure and collective action from students. Teaching is an act of love, and teaching on resistance and struggle has animated and oriented our praxis. The decolonial thinker Walter Mignolo (1999) reminds us that 'we are where we think' – that is to say, our thinking emerges from and remains embedded within our unique body- and geopolitics. To this, we might add that 'we are where we teach'.

We are deeply grateful for the communities, people and activists with whom we have collaborated over the years. In Nanga-Eboko, Kribi and Yaoundé, Cameroon the stories of activists and people fighting to survive decades of intergenerational slow violence wrought by large scale infrastructure has sustained Amber's political, epistemic and intellectual labour for over a decade. Likewise, she remains overwhelmed by and beholden to the activists and students who have spoken and shared their experiences in Addis Ababa and Jimma, Ethiopia. In Tanzania, Ng'wanza Kamata and Leiyo Singo deserve a special mention. Reciprocity is time-intensive and thoughtful; the work of recompense and cultivating decolonial and convivial relations continues.

Our editor, Jakob Horstmann, has been the ideal combination of patient with our work and family duties, and impatient to read more of what we meant by 'learning disobedience'. His support and insights have helped to make this book possible. Several colleagues have read and commented on drafts of our chapters, including Horace Campbell, Nokuthula Hlabangane, Nicholas Jackson and Chris Fratina della Fratina. We are grateful to the editorial team and staff at *The Singapore Journal of Tropical Geography*, particularly James D. Sidaway and Nura Aziz, for their kind invitation to deliver a plenary talk at the Royal Geographical Society's annual conference in 2022 on earlier iterations of our collaborative work on the importance of disobedient praxis in colonial institutions. Our work on defiant scholarship as the basis for dismantling coloniality in contemporary African geographies has been immensely enriched by subsequent commentaries and feedback from Christine Noe, Stefan Ouma, AbdouMaliq Simone and Maano Ramutsindela. We also thank David Mills, Natasha Robinson and Solomon Amare Zewolde for inviting us to speak about our disobedient teaching at the Centre for Global Higher Education's 2021 seminar series on *Racism and Coloniality in Global Higher Education*. Finally, our meaningful and critical exchange with colleagues and students at the *Oxford and Empire Network* in 2022 continues to inspire and guide this work. We are grateful to Gordon Barrett and colleagues for their encouragement to share our efforts to embrace disobedient teaching against empire at the lunchtime series. We are gratified to be part of this collective's important efforts to expose, critique and dismantle our institution's colonial violence, heritage and legacies. Some of our analysis of the significance of Thomas Sankara has been reworked from Amber's (2019) article, 'Between Assassination and Appropriation: Pedagogical Disobedience in an Era of Unfinished Decolonisation' in the pages of *International Journal of Social Economics*, Volume 46, Issue 11, pages 1319–1334. Four paragraphs of the empirical materials from digital protest in Cameroon and Ethiopia in Chapter 5 has been adapted from one of Amber's (2022) publications titled, 'A Decolonial Political Geography of Resistance and Infrastructural Harm in Cameroon and Ethiopia' in the pages of the journal *Globalizations*.

None of this work would have been possible without our families. For her part, Amber thanks Derogy, Malicia, Sankara and Mustafa Ndewa for understanding her many late nights and early mornings writing and reading for the book; and for their tolerance with her sudden bursts of vibrant dialogues about activism, videos on Tik-Tok about decolonization and the importance of working against the status quo at Oxford University. Her mother, Kristy Burnett, played a pivotal role by instilling in Amber a spirit of disobedience. Her mother-in-law, Marceline Njouongo, provided such crucial support in the last weeks of writing. Amber will be forever regretful that her maternal grandmother, Sharon Burnett, passed away unexpectedly before the book made it to print. Sharon was a powerful force for optimism and self-lessness, quietly supporting Amber's anti-imperial, anti-racist and Pan-African activism even when it estranged her from other members of the family. Patricia thanks Sule, Bovell, Samantha, Samone, Helon, Aunt Beryl, and especially her newly discovered siblings, Joan, Paul, Sandria and Norma whose entry into her life has brought the peace of mind that makes writing so much easier.

REFERENCES

Mignolo, W. (1999) 'I am where I think: Epistemology and the colonial difference', *Journal of Latin American Cultural Studies*, 8(2), pp. 235–45.

Introduction:
Learning Disobedience from
the Heart of Empire

(UN)LEARNING AND LEARNING DISOBEDIENCE
TO ABOLISH DEVELOPMENT

We take as our starting point the imperative for collective projects to abolish international development. Part of this struggle means abolishing development studies and a set of disciplinary specialisms, among them development geographies. We invite scholar-activists, students, organisers and practitioners to divest themselves and their institutions from the practices, ideologies and spaces of international development. For us, cultivating and learning disobedience is at the heart of the struggle for futures beyond development. The apparatus of international development is so thoroughly implicated within ongoing colonial and capitalist formulations of extraction, marginalization and exploitation that we cannot continue to even passively take part. Beginning with our refusal to take 'development' for granted as a feature of contemporary life, being-in-the-world and academic knowledge-making, we embolden ourselves to the tasks of repair, re-imagining and transformation beyond it.

As scholar-activists working within a sub-field entangled in colonial legacies, namely 'African development geographies' (Mercer, Mohan and Power 2003; Daley and Murrey 2022a), we strive to imagine and cultivate a new paradigm that addresses global inequalities, disrupts power relations, attends to ecological repair and emphasizes our common humanity – all starting from the ground-up. In so doing, we extend a rich and radical body of literature that critiques development (in its many iterations) as deeply embedded within the 'colonial matrix of power' (Quijano 2000): as Eurocentric, heteronormative, embedded within racializing thought and rooted in colonial logics. As consenting to capitalism and, often, as promoting neoliberal capitalism. In our pursuit of epistemic and political ruptures with development, we bring together a capacious and important

1

intellectual work on critique and struggle. We find solace in the more emergent projects to decolonize development thought and practice, particularly through meaningful and enduring solidarities. This book is our effort to open up the ways in which we have knowingly engaged in the unfinished project of abolishing development in our teaching praxis.

The project of abolishing development entails a double movement: undoing and dismantling international development, while simultaneously building solidarities and contributing to movements for reparative justice and healing that address and redress intergenerational harms perpetrated in the name of 'development'. In spaces and places impacted by coloniality, struggles to decolonize necessarily involve movements to repair colonial wounds and nurture forms of anti-imperial responsibility for harm by those situated in the Global North (e.g. Raghuram, Madge and Noxolo 2009), alongside creative and joyful political practice. We have come to understand decolonization as the collective and ongoing move to break with colonial systems (including, for example, racist and anthropocentric norms, institutions, values, built environments, technological dimensions, etc.) in ways that work towards realizing decolonial, anti-racist and queer futures. Abolishing international development is therefore an essential movement within the wider project of abolishing racial capitalism (Bhattacharyya 2018).

We are inspired by the prison-abolition movement and Ruth Wilson Gilmore's (2007) work on abolition geographies, which assert the need for the negation of the confinements, borders, structures and relations of carceral geographies to end the Prison Industrial Complex (see also Davis 2003; Vitale 2018; Elliott-Cooper 2021). Abolitionist perspectives can be directed generatively towards development. As our comprehensive engagement with international development here shows, we have had enough with superficial and cyclical reforms. For us, upending the elaborate systems of international development begins with the dismantling of our disciplinary and sub-disciplinary areas of focus. As activists, after all, we begin where we are already situated. This project begins with our active divestment in the hegemonies of knowing and practice fostered by international development actors, sectors, funding and epistemes. This freeing up of our labour, energy and political resources allows us to direct more attention to repair, reparations, justice and decolonial options.

DISMANTLING DEVELOPMENT, DISMANTLING COLONIALITY

To dismantle development, we work from decolonial thought. We situate our present world order as one of 'global coloniality' (sometimes referred to as the 'colonial matrix of power'). In the Peruvian sociologist Anibal Quijano's (2000a) seminal article outlining this concept, he works from the earlier intellectual traditions of dependency theory (Amin 1972) and world systems analysis (Wallerstein 1974) to assert the continuation of colonial relations of power and being beyond and in spite of formal (or 'flag') decolonization on a global scale. Reading Quijano's (2000a, 2000b) work, we understand that the colonial matrix of power has four interrelated domains:

1. control of the economy (land appropriation, exploitation of labour, control of natural resources);
2. control of authority (institutions, army);
3. control of gender and sexuality (family, education);
4. control of subjectivity and knowledge (epistemology, education and the formation of subjectivity).

For Quijano (2000a), race is the 'mental category of modernity', and coloniality is maintained through the establishment of racial difference. The decolonial feminist Maria Lugones (2008, 2010) amends Quijano's articulation so that it attends more fully to the centrality of sex and gender difference within the coloniality of power (see Chapter 6). The colonial matrix of power operates as a hegemonic ordering logic that configures economies, relations and epistemes but in ways that go unsaid, unacknowledged and unrecognized by most people. For this reason, decolonial scholars have been interested in understanding the epistemological functions of global coloniality and racialization, as it is through ideas, and the structuring of reality effected by those ideas, that coloniality is concealed. Decolonial thinker and sociologist Rolando Vázquez (2012) calls the effacement of coloniality by modernity 'the denial of the denial'. Coloniality operates rhetorically through a double negative that dispossesses and excludes the 'Other' and then invalidates, negates and disavows that very dispossession and exclusion.

3

Coloniality is what is erased by the classification and representation of 'modernity' – *plus the denial of that erasure* (Vázquez 2012). Working within anthropology, Francis Nyamnjoh (2017a, 2017b) has argued that the perpetuation of epistemic Eurocentrism (namely the inability to acknowledge the different ways of knowing by which people in the margins and beyond Europe and North America give meaning to their lives) has sometimes involved 'epistemicide' or the active killing of knowledge forms. There is a deep relationship between knowledge of the world, knowledge in the world and political and social justice. Motivated to push the conversation *beyond critique*, scholars like the Zimbabwean decolonial philosopher Sabelo Ndlovu-Gatsheni and decolonial feminist Rosalba Icaza have argued that decolonial options offer pluriversal and alternative epistemes for understanding and engaging with Euro-normative units of analysis and ways of thinking about our social and natural worlds.

In this way, 'decolonial options' (Mignolo and Escobar 2010) seek to move beyond critique (of the coloniality of power) to politically and ethically oriented action (see also Icaza and Vázquez 2017, 50). Mignolo (2010) and other decolonial thinkers have written of the sets of *possible pathways* beyond coloniality as 'decolonial *options*' as they are necessarily multiple and our engagement with them (within our communities of struggle) is influenced by our situatedness, and our body- and geo-politics. The work of decolonial scholars is therefore to imagine presents and futurities beyond the colonization of the future effected by colonial logics (which would deem the present state of affairs absolute and inescapable) – this is an imaginative work called 'gesturing'. Given our shared context of coloniality, we seek to craft generative courses of action that neither presume to escape our entanglement within the coloniality of power, nor to render us innocent (e.g. Tuck and Yang 2012).

Indigenous-inspired approaches emphasize an ability to work and be collectively without claims to either expertise or mastery. Decolonial notions of the pluriverse posit possibilities of co-existence and co-entanglement of multiple worlds and ways of being in the world. Calls for convivial, alternative and decolonial knowledge demand that intellectuals, and people more broadly, move away from binary imaginaries (Icaza and Vázquez 2017; Boidin, Cohen, Grosfoguel 2012, 2–3). These efforts seek to imagine *other ways* of expressing knowledge, shared and collective thinking, and creative processes.

4

Beginning from the perspective of decolonial options means that those scholarly lexicons taken-for-granted in the social sciences – gender, the nation-state, territory, the normative individual, culture and more – are unsettled as analytical frames of reference (Kothari et al. 2019). Decolonial options are more than supplementary components to be merely added upon pre-existing terms and frames: to take the project of decolonizing development and reworlding seriously, a new vocabulary, a decolonial language, is indispensable. Projects of re-founding the university demand attention to forms of epistemic injustice and violence; thus, necessitating forms of disobedience in our learning, unlearning and knowledge practices. For us, this entails active disobedience in turning away from the illusions of universal knowledge towards pluriversal knowledge.

'WHITESTREAMING' AND THE (MIS)APPROPRIATION OF DECOLONIZATION

As we write this book, international development has not yet been abolished. We are at (yet another) colonial impasse (Schuurman 1993; Booth 1985) in which long-established and prevailing formulas of development have been exposed as enacting forms of subjection, exclusion and dispossession. In the last decade, we have witnessed a proliferation of publications, workshops and conferences on themes related to decolonization. So much so that some have argued that the current tenor of the university has taken on the form of a 'decolonization industry' (Táíwò 2022) – so named to critique the ways in which a discourse of 'decolonization' has been mainstreamed (as well as appropriated and emptied of concrete political meaning) within academic business-as-usual. The drumbeat of inclusion and equity has not, however, led to structural change within our institutions; we know from the work of feminist scholars such as Sara Ahmed, Patricia Noxolo, Farhana Sultana and others that these provisional projects of diversification have in fact amounted to ongoing forms of alienation for scholars of colour. 'Inclusion and equity' would resign our political projects as merely additive to the existing system. Decolonization, rather, calls for a radical transformation of knowing, being, relating and praxis (Bhambra, Gebrial, Nişancıoğlu 2018).

The mainstreaming or, we might more appropriately say, the 'white-streaming'[1] of decolonization, has done a disservice to the political project of decolonization. In the context of international development, Themrise Khan (2021) notes that not only does decolonization often fail to translate across and between languages ('in many other languages, from Arabic to Spanish, only a loanword exists'), but that this lack demonstrates how Anglocentric such contemporary discussions are.

Writing and speaking in 2016, we predicted that 'decolonization' would be appropriated by hegemonic financial and developmental institutions (we specifically named the World Bank) to sabotage and curtail radical projects (Murrey 2016, 2019). Tuck and Yang (2012) give a name for the phenomenon of well-intentioned 'decolonizing' scholars who impede Indigenous struggle for land, sovereignty and dignity through their claims of decolonization: these are 'moves to innocence' that would absolve settler guilt and reify white saviour paradigms. The permanent misappropriation of defiant language by colonial forces remains a shameful practice of corporate and colonial actors (see also Daley, in Hughes and Murrey 2022). As such, it is a wicked problem that we must constantly address in our journey of disobedient learning (Murrey 2019). This feature of ongoing coloniality enacts fresh epistemic violence against communities of intergenerational struggle.

Here, *coloniality* is a name for the enduring forms of colonial relations, logics and structures beyond the moment of official (juridical or 'flag') decolonization (Quijano 2000). Colonial logics mystify the continued practices of political and economic violence, often by labelling them with the language of emancipation (Escobar 1995). These logics undermine existent and emergent solidarities by casting doubt, fostering scepticism and hesitation, and dismissing genuine attempts at decolonization as dangerous facsimiles. For a variety of reasons, the relative explosion in projects of decolonization in the present are summarily dismissed as another 'fad' and 'fashionable' project. For scholar-activists and activists

---

1. Here we work alongside Grande's (2003) criticism of hegemonic forces within academic feminism as 'whitestream', a phenomenon they describe as 'a feminist discourse that is not only dominated by white women but also principally structured on the basis of white, middle-class experience; a discourse that services their ethno-political interests and capital investments... whitestream feminism [also] include[s] a heavy dependence on postmodern/poststructuralist theories, a privileging of "academic feminism" over the feminist political project, and an undertheorizing of patriarchy as the universal oppression of all women' (Grande 2003, 330).

– particularly queer and women of colour scholar-activists – who have struggled and worked for decades in these areas, more emergent moves to decolonize from and by hegemonic institutions and people signal yet another form of appropriation, glossing over and consuming the time, labour and love of intergenerational struggles (in long, protracted and historically patterned ways). The institutionalization of 'decolonization' – the rendering of a project into an industry both in academia and development – permits yet another false narrative, yet another misguided kind of white 'help' and 'aid'.

Within academia, there is a tendency to superficially apply and dangerously misappropriate critical concepts that emerge from the labour and energy of Indigenous, Black and marginalized scholars (Tuck and Yang 2012; Roy et al. 2020). The appropriation without citation of women of colour scholars has been an endemic feature of the coloniality of knowledge within the operations of the university (Rivera Cusicanqui 2012; Tilley 2017). Feminists have long asserted that our words are life – that our words, our terms and our concepts carry political, social, economic and geographical significance (Brand 1990). The theft and misappropriation of ideas occurs within and brings attention to the concurrent and permanent orders of racialized and gendered violence that are simultaneously standardized within racial capitalism (Smith 2022), with each violence building upon and also only occurring within and because of the multiplicity of colonial racialized violence. Roy (2020) writes powerfully of the ways in which the work of postcolonial, queer and feminist scholars in the discipline of geography are held up as evidence that the discipline is diversifying – thus providing forms of 'citational alibis' – even as they simultaneously remain decentred, seen as 'specialized fields of inquiry' and as actively depoliticized (Roy 2020).[2]

For some bad faith actors (including openly fascist and racist public intellectuals as well as more 'moderate' neoliberals), recent movements for decolonization have been dismissed as shallow posturing. Through this, we see that bad faith actors modify and exaggerate the purposeful critique of decolonization first crafted by Indigenous scholars (Tuck and Yang 2012) in ways that would discredit anti-racist and anti-colonial

---

2. Against this kind of gesturing 'respectability politics' within academia, Roy (2009, 2011) argues for the need of 'new geographies of theory' that compels a 'reworlding' of the discipline.

movement-making. Other bad faith actors argue that decolonization is entirely misguided: based on either 'bad science' or overburdened with 'identity politics' that presume forms of racial purity that are inherently divisive and essentializing.

Given this milieu, you might wonder why we *knowingly* persist in using the concept to describe the project within which we collaborate. This is because, for us, decolonization continues to have an active traction; it is valuable particularly in teaching and recognizing the ongoing contours of the settler–slave-Indigenous relationship within development studies/geographies (Curley et al. 2022). Decolonization speaks to our aspirations in teaching pedagogies and praxis (Sultana 2019), and it provides a useful emboldening agenda for us, our students and our readers as we consider the possibilities and potentials of teaching against our own institution, and therefore unlearning dominant frames of being and knowledge. Our usage of the term is done in the ugly context of its systematic sabotage and appropriation by institutional actors, with an awareness of our liminality and our weaknesses (including our mindfulness that we have weaknesses that we are not yet aware of).

PEDAGOGICAL DISOBEDIENCE

Drawing from a transdisciplinary body of thought on decolonizing the university and decolonizing pedagogy though grounded, pluralistic and holistic praxes, we think through our practice of 'pedagogical disobedience' as one through which educators, students and activists can work to unlearn – with lucidity and humility – the colonial logics within international development, while supporting decolonial options for futures both beyond and outside mainstream development models. Our use of disobedience draws from Mignolo's (2009, 2011) arguments on the importance of 'epistemic disobedience' in dismantling coloniality (we trace the longer legacies of this thought elsewhere; see Murrey 2019 on 'disobedient pedagogies'; Daley and Murrey 2022a, 2022b on 'defiant scholarship'). Learning how to be intellectually disobedient to the multi-headed hydra of racialized capitalism is an active, collective and ongoing ambition. Dismantling and divesting our selves, our labour, our communities and our institutions from development fictions and structures – through practices of epistemic and pedagogical disobedience – is fundamental to our yearning for flourishing and joyful collective lives.

While this is a co-authored book that draws from our experiences creating, co-teaching and learning over the past five years, at Oxford University's School of Geography and the Environment, our reflections cull from our multiple decades of wider and richer experience of teaching and learning in and against 'international development' in the social sciences, including at institutions in the UK, US, Cameroon, Egypt and Ethiopia. To do so, we build from a powerful existing scholarship to demystify the fluctuating colonial logics undergirding international development for the last 75 years, including Euro-normativity, heteronormativity and white supremacy in development studies and development practice. As anti-racist educators, we seek to learn *with* and to build important relations, connections and curriculums in the watershed moment of projects to decolonize knowledge to nurture flourishing and thriving worlds. Inspired by the promises of Pan-African, decolonial and pluriversal options, it is not sufficient to work against the doxa of Eurocentric 'canons' of thought – we must imagine new, liveable and dignified futures.

Whose knowledges and perspectives have, do and should inform and shape international development policy and programming? How do we actively set out about a praxis of (un)learning as educators, as students, and as activists? In our responses to these questions, we build from the scholarship on decolonizing pedagogies, which (a) centres Indigenous and decolonial ontologies and epistemologies; (b) is purposefully oriented to abolition; (c) critiques the role of coloniality in informing human/nature relations; and (d) is place- and land-based (McCoy, Tuck and McKenzie 2017). Working from Eve Tuck's (2019) challenge, 'to work purposively to create healthy decolonized academic spaces', we aim to be thoughtful in seeking a holistic consideration of decolonizing praxes and curricula (Murrey 2019; Sultana 2019). Tuck and Yang (2012: 21) explain that 'the colonial apparatus is assembled to order the relationships between particular peoples, lands, the 'natural world', and 'civilization'. Colonialism is marked by its specializations. While we are both working within the sub-fields of decolonial political geography and feminist political ecologies within a British university, in our teaching we intentionally pull from an eclectic and wide range of materials, including music, video, social media posts and popular sources like blogs and interviews. Our purpose in writing this book is to carve out the space to sincerely sit with our own co-teaching and (un)learning practice, so as to enrich it and to trace generative connective tissues (including contributing helpful examples) for activists, students and educators committed to the project of decolonizing development.

Within the tradition of decolonial geographies, 'liminality' is a particularly important concept as it admits the modesty and transience of our scholar-teacher selves. We are always in transition, always becoming, always unlearning and learning. Something that remains a particularly instructive prompt for us, especially while we are at the University of Oxford, is to think about how we, as educators, have been inculcated and socialized by and through colonial thought. The project of colonial unlearning requires cultivating a critical awareness of how our own knowing, training, teaching and research practices reinforce systems of oppression (Jackson 2017). How do we set about un-thinking the boundaries of our knowledge projects? Part of this includes deliberately upsetting taken-for-granted parameters regarding the world, interspecies and interhuman relations, and more – the project to decolonize international development entails decolonizing the nation-state, queering our thought (see Alqaisiya 2018), engaging in decolonial praxis, rethinking transnational solidarity, and more.

The project of unlearning and rebuilding is a useful counterpoint to the focus on critique within the Western university, which often takes the form of critique-as-destruction or critique-as-disengagement/dismissal. One thing we remind our students and readers – and one thing we see in ourselves and our own disciplinary training – is that deconstruction can be quick and relatively easy. It is much easier to read a paper and 'identify the weaknesses' (as we are often trained in the Western university) than it is to imagine, write and create. Creation and imagination are challenging, painstaking and sometimes dangerous work. This phenomenon presents challenges for decolonial scholarship, centred as it is in reimagining and creating beyond the ideas of modernity and coloniality. Not only will our task be time- and labour-intensive, but within the university we oftentimes default to critique *even in projects that centre upon reimagining*. We have seen this in our classrooms, for example, when we ask particularly imaginative questions for which there will be no quick response (and no solution-oriented answers). Our students will sometimes defer to, unpacking, the question, identifying its framing implications or critiquing the specific terminologies and linguistic patterns. The work of critique is important! As Carlos Rivera Santana and Graham Akhurst (2019: 2) explain, 'decolonial work has simultaneously been diagnostic –

to expose and discredit coloniality – as well as imaginative-futurities – to expose and realize decolonial options within the pluriverse'. Yet, disobedience in the colonial university requires both anti-colonial critique and decolonial imaginaries.

This book is intentionally provocative in articulating disobedience as central to decolonizing development studies. We embrace the objective of learning disobedience in refusing to abandon the project on the basis of uncertainty – that is, we know that we do not yet know *how* what we name 'decolonizing development' will come to fruition (Sultana 2019; Daley and Murrey 2022b). But we remain disobedient in the face of capitalist, extractivist and colonial paradigms by insisting that *it is possible*. In the face of intellectual projects that would shore up and dismiss decolonial work and decolonizing projects as unconvincing or improbable because they are unfinished (Nyamnjoh 2017a, 2017b), we propose a knowing defiance, a knowing disobedience. We draw from a transdisciplinary body of decolonial work to historicise coloniality and situate it alongside activist and scholarly projects to imagine new and more dignified post-capitalist, post-extractive and post-heteropatriarchal futures.

OUR CODES OF BEHAVIOUR IN THE ARTICULATION AND PRACTICE OF DISOBEDIENT PEDAGOGIES

Refusing to seek legitimation by colonial epistemologies, defiance can be a tool for dismantling coloniality in African development geographies. Working towards pedagogical disobedience is a relational and constant project, one which requires a thoughtfulness and labour that is often not allotted within neoliberal universities. For us, there are several dynamics central to our articulation and practice of disobedient pedagogies:

(1) humility;
(2) unlearning;
(3) learning in-place;
(4) a decolonial ethic; and
(5) attention to power.

Humility is a starting component of disobedient pedagogies. It enables critical reflection on our positionalities and the epistemic violence that informs how and what we were taught in the academy and how those pedagogies may continue to shape the ways in which we approach the teaching of development. Having first questioned these hegemonic pedagogies, we then embark on a process of unlearning.

Through **unlearning**, we highlight the importance of recognizing the violence(s) of development projects and its epistemological branch through development studies and focus on teaching radically alternative approaches, including post-development, anti-imperialism, dependency theory, indigenous studies, decolonial futures and pluriversals.

Through **learning in-place**, we encourage teachers, students and activists to engage with their local spaces, communities and institutions. Learning *in-place* and *with-place* is a fundamental practice of any disobedient pedagogy. We therefore reflect upon the particular role of our institution, the University of Oxford, within colonial and capitalist development. Pedagogic disobediences are vital at hegemonic institutions like Oxford, which continue to operate as nuclei for global economic and political hubris. We remain vigilant to these **power asymmetries**. Working within a **decolonial ethic**, we frame our teaching and coursework so that students think critically about what it means to learn and study Africa from Oxford, what it means to aspire to 'do' development 'work', what it means to read, study and observe places elsewhere. Within a disobedient pedagogy, the way to learn 'development' is to fundamentally unlearn it; to interrogate the imperial arrogance in the premise of cyclical historical intervention; to decolonize development by working to end it and engaging in other sets of relations with the human and non-human worlds, engaging in decolonial solidarities and horizontal political projects.

(UN)LEARNING FROM THE UNIVERSITY OF OXFORD

We remain alert to the colonial ground upon which we stand at Oxford, even as we seek to gesture towards decolonial futures of ecological co-existence. We situate our starting point from Oxford, a city with outsized policy importance in terms of setting the tone for international development policy and for the university's role in condoning colonial knowledges and patrimonial relations with the Global South. Oxford has a long tradition of educating the British ruling elite and providing a space for the development of colonial ideas and strategies, including the legal premises for enslavement and the expropriation of native land and property (John Locke, etc.) and the acquisition of knowledge and artefacts through conquest and coercion. Sarah Stockwell (2018: 93) describes the roles of Oxford and Cambridge during the late colonial and early postcolonial era as aiming to 'teach what "the Natives need to know"'.

The civil rights lawyer and legal scholar Michelle Alexander (2010) writes powerfully about the roles of 'race-making institutions' within systematic anti-black racism. Racial and gendered representations, formal legal policies and taxonomies of power shift over time, yet dominant 'race-making institutions' operate in ways that continue racial hierarchization and violence. While Alexander writes in the context of the US prison-industrial-complex and what she terms the 'new Jim Crow' (or the ways in which contemporary organizations perpetuate racial segregations similar to those more formalized during the late nineteenth and early twentieth centuries Jim Crow period), her elucidation of certain hegemonic institutions as 'race-making', or systemically (re)materializing forms of racial violence, is an important starting point for our consideration of co-teaching and (un)learning from the University of Oxford.

The imperial underbelly of British geography implicates all of us that work at Oxford, including those of us who wish to work against it. The British colonialist and founder of the De Beers diamond firm, Cecil Rhodes, described colonialism in the former colonial territory of Rhodesia (now Zimbabwe and Zambia) in Southern Africa in the following terms: 'imperialism was philanthropy plus a 5 percent dividend on investment' (Rhodes, quoted in Lawlor 2000: 63). In eighteenth-century England, plantation owners in the so-called 'New World' of the Americas and the West Indies amassed the money that enabled the financing of institutions of higher education, factories and industry in the imperial core. The Cameroonian political philosopher Achille Mbembe argues that the colonial system and the slave system 'represent modernity's and democracy's bitter sediment . . . driving it towards decomposition' (2017, 20). Meanwhile, one of our colleagues at the School of Geography and the Environment, Professor Danny Dorling (2020) argues that the

[p]urpose of geography originally [was] as a subject of Empire: to know about the empire before going out and serving in it . . . Geography has its origins with people like Halford Mackinder who cared deeply about the British Empire: the purpose of geography was to produce colonial officers.

At the behest of the Vice President of the Royal Geographical Society, who appealed to the Vice Chancellors of the universities of Oxford and Cambridge in 1886, Halford John Mackinder was appointed Reader in Geography at the University of Oxford (in 1887) and became the School of Geography's first director (in 1899). The school was established in 1899, with a lineage directly traced to Mackinder's ascent up Mount Kenya. Mackinder would maintain the post of Reader in Geography from 1887 to 1905.

It was in 1899 that Mackinder led an expedition to Mount Kenya in an attempt to become the first white man to scale Africa's second highest peak. The members of the expedition consisted of 99 Kikuyu, 66 Swahili and two Maasai porters and guides, alongside six Europeans. The journey was marked by violence from the beginning. Mackinder used enslaved Swahili labourers as porters, who he compared to animals in his diaries (calling them, for example, his 'faithful dogs'). East African labourers were disciplined and intimidated with the whip and the firearm, including by Mackinder himself. Mistreated and facing possible starvation, a group of labourers sought to escape. Eight porters were 'shot by orders'. The historical records remain debated, in part because of Mackinder's own silence about the killings. Yet, most scholars are confident that these executions were for 'insubordination' or desertion, following deplorable treatment and conditions. As the geographer Gerry Kearns (2009) explains, 'Mackinder and indeed empire remains part of the historical and epistemological legacy of British geography . . . Mackinder's geography was not only a science of empire, it was also a way of promoting the cause of Empire'. Nowhere is this truer than in the halls of the Oxford's School of Geography and the Environment.

When Mackinder departed Kenya, he is said to have returned to Oxford with a rock that constituted the uppermost piece of the summit of Mt. Kenya. This small rock remained on display on his desk throughout his tenure and remained somewhere in the School of Geography and the Environment as recently as 2009. In 2021, we began a sustained search for the object, reaching out to colleagues, administrators and maintenance personnel. In the course of teaching on a collaborative postgraduate course entitled 'UNISA-Oxford Decolonising Research Methodologies' in 2020, with students from universities across the African continent, we sought to locate the rock and ultimately repatriate it to the University of Dar es Salaam as a means of speaking to and acting against the colonial legacies of our subject at Oxford. The removal of the rock at the summit of Mount Kenya and its blasé display in our department fits within the wider paradigm of colonial dispossession and theft, often in the name of universal 'knowledge' and 'human betterment' (see Smith 1999).

We corresponded with Benezet Rwelengera, a PhD student in the Department of Geography at the University of Dar es Salaam. Our task was rendered more difficult insofar as we did not know quite what the rock looked like. One of our former colleagues, the economic geographer Gordon Clark, told us that he was aware of its (supposed) provenance and had seen the rock about fifteen years ago, sometime between 2008 and 2009. Gordon described it as small ('approximately two thumbs in size') and 'blue-brown in colour'. To his recollection, it was 'kept in a little box' with 'no tag or label'.

In our search for the rock, Oxford maintenance staff pulled boxes out from storage containing Mackinder's loot. We uncovered and analysed several of Mackinder's various 'trophies'; the animal skulls, furs and remains which were being stored, without labels or identifying tags, in the basement of our building on South Parks Road. Yet nowhere did we locate the elusive rock. We perused the electronic files and scans of Mackinder's work in Oxford's Bodleian Library and learned that Mackinder's original trunk had been 'disposed of' when his objects were transferred from the Mansfield Road building to the library for digitization and permanent archiving.

What began as a project to repatriate the rock from the summit of East Africa's second highest peak to the University of Dar es Salaam, ended anti-climactically, without event and, significantly, without the rock. Things had been put in the bin, others left to collect dust and fragment in dark basements, and others basically vanished. The disordered handling of the objects taken by Mackinder from East Africa reflects some of the strange modifications over time between empire and our university: from the height of colonial removal to the quieter colonial apprehensions and hegemonic effacements of the post-colonial[3] moment. The main lecture

---

3. We employ the hyphenated term 'post-colonial' to refer to the historical period following formal decolonization in the second half of the twentieth century; 'postcolonial' is used in reference to the body of critical scholarship critiquing colonialism (that is, postcolonial studies). Postcolonial scholarship has revealed the lack of an absolute break or rupture between the colonial and post-colonial periods (see Chapter 1).

theatre, for example, in Oxford's School of Geography and the Environment had been named the 'Halford Mackinder Lecture Theatre' in the early years of the twenty-first century, as each of our rooms was named after a geographer of note. (Significantly, only one room was named in honour of a woman geographer at the time: the staff coffee and break room was named after the geomorphologist Dr Marjorie Sweeting. We often remarked that the only 'kitchen' space in the building was named for a woman). Then, in May 2020, after some internal debate, the school's teaching and research staff voted to remove Mackinder's name from our main lecture theatre. Subsequently, in the early months of the Covid lockdown, every room in the building was quietly renamed to reflect seemingly apolitical and noncontroversial geographical themes: we now teach in awkwardly named rooms like the Atmosphere Room, the Village Room, the Space Suite, the Diversity Room and so on.

That our department, as far as we can tell, lost this rock is in keeping with the imperial debris and colonial hauntings of the university. One of our students, for example, recently shared a rumour that the foundation of the building housing the Department of Physiology, Anatomy and Genetics (DPAG) contains the bones and remains of indigenous peoples, illicitly removed and stolen for medical research. In 1945, the university established the Institute of Colonial Studies (ICS) to educate colonial officers and administrators – today, this institute has been renamed the Department of International Development.[4] In the post-colonial period, 'courses [initially] created for British [Colonial Administrative Service] probationers developed into training programmes aimed wholly at overseas civil servants in independent countries . . . [these appointments were seen] as "key" because they were aimed at high fliers likely to become department heads . . . [and thus would] advis[e] their governments on policy' (Stockwell 2018: 94). The earlier colonial names of buildings and knowledge programmes have slowly been painted over, but the legacies of empire remain embedded within the materials, practices and discourses of our 'race-making institution'. Within present-day coloniality, colonialism has been transformed rather than eliminated. Even

---

4. For more on the colonial history of International Development at Oxford, readers may wish to consult the 2016 Oxford and Colonialism project and webpages, for example https://oxfordandcolonialism.web.ox.ac.uk/department-international-development.

as critical notions are increasingly taken up within a geographical tradition influenced by postcolonial, decolonial and anti-racist thought, most scholarship is still written and published by white academics from the Global North, working in Western universities and institutions. The anti-racist geographers James Esson and Angela Last (2020) explain that whiteness (as a location of structural advantage and an unacknowledged normative positionality) remains standard in British geography departments. Decolonial pedagogical praxis thus necessarily and defiantly takes on the structures and institutions of contemporary geography (Esson et al. 2017: 385; Daley and Murrey 2022a).

The age-old idea of the university as an 'ivory tower' removed from the world and messy geopolitics is not only incorrect, but dangerous. Part of our purpose in writing this book is to embrace a teaching praxis that refuses to sequester ideas behind 'ivory towers'. The classroom is a battleground in the struggle to decolonize development. Inspired by Alyshia Gálvez (2020) and other critical pedagogists, we ask, 'How is [our] understanding of what is necessary to read, write and know in this course shaped by white supremacist ideas about whose work matters?' The university and our intellectual practices within and beyond it contribute to public debate and action. The university is a site for the socialization, formation and training of countless public figures and leaders. Those who do not attend formalized post-secondary education are nonetheless influenced by the primary school teachers, journalists, pundits, authors and researchers trained within their walls. Some 75 per cent of all British Prime Ministers (57 in total) have been educated at the University of Oxford and the University of Cambridge alone (Dorling and Tomlinson 2019). The university where we teach and research holds a significant position for configuring conversations around (and conceptualizations of) colonial violence, economic (in)justice, racial repair, ecological restoration and dignified futurities.

We therefore ask our students and readers to think about why a consideration of our situatedness at Oxford is important and how it does (or should) structure our conversation, our study and our unlearning differently. What are our unique responsibilities as differentially positioned and differently racialized scholars in the United Kingdom and in Oxford? The Liberian scholar of public policy, Robtel Neajai Pailey (2020), speaks of the need for holistic approaches to decolonization which centre upon rethinking knowledge itself – demanding that we rethink our very imaginaries.[5] How do we take up Pailey's (2020) urgent demand, in the classroom and beyond, to de-centre the colonial and white gaze of development? In our defiant and disobedient teaching praxis, we seek to remain aware of how students and educators at Oxford encounter particular responsibilities and challenges in the study and (un)learning of international development within the 'colonial matrix of power'.

TEACHING FROM THE INTELLECTUAL CENTRE OF EMPIRE

It is important to understand Oxford's simultaneously prominent and concealed position and function within the British colonization of, and extractive corporate practices within, Africa, Asia and the Americas; and to supplement this understanding with self-reflection and decolonial ethics. We have intellectual and activist networks across the African continent and, throughout this book, will often draw from our experiences teaching and learning in Ethiopia, Egypt, Tanzania and Cameroon. Our collective teaching practice is motivated and imbued with a decolonial ethics, in which we are in the university but not *of* the university (Harney and Moten 2013), and in which our accountability and responsibilities are to the people in the communities where we work. We make a case for researchers to practice an ethic of responsibility that involves adopting the stance of 'guerrilla intellectuals' as articulated by Walter Rodney (1990), where we recognize that the legitimacies of modern universities are too often derived from Eurocentrism, elitism, capitalism and white supremacy. Our aim is to enact a struggle against those ideas, rather than to legitimize them.

The institutional setting that is Oxford fosters all sorts of colonial illusions in the present-day. We are endlessly pressed within certain moulds of coloniality, including the discriminatory and hidden demands to present in specific ways and formulas (for example, to assert the title of 'recognized knower' or 'expert') (see González and Harris 2012). We seek to unthink and reject the title of 'expert' from within. Both of us, for different reasons, are not automatically recognized as expert 'scholars' who

---

5. We recommend listening to Pailey's comments on decolonizing international development in an episode of "ODI Bites" from October 2020, available here: www.youtube.com/watch?v=liyeK8wnsIo.

merit respect in our immediate institutional setting (unlike many of our older white female-presenting colleagues or our male-presenting colleagues of most any age). We teach with and through these differences. We have been frequently overlooked and dismissed by colleagues, students and maintenance and security staff, although for different reasons. We situate our (un)learning from the imperial remains of Oxford, and we situate our teaching from our bodies.

One of us (Patricia), was appointed as the first Black permanent member of teaching staff in the University of Oxford's some thousand-year history in 1991. Patricia, coming from rural Jamaica and a London working class background, faced classism, racism and sexism simultaneously. But equally important were the challenges she encountered as a diaspora African studying and researching on Africa amongst white Africanist colleagues who sought to delegitimize her contributions by labelling them 'Afrocentric' and to marginalize her in the spaces of the university to avert competition for funding and status. One of us (Amber) is a white, first-generation and immigrant scholar, also from a rural background in the mountains of the US Pacific Northwest. Amber is neurodivergent and teaches as a dyslexic scholar, a reality that is at once enriching and marginalizing. Dyslexia can foster numerical confusion and anomic aphasia or an inability to recall names, but it can also allow scholars to see connections, contours and big picture phenomenon with incredible clarity of vision.

Our co-teaching has been focused on interrupting the colonial and capitalist logics embedded within development scholarships and development geographies. Our co-teaching is grounded on our relationship and mutual accountability, our relations with our students (who propel us with vigorous insights and robust questions) and our excitement regarding decolonial work and how we might *gesture* towards anti-racist, anti-imperial and Pan-African pathways.

Thus, we are simultaneously keenly privileged for being within the 'belly of the beast' (Oxford) and relegated within this colonial space in everyday and mundane ways. This dual-being structures our teaching. More than one reviewer of our work has asked if we 'can ever even say that we do anything akin to decolonization while employed by the University of Oxford'. To this, we respond firstly with comprehension: making unfounded claims of collaboration would be tantamount to the worst forms of moves to innocence (see Tuck and Yang 2012); for both of us, our political commitments to Pan-African, collaborative and solidarity work is as long as our intellectual trajectories. These are not new or careerist endeavours for us, but lifelong commitments that began much earlier than our employment at Oxford. Secondly, the institution of Oxford is too important within British imperial politics to leave either unchallenged or unchanged. We refuse to be debilitated or demobilized by the numerous, real imitations that we encounter (daily and via structural means to contain and limit the work of decolonizing). As activists and political intellectuals, we work where we are and where we are shapes our work. In the context of international development, Oxford continues to play an important role as an institution that contributes to setting the parameters of dominant thought and practice, including through naming and analysing people and places in publications, teaching and seminars. These intellectual practices are transformed into policy-making and grounded action (see Escobar 1995: 41) by students and intellectuals who graduate and continue on to become corporate 'flexians'[6] and officials, Prime Ministers and planners.

We have no illusions of scholarly or political purity, and our situatedness within this imperial institution marks our knowledge projects differently. As Burman (2012: 117) rightly notes, 'there is no way we are going to intellectually reason our way out of coloniality, in any conventional academic sense. There is no way we are going to publish our way out of modernity. There is no way we are going to read our way out of epistemological hegemony'.

At times, the topics of our research and teaching have subjected us to forms of institutional ostracization and isolation. We have organized talks on 'defiant scholarship in Africa' at the University of Oxford. We know that some of our work has been received with confusion or condescension. Within geographical circles, work in decolonial African

---

6. Flexians is a term coined by Anthropologist Janine Wedel to refer to groups of educated, affiliated and connected people within the 21st Century who maintain multiple roles and positions of influence in global capitalism. These people move in and out of institutions – for example, holding visiting fellowships at the world's leading universities, while sitting on corporate advisory boards, and authoring government policy. The multiple affiliations are frequently changing, often opaque and render responsibility difficult to determine (see also Jackson 2019). For people interested in working together against capitalist exploitation and extraction, understanding the manoeuvrings of these actors can be essential to exposing motivations and entrenched networks of power.

political geographies has often been oddly situated outside conversations in Black geographies, an important sub-field of heterogeneous Afrodiasporic thought within the powerful Black Atlantic traditions, focused on the spatial, place-based and embodied experiences of blackness as multiple, creative and resurgent (McKittrick and Woods 2007; Noxolo 2022); and yet also often separate from decolonial geographies (which has focused more centrally on epistemic and political communities of Latin America). Our teaching is thus an enactment against geographical segmentation. As the powerful scholarship within the remit of epistemologies of the South has made clear, knowledges in and of Africa are not confined to 'area studies' (Zeleza 1997) – or forms of knowing 'merely' interesting or applicable within their particular areas or regions (see also Sidaway et al. 2016 on thinking against the geographies of 'areas') – but have global significance. Thinking with and from African geographies is an element of our disobedient pedagogy, pushing against wider trends to separate and hyper-marginalize African epistemologies within the Westernized university (i.e. the Euro-Anglocentric colonial university system; see Grosfoguel 2013). Centring African societies within our decolonial teaching praxis is a facet of working against forms of intellectual and 'academic imperialism' (Ake 1996; Alatas 2003), which continues to foster 'epistemic exclusion, cultural mismatch and epistemic extractivism' (Readsura Decolonial Editorial Collective 2022). It is an act of solidarity with global African peoples. Critical geographical scholarship has much to contribute to the project of decolonizing development. Yet, as the title of the book connotes, the social science of development we engage with is broader and wider than African development geographies and, in elevating decolonial transdisciplinary praxis, we are not fixedly loyal to geography as a discipline of thought (see also Daley and Murrey 2022a, 2022b).

At other times, our anti-racist and anti-imperial work has been heralded and arrogated by institutional actors in ways that would 'take credit' for labour often done against and in spite of institutional structures (we are aware of this risk with the publication of this book, for example). This public-facing appropriation of small-scale decolonizing projects within the university can disguise the ongoing injustices of our institution, as it simultaneously defers the radical or militant energies of students, staff and educators to press for substantive change. The fracturing of dissent has been particularly pernicious in the formation of committees (and subcommittees) to address targeted tasks in response to student-led pressures to decolonize the university (see also Ahmed 2008). At Oxford, we are not (yet) working within holistically anti-imperial collaboratives. This inevitably marks our teaching in the minds and experiences of our students and for our capacities to move against coloniality. Part of our job has been to reveal the inner workings of institutional power with and alongside our students, not as uniform or omnipotent aligned forces, but as ever-evolving sets of seizures, dismissals and seductions by hegemonic actors (see also Murrey 2019). We have often responded in real-time to the (anticipated, sometimes random and capricious) enclosures and misappropriations of radical scholarship in the service of colonial stabilization and capitalist reproduction. Defiant scholars like Sara Ahmed, Patricia McFadden, Stella Nyanzi, Olivia U. Rutazibwa, Sara Salem, Lisa Tilley and Farhana Sultana (there are too many to list!) steadily cultivate scholarly praxes that refuse the university's misuse and commodification of their knowledge. As we seek to 'learn how to live with difference in damaged heterogeneous worlds' (*Common Worlds Research Collective*), our work has sometimes felt fragmented and piecemeal. Indeed, elsewhere we have likened our decolonial praxis to a form of 'hustling' (see Daley and Murrey 2022b); it is a state of continuous manoeuvring and relation-making, guided by a decolonial ethic grounded in the commitment to collaboratively work for dignified futures. In the spirit of Nyamnjoh's (2017a) 'case for conviviality', we ask what it means for our scholarship to be decolonial and 'disobedient' to colonial and capitalist epistemes (Daley and Murrey 2022a).

Colonial legacies and colonial logics continue to shape the ways in which land, wellbeing, progress and development are conceived of and practiced. How do we, through our classroom and activist practices, work collaboratively to create the radical imaginaries and practical scaffolding we need for decolonizing development? Given the centrality of forms of expertise in fostering and legitimizing histories of Eurocentric development practice, we argue that the classroom is a key domain in the larger struggle to decolonize development. Employing a practice that we call 'pedagogical disobedience', we chart a critical interdisciplinary approach to unthinking, unlearning and decolonizing international development studies. Through pedagogical disobedience, we develop a critique of the longstanding colonial practice of 'incorporating' marginalized people within dominant development paradigms (like projects to 'diversify' that do not alter structural relations of racialized empire and coloniality nor the material conditions of domination); these forms of 'diversification' can condone or even exacerbate capitalist exploitation. Rather, epistemic, racial and ecological justice are praxis-oriented: we actively imagine and construct liveable futures, foster dignified obligations as part of our reworlding (Spivak 1988; Ndlovu-Gatsheni 2023). Our teaching is part of our wider web of relations. What is meaningful in the classroom is meaningful beyond it.

In developing our teaching praxis throughout this course and over time, we have sought sustenance and gained momentum from Pan-African, anti-racist and decolonial collectives and forms of resurgence. In our citational and elevational practices, we seek to cultivate forms of reciprocity for the scholars who have both formed and informed us. We have learned from many different decolonial teaching collectives, who importantly have a rich plethora of open-source materials available online. We are accompanied in this project to unthink and unlearn development geographies with pluriversal possibilities. So much important work has set the stage for our intervention.

The digital commons nurtured by Convivial Thinking has done important work gathering materials on decolonial and anti-colonial rejoinders to development and publishes thoughtful, experimental blog posts, poems, songs and podcasts. The Earth Unbound Collective meanwhile prioritizes forms of 'unbuilding' ongoing colonial violence; 'undoing' frameworks that 'celebrate, exoticize or extract "minor" knowledges' and 'address . . . fear, guilt and anxiety'. For their 'commoning pedagogies', the Common Worlds Research Collective finds inspiration in Donna Haraway's interspecies notion of 'worlding' to name the co-making of 'common worlds [as] an inclusive, more than human notion'. Commoning pedagogies begin with the awareness that 'we inherit worlds already damaged in the name of human progress and development, e.g. by colonisation and extractive capitalism'; therefore, communing pedagogies entail 'shifting from the current focus upon individual human learners learning facts about the world (out there), to following and enabling collective, productive and pedagogically worldly relations'.

The Gesturing Towards Decolonial Futures collective are a powerful source of provocative projects and activities for those committed to turning away from coloniality and the coloniality of being. They describe their decolonial practice as

multi-layered and rather difficult to explain . . . it is about compost-
ing our individual and collective shit with humility, joy, generosity and
compassion . . . it is about facing our complicity in violence . . . and
its implications with the courage of really seeking to connect with the
collective pain, past, present and future . . . it is about recognizing and
taking responsibility for harmful modern-colonial habits of being . . .
that cannot be stopped by intellect, by good intentions and by spiritual,
artistic or embodied practices alone (Gesturing Toward Decolonial
Futures n.d.)

Their exposure of the pretences and illusions of academic practice is both
thorough and deeply humbling. A decolonial praxis demands that we recognize and deliberately destabilize our desires for self-aggrandisement,
recognition and authority, instead fostering spaces for 'accountabilities,
for response-abilities, for exiled capacities and for deeper intimacies'.
(Ibid) This is a collective state of being-in-the-world with the capacity to
learn with difference so as to mourn, grieve, heal, digest and metabolize,
so as to see ourselves as 'cute and pathetic, so that the wider metabolism can breathe and move more easily within and around us'. (Ibid) The
Gesturing Towards Decolonial Futures collective has a deck of playing
cards which raises questions and topics for people compelled by 'decolonial options'. Many of their questions burn in our minds as we write this
book, and as we have taught and engaged with complex colonial, capitalist and racial questions.

PAN-AFRICAN DEFIANCE, JOY, HOPE AND SONG

Patricia's defiance owes much to her maternal grandmother and aunts –
phenomenal women who worked as housewives, nursing assistants, care
workers, peasant farmers and domestic workers. At a breakfast in her
honour organized by black female students from Oxford's Africa Society[7],

---

7. 'The Daley Breakfasts' were three interrelated events organized between 2018 and
2019 to celebrate the contribution of Black women in Oxford. The first event focused
on the career and activism of Patricia Daley; the second event was on non-conformity,
space-making and the politics of Black hair, with Amber Starks of 'Conscious Coils';
the final event celebrated the work of the Zimbaabwean journalist and author Panashe
Chigumadzi and was titled, 'Black as I am, Black as we are'.

she spoke of how the women in her family survived where they were not meant to even thrive, created citizenship in marginal spaces, ensured a sense of belonging that transcended generations – how they made family life, laughed, clapped, sang and danced. Her intellectual flourishing occurred outside the academy and from reading Pan-Africanist women writers, poets and artists such as Maya Angelou (1969), Dionne Brand (1990), Grace Nichols (1984), Loretta Ngcobo (1990), bell hooks (1986, 1994) and Ifi Amadiume (2007), all of whom possessed heightened awareness of injustices and intersecting oppressions. These theoreticians were unafraid of disrupting, constantly creating new concepts and vocabularies to express the specificities of their condition, to articulate their resistance, and to communicate their imaginations of a better future.

Together, we draw inspiration from and are motivated by the student-led Rhodes Must Fall (@RMF_Oxford) campaign in our city; this is a struggle that both of us have joined in the classroom and on the streets (see Daley 2018). One of us (Amber) gave the inaugural talk at the Rhodes Must Fall Freedom Summer Teach-in in the streets of Oxford in 2020, on 'Pedagogies of Disobedience and the "Dangerous" Ideas of Thomas Sankara'. With hundreds of students and activists gathered at Oriel Square, Amber spoke about the significance of unrelenting pressures on the university and its associated colleges. She described how the Pan-Africanist revolutionary Thomas Sankara galvanized and embodied a militant decolonial praxis in the 1980s, before we even had a label for 'decoloniality' (see Biney 2018). His people-centred practices provide a powerful illustration of the political possibilities for community flourishing, and yet also expose the endangerments of neo-imperial racialized violence (see Chapter 2).

To provoke and incite you (our readers), we have integrated critical materials from a wide range of sources, built in possible activities and offered questions for further thought as you continue to ruminate on your journey to untangle the colonial matrix of power, nurture anti-colonial solidarities and co-create life-affirming relations. In our invitation to take up the project of fundamentally breaking away from the promise and illusion of development imaginaries, violence and practice, we acknowledge that theorization does not occur exclusively in the spaces of the academy. The theorization of power, the critique of coloniality, heteropatriarchy and racism, and the fostering of other ways of being, knowing and acting has long been best championed amongst activists, songwriters, musicians, poets, writers, visual artists and storytellers, who, in whatever medium they use, provide incisive analysis of the conditions of life in the Global South and articulate visions of alternative lifeworlds.

Thus, at the beginning of each chapter in this book, we seek to provoke and move you with short decolonial and anti-colonial musical playlists. Songs are a powerful force for transformative socio-political change. We have selected these songs because they have moved our own work, they have challenged us and they provide moving and insightful artistic and musical commentaries on the subjects and themes about which we write. Students and readers might listen to one or two (and watch the accompanying music videos) before immersing themselves in the reading materials. We hope educators reading our book will, in their teaching practice, add to these playlists music from their own communities of struggle, imagination and being. We hope they will encourage readers to appreciate knowledge creation beyond Euro-America, including cultural forms that 'speak back' to the empire, in the tradition of bell hooks (1986). As hooks (1986: 123) explains, 'to speak when one [is] not spoken to [is] a courageous act – an act of risk and daring'. As with all cultural arte-facts, songs are not unproblematic. We invite readers to sit with – rather than turn away from – discomforts provoked by these playlists and by our words. Discomfort is one important component of anti-racist and deco-lonial unlearning, just as 'there is much to learn from joy and pleasure' (Eaves et al. 2023: 3). Within feminist political geographies, an

> intentional . . . engage[ment] with discomfort plants] "a seed that provokes questions" about power, difference, and authority . . . [it is important to think about] what occurs when you feel discomfort, revulsion, abjection, or a sense of unbelonging – [sometimes] at the very instant you are told you are being cared for? (Eaves et al. 2023: 3).

A critical and knowing engagement with discomfort is part of a wider project of refusing the imperial fostering of comfort within the university, which is too often at the expense of marginalized people and communi-ties of colour (Ahmed 2017).

TEACHING, (UN)LEARNING AND BECOMING TOGETHER

Our book begins with the emergence of imperial claims to benign humanitarianism within colonial projects and engages in a broad survey of the diverse and complex ways in which (multiple) ideologies of race are foundational to various forms of development through the cultivation of a particular (victimized, disposable, criminal, rights-deficient) 'Other' (Chapter 1). A critical interdisciplinary approach to development does not mean uniformly tracing failures or problems within development, rather we consider development as a collection of ideas that emerge from specific social, historical and geographical contexts, with often unintended outcomes that reflect complexities on the ground. We consider critical development studies and post-development literatures alongside examinations of the political, social and ecological contexts of development in order to address critical global issues: political ecologies of aid; the relations between humanitarianism, violence and militarism; the corporatization of NGOs and the NGO-ization of the corporation; digital media and social justice movements; 'decolonizing development' (Sultana 2019) and indigenous struggle outside of official or mainstream development frequencies. Through context-specific analyses of development we are attentive to dissimilar people and communities too frequently marginalized bydevelopment practice: women, non-binary, LGBTQI, Indigenous and differently-abled people from across the Global South, especially Africa. We hope that our book contributes to the collective labour and energy of engaged and critical learners who are interested in (un)learning together to abolish development as a set of material and ideological practices . . . this is a struggle that continues.

QUESTIONS FOR FURTHER THOUGHT

We invite you to sit with the argument that the project of decolonizing geographical knowledge could do 'more harm than good' (Esson et al., 2017, p. 384). Why is this so and how might it guide your reading of this book, and the wider projects with which you collaborate?

REFERENCES

Ahmed, S. (2008) *On being included: Racism and diversity in institutional life.* Durham, NC: Duke University Press.

Ahmed, S. (2017) *Living a feminist life.* Durham, NC: Duke University Press.

Ake, C. (1996) *Democracy and development in Africa.* Washington D.C.: The Brookings Institution.

Alatas, S. F. (2003) 'Academic dependency and the global division of labour in the social sciences', *Current Sociology*, 51(6), pp. 599–613.

Alexander, M. (2010) *The new Jim Crow: Mass incarceration in the age of color-blindness*. New York: New Press.

Alqaisiya, W. (2018) 'Decolonial queering: The politics of being queer in Palestine', *Journal of Palestine Studies*, 47(3), pp. 29–44. DOI: 10.1525/jps.2018.47.3.29.

Amadiume, I. (2007) *Voices draped in black: Poems*. Trenton, N.J: Africa World Press.

Andreotti, V. (2021) *Hospicing modernity: Facing humanity's wrongs and the implications for social activism*. Berkeley, Calif.: North Atlantic Books.

Angelou, M. (1969) *I know why the caged bird sings*. New York: Random House.

Biney, A. (2018) 'Madmen, Thomas Sankara and decoloniality in Africa' in *A certain amount of Madness: The life, politics and legacies of Thomas Sankara*. Murrey, A. ed., pp. 127–46. London: Pluto Press.

Boidin, C. and Cohen, J., Grosfoguel, R. (2012) 'Introduction: From university to pluriversity: A decolonial approach to the present crisis of Western Universities', *Human Architecture*, 10(1), pp. 1–6.

Booth, D. (1985) 'Marxism and development sociology: Interpreting the impasse', *World Development* 13(7), pp. 761–87.

Brand, D. (1990) *No language is neutral*. Toronto: McClelland and Stewart.

Burman, A. (2012) 'Places to think with, books to think about: Words, experience and the decolonization of knowledge in the Bolivian Andes', *Human Architecture* 10(1), pp. 101–19.

Curley, A. and Gupta, P., Lookabaugh, L., Neubert, C., Smith, S. (2022) 'Decolonisation is a political project: Overcoming impasses between Indigenous sovereignty and abolition', *Antipode* 54(4), pp. 1043–62.

Daley P., Murrey A. (2022a) 'Response to commentaries on Patricia Daley and Amber Murrey's "Defiant Scholarship: Dismantling Coloniality in Contemporary African Geographies"', *Singapore Journal of Tropical Geography*, 43, pp. 194–200.

Daley P., Murrey A. (2022b) 'Defiant scholarship: Dismantling coloniality in contemporary African geographies', *Singapore Journal of Tropical Geography*, 43, pp. 159–76.

Daley, P. (2022) 'Linguistic defiance: Language mobilization and new spaces of resistance' in Hughes S., Murrey A., et. Al. Interventions on the political geographies of resistances: The contributions of Cindi Katz. *Political Geography*, 97(1). DOI:10.1016/j.polgeo.2022.102666

Daley, P. (2018) 'Reparations in the space of the university in the wake of Rhodes Must Fall' in Chantiluke, R., Kwoba, B. and Nkopo, A. (eds.) *Rhodes Must Fall: The struggle to decolonise the racist heart of empire*. London: Zed Books, pp. 74–89.

Davis, Angela Y. (2003) *Are prisons obsolete?* New York: Seven Stories Press.

De Sousa Santos, B. (ed.) (2007) *Cognitive justice in a global world: Prudent knowledges for a decent life*. New York: Lexington Books.

Dorling, D. (2020) 'Empire with Danny Dorling, an interview on Greenbelt Volunteer Talks'. Available: www.youtube.com/watch?v=83BfemZxqyg.

Dorling, D. and Tomlinson, S. (2019) *Rule Britannia: Brexit and the end of empire*. London: Biteback Publishing.

Eaves, L. and Gökariksel, B., Hawkins, M., Neubert, C. and Smith, S. (2023) 'Political geographies of discomfort feminism: Introduction to the themed intervention', *Gender, Place & Culture*, [online first].

Elliott-Cooper, A. (2021) *Black resistance to British policing*. Manchester: Manchester University Press.

Escobar, A. (1995) *Encountering development: The making and unmaking of the Third World*. Princeton: Princeton University Press.

Esson, J. and Noxolo, P., Baxter, R., Daley, P., Byron, M. (2017) 'The 2017 RGS-IBG chair's theme: Decolonising geographical knowledges, or reproducing coloniality?', *Area*, 49(3), pp. 384–88.

Gálvez, A. (2020) 'How I've implemented an anti-racist approach in my teaching'. Blog post. www.alyshiagalvez.com/post/how-i-ve-implemented-an-anti-racist-approach-in-my-teaching.

Gilmore, R. W. (2007) *Golden gulag: Prisons, surplus, crisis and opposition in globalizing California*. Berkeley: University of California Press.

Grosfoguel, R. (2013) 'The structure of knowledge in Westernized Universities: Epistemic racism/sexism and the four genocides/epistemicides of the long 16th century', *Human Architecture: Journal of the Sociology of Self-Knowledge*, 11(1), pp. 73–90.

Harney, S. and Moten, F. (2013) *The undercommons: Fugitive planning and black study*. New York: Autonomedia/Minor Compositions.

hooks, b. (1986) 'Talking Back', *Discourse*, 8, pp. 123–28.

hooks, b. (1994) *Teaching to transgress: Education as the practice of freedom*. New York and London: Routledge.

Icaza, R. and Vázquez, R. (2017) 'Notes on Decolonizing Development' in Estermann, J. (ed.)., *Das Unbehagen an der Entwicklung: Eine andere Entwicklung oder anders als Entwicklung?* Aachen, Germany: CoMundo, pp. 47–62.

Kearns, G. (1997) 'The imperial subject: Geography and travel in the work of Mary Kingsley and Halford Mackinder', *Transactions of the Institute of British Geographers*, 22(4), pp. 450–72.

Kearns, G. (2009) *Geopolitics and empire: The legacy of Halford Mackinder*. Oxford: Oxford University Press.

Khan, T. (2021) 'Decolonisation is a comfortable buzzword in the aid sector', *Open Democracy*, 15 January. Available: www.opendemocracy.net/en/decolonisation-comfortable-buzzword-aid-sector/.

Kothari, A., Salleh, A., Escobar, A., Demaria, F., Acosta, A. (eds.) (2019) *Pluriverse: A post-development dictionary*. New Delhi: Tulika Books.

Jackson, N. A. (2017) '"Social Movement Theory" as a baseline legitimizing narrative: Corporate exploitation, anti-hegemonic opposition and the contested academy', *Human Geography*, 10(1), pp. 36–49. https://doi.org/10.1177/194277861701000104.

Lugones, M. (2008) 'The coloniality of gender', *Worlds & Knowledges Otherwise*, 2(2), pp. 1–17.

Lugones, M. (2010) 'Toward a decolonial feminism', *Hypatia: A Journal of Feminist Philosophy*, 25(4), pp. 742–59.

Mbembe, A. (2017) *Critique of black reason*. Translated by L. Dubois. Durham, NC: Duke University Press.

Mercer, C. and G. Mohan, M. Power (2003) 'Towards a critical political geography of African development', *Geoforum*, 34, pp. 419–36.

McCoy, K., Tuck, E. and McKenzie, M., eds. (2018) *Land education: Rethinking pedagogies of place from Indigenous postcolonial, and decolonizing perspectives.* London: Routledge.

Mignolo, W. (2009) 'Epistemic disobedience, independent thought and decolonial freedom', *Theory, Culture & Society*, 26(7–8), pp. 159–81.

Mignolo, W. (2011) 'Epistemic disobedience and the decolonial option: A manifesto', *Transmodernity*, 1(2), pp. 44–66.

Mignolo, W. and Escobar, A., ed. (2010) *Globalization and the decolonial option*. London: Routledge.

Muhs, G. G. and Harris, A. P., González, C. G., Niemann, Y. F. (2012) *Presumed incompetent: The intersections of race and class for women in academia.* Salt Lake City: Utah State University Press.

Murrey A. (2016) 'The emotional geographies of slow resistance', *Singapore Journal for Tropical Geography*, 37(2), pp. 224–48.

Murrey A. (2020) 'Between assassination and appropriation: Pedagogical disobedience in an era of unfinished decolonisation', *International Journal of Social Economics*, 46(11), pp. 131934.

Ngcobo, L. (1990) *And they didn't die*. London: Virago Press.

Nichols, G. (1984) *The fat black woman's poems*. London: Virago.

Nyamnjoh, N. (2017a) 'Incompleteness: Frontier Africa and the currency of conviviality', *Journal of Asian and African Studies*, 52(3), pp. 253–70.

Nyamnjoh, N. (2017b) *Drinking from the cosmic gourd: How Asmos Tutuola can change our minds*. Buea, Cameroon: Laanga Press.

Pailey, R. (2020) 'De-centring the 'white gaze' of development', *Development and Change*, 51(3), pp. 729–45.

Quijano, A. (2000a) 'Coloniality of power, Eurocentrism, and Latin America', *Nepantla: Views from South*, 1(3), pp. 533–80.

Quijano, A. (2000b) 'Colonialidad del poder y clasificación social', *Journal of World Systems Research*, 6 (2), pp. 342–86.

Raghuram, P. and Madge, C., Noxolo, P. (2009) 'Rethinking responsibility and care for a postcolonial world', *Geoforum*, 40, pp. 5–13.

Rivera Cusicanqui, R. (2012) 'Ch'ixinakax utxiwa: A Reflection on the Practices and Discourses of Decolonization', *South Atlantic Quarterly*, 111(1), pp. 95–109.

Rivera Santana, C. R. and Akhurst, G. (2019) 'Critical creative pedagogies: A decolonial and indigenous approach using visual arts and creative writing', *The Australian Journal of Indigenous Education*, 50(1), pp. 47–54.

Rodney, W. (1990) *How Europe underdeveloped Africa*. London: Bogle-L'Ouverture Publications.

Roy, A., Wright, W. J., Al-Bulushi, Y. and Bledsoe, A. (2020) '"A world of many Souths": (anti)Blackness and historical difference in conversation with Ananya Roy', *Urban Geography*, 41(6), https://doi.org/10.1080/02723638.2020.1807164.

Schuurman, F.J. ed. (1993) *Beyond the impasse: New directions in development theory*. London: Zed Books.

Sidaway, J. D. and Ho, E., Rigg, J. D. Woon, C. Y. (2016) 'Area studies and geography: Trajectories and manifesto', *Environment and Planning D: Society and Space*, 34(5), pp. 777–90.

Smith, L. T. (1999) *Decolonizing methodologies*. London: Zed Books.

Spivak, G. (1988) 'Can the subaltern speak?', *Die Philosophin*, 14(27), pp. 42–58.

Stockwell, S. (2018) *The British end of the British empire*. Cambridge: Cambridge University Press.

Sultana, F. (2019) 'Decolonizing development education and the pursuit of social justice', *Human Geography*, 12(3), pp. 31–46.

Táíwò, O. (2022) *Against decolonisation: Taking African agency seriously*. London: Hurst.

Tilley, L. (2017) 'Resisting piratic method by doing research otherwise', *Sociology*, 51(1), pp. 27–42.

Tuck, E. and Yang, W. (2012) 'Decolonization is not a metaphor', *Decolonization: Indigeneity, Edcuation & Society*, 1(1), pp. 1–40.

Zeleza, P. T. (1997) 'The perpetual solitudes and crises of African studies in the United States', *Africa Today*, 44(2), pp. 193–210.

Zhao, W. and Popkewitz, T. S. (2022) 'Introduction: Critiquing the onto-epistemic coloniality of modernity in/beyond education', *Discourse: Studies in the Cultural Politics of Education*, 43(3), pp. 335–46. DOI: 10.1080/01596306.2022.2041327.

Vitale, A. (2018) *The end of policing*. London: Verso Books.

1

Coloniality, Racial Logics and the Ethos of International Development

Here we begin to analyse and critique, in order to unlearn, the discourse of international development and development geographies. We do this in the only way that we feel is possible from the vantage point of the twenty-first century, and from within an institution such as the University of Oxford: *with fire* (see Johnson et al. 2018).

We are cognisant of, and attempt to respond to, urgent demands from activists and intellectuals about the history, intent, form and production of international development as an interventionist machine and a regime of global significance that perpetuates considerable material and symbolic violence. After decades of cyclical failures from within the field of international development to foster social, economic or ecological justice, we wish to contribute to the political project of abolishing development. In the long tradition of anti-colonial and anti-imperial defiance and disobedience, we assert that a total dismantling of international development is required. Or, to return to the fire metaphor we used to open this chapter, we want to participate in the culling of dead debris and underbrush of development through the blaze of an active fire.

The material and ideological challenges facing us are real. It is therefore necessary to conduct this controlled burning of dangerous, harmful and restrictive colonial-racial ideas and exercises, as we simultaneously try to foster the necessary modes of life-making and social relations that will be able to take seed beyond the violence of capitalism and coloniality. At the core of our shared conversation in this book is the question of how to imagine liveable futures against and beyond the dominant international development ethos, while our lives reside – and thus remain structured within – pervasive forms of the 'coloniality of power' (Quijano 2000a, 2000b). This initial chapter is thus an invitation to our readers to critique the colonial logics at the heart of the development ethos, and to take up the radical collective project of pursuing pluriversal pathways towards intersectional, interspecies and intergenerational justice.

First, we address the ways in which colonial relations and the coloniality of power have been perpetuated beyond the post-independence period. Colonial relations have persisted in and through economic and political relations and social and cultural representations. Within the nexus of coloniality, international development has (a) consistently restricted radical possibilities of 'otherworlds' and (b) facilitated the maintenance of certain forms of coloniality.

Next, we consider the function of 'whiteness-as-benevolence', or alternatively 'whiteness-as-expertise-and-authority', and the ways in which (a) this phenomenon is erased from popular discourse and (b) this conception of whiteness depends on spectacles of the racialized Other. To expose the complex ways in which colonial racializations work within the international development ethos (often in obscured forms), we look at the international Save Darfur Campaign and the Kony2012 Campaign. We engage with humorous and comedic critiques of the development ethos that demystify its racialized and colonial logics. We further question how activists and intellectuals gaze back at the empire, and accordingly at the practitioners of development.

ANTICOLONIAL AND DECOLONIAL SOUNDTRACK

We begin our consideration with aspiration, with dreaming, with fire in the gut. A wonderful song which captures this energy is 'Mon Souhait' ('My Hope') (2012) by the Cameroonian reggae group Sumanja. In this song, Soumalek sings in his characteristic bass that, 'my dream is that joy reigns the world . . . that misfortune transforms into happiness': https://open.spotify.com/track/2Z1gR6ozRxJzMWTVqYp2HG

A NOTE ON TERMS

We begin below with what may appear to be an intimidating or confusing set of terms: 'coloniality', 'the coloniality of power' and 'racializing logics'. We understand that these terms may be challenging or intimidating to some readers. Their significance may entail, for certain readers, an unlearning of long-held, and often hidden, beliefs about themselves or their communities and countries. For other readers, this discussion may reinforce the kinds of knowledge that they bring to this conversation, including intergenerational experiences of the violent belief systems that permitted and enacted real and epistemic violence against themselves and their communities. We ask you to stay with the conversation even if it provokes discomfort and unease. As you encounter these terms, allow yourself to feel the fullness of your response, in all its complexity, as well as to engage deeply with the histories and the worldview imparted through them. It is necessary to think, on an ongoing basis, about how your engagement with these terms might reveal aspects of your own experiences to you, and mirror and build on your education more broadly, or to stand in contradiction to what you have learnt elsewhere.

This book should not be a dispassionate read. Dispassionate readers tend to lose clarity about what is at stake in critical conversations about the uneven geographies of international development. Even if you are compelled to read this for work or study in a neoliberal university – for an exam or for assessment (and therefore as a constitutive part of your entrance into the bourgeois class!), we encourage you to practice reading and thinking *against* the dominant demobilizing patterns that would render reading into a static, solitary and emotionless practice. As you read these conversations, keep in mind the real, material impact of ideas. Although these are words on a page, *you are reading about real people*. Do not forget that we are writing about people's lives, nor that we, Amber and Patricia, are communicating ideas with you as individuals with politicized bodies and identities. We are neither above nor outside the coloniality that we critique here, a coloniality that structures and contours our institutional and personal selves.

It is essential that our decolonial vocabularies do not become abstracted from the material conditions of people's lives and from struggles for decolonial justice. Decolonial theories are not detached concepts to be mapped onto abstract truths. Action is directed through words and concepts, which is why they are important. Power is exercised through discourse, including the power to *determine the possible*. The production of discourse under conditions of unequal power is what Chandra Mohanty (1984) calls 'the colonialist move'. The instrumentalization of particular concepts within the hegemonic discourses of international development occurs within a system in which the Global North maintains a certain dominance over the rest of the world. Words and concepts therefore have profound political, economic and cultural effects.

Language is a powerful tool that we can use collaboratively to build towards and fight for liveable futures. We choose our words carefully here, because we hold ourselves accountable to communities of struggle, and because we refuse to endorse colonial practices of dispossession, extraction, land enclosure and exclusion. We therefore choose to interrogate and move away from the use of certain terms. Dominant institutions, as well as regressive and oppressive individuals, are often adept in their use of language and have the capacity to appropriate the radical language of dissent and to foster confusion and mistrust within progressive alliances. The economic geographer Gillian Hart (2009: 121) writes that, '[d]evelopment can operate as much as a discourse of entitlement as a discourse of control'. As (un)learners and students of and against international development, we have a responsibility to read with keen passion, and with rage and sorrow, and to challenge the misappropriations of radical and decolonial language and projects that continue within long-established hegemonic structures.

COLONIALITY, THE COLONIALITY OF POWER, AND COLONIAL VIOLENCE

Our definition of 'coloniality' draws from post-colonial scholarship, post-development scholarship and critical decolonial analysis of the 'coloniality of being'. The 'post-colonial moment' is characterized by the persistence of colonial violence into the present. The idealizing promises of development played an important part in obscuring the ongoing violence at the core of development ideologies and the colonial metropoles, while alluding to a better future on the horizon for people in colonized or formerly colonized nations. The coloniality of power refers to the structures of power, control and hegemony that have emerged in our contemporary epoch, and that lock states into perpetual trajectories of neo-colonial relations. The coloniality of power delineates the differential organization of people and places along racialized lines to fulfil the requirements of capital, and principally capital accumulation (Quijano 2000a).

International development cannot be understood through discourse analysis alone. Arturo Escobar (1995) encourages us to understand the emergence of 'development' in the 1940s as a phenomenon accompanied by 'specific forms of modernized violence' (see Chapter 3). Some of the foundational characteristics of development align with those forms of racialized violence that emerged around 1493, at the colonial moment of

35

contact. International development emerged within and as a mechanism of the coloniality of power, and it has been instrumental to the fostering of a discourse of modernization, by which we mean the illusion of a path for human and planetary wellbeing via endless capitalist growth and expansion, the hierarchization of social groups and the emergence of different kinds of 'techno-utopia's. Mainstream development discourse maintains that poverty is an apolitical and often ahistorical phenomena that can be mitigated through corrective financial calculations, socio-environmental equations and external interventions (see also Chapter 3). The development ethos functions on the reverse-side of the material violence of the modern 'coloniality of being', or what the Argentinian decolonial scholar Walter Mignolo (2011) has termed the 'darker side of modernity'. This concept names the sanitized modern version of global history, which maintains a conviction that infinite economic growth is not only possible but imperative, and that social wellbeing and 'modernity' can be achieved only through continuous economic growth. The study of international development is therefore the study of particular but kaleidoscopic forms of complex violence that underpin globalized racial capitalism today.

These ideas are explored further in Chapter 3, where we consider Cameroonian scholar Achille Mbembe's 'necropolitics' – a concept he refines to capture the ways in which colonial politics and pathologies, including its fears and violence, are contemporaneous. Mbembe argues that vast majorities of the post-colonial world have long been governed by 'necropolitics', which names the structural and historical vulnerabilities shared by colonized and marginalized groups, and which are undergirded by ever present threats of annihilation (see Chapter 3). Colonial power is not, however, solely in the hands of the colonizer, nor is it unidirectional. Frantz Fanon, for instance, understood the psychological harms of the relationship between the colonizer and the colonized to be mutually destructive. People have historical agency, and decolonial resistance to development studies seeks to recover possibilities for development outside modern, Eurocentric frameworks (as we explore in Chapters 5, 6, 7 and 8).

THE RACIALIZING LOGICS OF DEVELOPMENT AND ITS WHITE GAZE

In 2018, stories began circulating online about Renee Bach, an eighteen-year-old white American woman who had been living in Masese,

Uganda. Bach was a high school graduate, a missionary, and a 'health-saviour' who worked with the American non-profit organization, Serving His Children. This religious organization claimed to combine child malnutrition awareness programming and treatment with the 'love of Jesus'. Bach, known locally as the '*mzungu* doctor' (the 'white doctor'), had no formal medical training but had nonetheless been performing medical procedures on young children and posting her reflections about these experiences online. In January 2019, Bach was sued by Brenda Gimbo and Annet Kakai, two mothers whose children died while in Bach's care. Bach has since returned to the USA, and the legal case is ongoing. This is just one example from among many that demonstrates the ongoing material urgency of issues that arise from the intersections between racism, whiteness (including whiteness-as-expertise) and knowledge in development geographies.

Nonetheless, even today, it continues to be unusual for a development studies course to open with a discussion of the significance of racialization, racial difference and racial logics in international development discourse and practice (Murrey 2019; Patel 2020). Uma Kothari powerfully criticized the silence surrounding questions of race and power in development in 2006, calling out the figure of the white humanitarian who gets to define what constitutes the Other and sets the parameters for the problem to be addressed inevitably imagining the humanitarian subject as the '(only) solution'. Following Kothari's prompting, the development studies scholar and anti-racist practitioner Kamna Patel (2020) examined the frequency – or, rather, infrequency – of the use of the terms 'race', 'racial' and 'racism' in 9,280 peer-reviewed journal articles in development studies in English in the thirteen years since 2006, when Kothari published the call for more attention to be paid to race in development studies. Less than 1 per cent of the papers surveyed mention or engage with race and racism (a mere 24 of 9,280). Patel (2020: 1473) writes:

The implications and danger of this [ongoing silencing of race], especially in light of an institutional reluctance to intertwine material and discursive race-work in moves to 'decolonise the centre', is a hollow skirting with decolonisation and the parsing of deep engagement with the power of whiteness in shaping the content of our disciplinary discussions and the environment in which knowledge is produced and valued.

Racialization and racism have tended to be erased from, or to reside only at the margins of, the practice and the study of development for most of its disciplinary lifespan. This has, in consequence, produced a certain degree of ignorance towards the ways in which racial difference and racialization influence development's structures and forms. In contrast, racialized thinking and racial difference are central to our discussion of critical development geographies, and constitute the first theme that we address with our students and readers.

Race shapes material structures of power and the distribution of resources. In Chapter 2, we look at the ways in which poverty does not emerge statically, but is in fact actively produced. Racial ideologies are foundational to various forms of development through the cultivation of the 'Other'. This Other is racialized as non-white and non-Western, and is variously victimized, rendered disposable, criminalized, deprived of rights, or defined as corrupt. The French philosopher Étienne Balibar (2005) describes this form of modern socio-cultural racism as a 'racism without races', where terms such as 'culture' and 'ethnicity' are used to allude to race, but race itself is never explicitly named (see also Elliott-Cooper 2021). Terms such as 'overpopulation' and 'illiterate', for instance, often function as racialized signifiers within the discourse of international development (Pierre 2019; Tilley and Ajl 2022).

Many scholars, activists and practitioners are building an anti-racist praxis within development studies, including a critique of the roles and functions of whiteness. The coloniality of power organizes people with differential and racializing effects, and in so doing entrenches structures of racialized privilege and power (Quijano 2000; Ndlovu-Gatsheni 2023). Here, we return to the colonial archive to address historic expressions of the development ethos that remain present today, including the central racialized subjectivities and categories that continue to orient actions, thinking and beliefs in development, namely, spectacles of suffering and notions of white benevolence. These constitute a foundational myth in the justification for colonial projects as so-called 'civilizing missions'.[1] Framing violent colonial expansion as a 'civilizing mission' means

---

1. The 'civilizing mission' (in French 'la mission civilisatrice' and in Portuguese 'missão civilizadora') arose from the idea that Western society was the most advanced in terms of human development and was used to justify colonialism. Europeans and later the US would argue that colonization was not about economic extraction but had a higher purpose: that was to 'civilize' the indigenous peoples.

that colonialists have propagated the idea that colonial domination has benefited native and colonized peoples. Imperial claims to benign humanitarianism and development emerge through this European colonial discourse.

Daybreak in Udi (1949), the first Nigerian film to win an Oscar, is a compelling example of the kind of racialized-colonial thinking that privileges whiteness and celebrates colonial subjects who are (seemingly) receptive to forms of colonial intervention. According to the film's description, *Daybreak in Udi*:

> highlights the effort of a small community to build a maternity centre amidst the opposition of some village men. The British colonial officer in charge of the Udi . . . District was asked to help in the project. He helped and provided materials and motivation for the community. But in the end, it was the villager's willingness to bring change and improve their community that triumphed.

The film perpetuates the myth of a paternalistic relationship between the people and the colonial officer. Many of the Nigerians in the fictional film embody the trope of the 'good' colonial subject, who wish to Westernise and have internalized colonial ideas of 'progress'. In the film, these people are pitted against other members of the community who are cast as 'traditional' and 'backwards', and against those who actively seek to disrupt the projects of the 'well-behaved' and 'ideal' colonial subjects. Colonial logics maintain a hierarchy of the human that has been legitimized through racialized dichotomies of the modern against the traditional, and the civilized against the barbaric. Interventions in the name of development were endorsed by the explicit and implicit hierarchies that positioned Eurocentric approaches to social advancement as superior. Pervasive racializing logics have enabled these colonial classifications of difference to be carried through into contemporary development practices. This phenomenon, however, is not always straightforward nor easy to identify, precisely because modern coloniality operates by obscuring and denying the significance of racializing processes in global capitalist society. The premise of 'underdevelopment' is that there is a *lack* or a *negation* that needs to be addressed or countered, and that this can take place most effectively through the 'aid' of an external 'expert'.

The documentary film *Concerning Violence* includes colonial archival footage from Moshi, a town in northern Tanzania. Some of the foundational forms of racial difference that are embedded within colonial projects and presented as 'civilizing' are evident from certain scenes. The documentary takes its name from the chapter in Frantz Fanon's *The Wretched of the Earth* titled 'On Violence' and is narrated by Lauryn Hill. In one scene, two white Dutch colonialists are asked about the aims of their Christian mission, and about any religious developments that they have noticed in the country. Throughout the scene, Tanzanian labourers can be seen in the background digging trenches for the foundation of a new church. The visible material discrepancies between the clean clothes of the missionaries and the men and children labouring in the background, are unaddressed by the clip, which we will return to below.

The narrative of the 'civilizing mission' was consistently employed to justify colonial occupation, extraction and racial violence. David Jefferess (2015: 5) argues that '[h]umanitarianism can be understood as an orientation of whiteness, in part because it affirms the caring subject while refusing to recognize the racialized trajectories of global material inequality and its apparent solution, humanitarianism'. While colonial-developmental Othering occurs across post-colonial societies, it has been especially destructive within African geographies. Violent European intervention along the North, Central and West African coasts signalled the origins of modern coloniality. We cannotprovide an extensive world history, however, a brief reference to colonialism's historical origins is useful here. The beginning of the *longue durée* of coloniality is generally dated to August 6, 1444, when six ships, chartered by the Portuguese Lagos Company, captured 240 West and Central Africans and forcibly transported them to Lagos, Portugal, under the patronage of Prince Henry. In the fifty years prior to Columbus's voyage, Portugal was already importing between 1,000 and 3,000 enslaved Africans a year. The Cameroonian film-maker Jean-Marie Téno captures the reality of post-colonial life in Africa in his 1992 film, *Afrique, je te plumeria* ('Africa, I Will Fleece You'). In the classroom, this film can be screened to illustrate the longevities of coloniality and colonial modes of violence into modern societies.

The 'ethos' of international development – what Escobar (1995) calls the 'desiring machine' – developed throughout the colonial period and persists under present-day forms of coloniality and racial capitalism. Kothari's (2005, 2006) work traces the ongoing relationship between colonial forms of rule and governance and the purpose and practice of development, encouraging us to see the transition from 'colonialism' to 'development cooperation' not as a rupture but as a progression, where new language and talking points might be employed but power inequalities and the unequal violence(s) of global geopolitics remain. She writes, 'traces of colonialism . . . pervade the workings of the post-independence international development aid industry' (2005). Colonial relations persist in representations of development and in development practices. International development discourse has universalized the 'Global South' and the majority world into a homogenous group (Chapter 4). This is evident today in child or village sponsorship advertisements, for instance, where despite humanitarianism purporting to be 'colour-blind', racialized children are rendered spectacles of suffering that both reflect an 'ideal of universal childhood, [but] yet their "need" is distinguished in part by how they must look "different" or "ethnic" to show that they are "Other" children' (Kothari 2016). However, as Kothari (2016) writes:

> it would be a mistake to suggest that present-day development discourse is simply a reworking of a (neo) colonial one since development is not always and inevitably an extension of colonialism . . . however, we [also] need to be wary of histories of development that deny this colonial genealogy and attempt to create distinct and artificial boundaries between the exploitation of empire and the humanitarianism of development.

The 'development ethos' is thus constituted by the ideologies, institutions and practices associated with the distinct project of intervention in the Global South, and with the so-called 'will to improve' (Li 2007), or particular condition within neoliberal capitalism in which postcolonial peoples self-subject to the whims and wills of capital growth (Kothari et al. 2005; Livingston 2019). This abiding by the ills and wills of capital is perhaps its most nefarious form. This is a seeming conundrum that must be approached in any serious classroom of the colonial condition: what does it mean when the illusions of development become part of the nostalgia of the people in the post-colonial world? Development's stated central rationale is that intervention improves welfare, encourages growth, and instigates progress. There is an important distinction, however, between the stated and unstated rationales of the sector, because international development entails managed and unmanaged adjustment, conversion and transformation (Shivji 2006). To understand the unmanaged or unanticipated aspects of international development, the work of postdevelopment and anti-imperial thinkers is useful to show how the 'good intentions' of development work often does not fulfil those intentions (Forte 2014). However, this work *does* affect other changes – it does *do* something (Maren 1997; Ferguson 1990). Tracing these things becomes the task for the prudent student (un)learning development.

RACIALIZATION AND COLONIALITY IN THE 'SAVE DARFUR' CAMPAIGN

The Ugandan political theorist Mahmood Mamdani engages with developmentalist interventions in *Saviors and Survivors: Darfur, Politics, and the War on Terror* (2009). Here, Mamdani traces the artificial tribalization of groups and governance in Darfur by British colonizers, who created hierarchies of indigenous peoples through their implementation of specific administrative practices, bifurcating groups between the settler Arabs and native African (Zurga) races, and effectively pitting them against one another in a common colonial strategy called 'divide and rule'.

The 2003 Darfur conflict, which Mamdani presents as a bloody and brutal counterinsurgency, was a consequence of this earlier tribalization of political and cultural identities. Mamdani argues that, despite the significant and Western colonial rule for the political conflict in the region, Western humanitarian agencies and groups – under the auspices of the Save Darfur Coalition – quickly declared the conflict a 'genocide', framing the struggle in moral terms, because it was politically expedient for them to do so.

Mamdani's analysis demonstrates that claims that the conflict was a genocide were bolstered by misleading, and sometimes even fictional, data on mortalities. These claims were necessary to condone military intervention, including an increase in defence spending, and to further underwrite the US creation of US Africa Command – the military command base that oversees the African continent – which was being rolled out at precisely this time to address US energy and resource needs and to confront competition with China. In the Save Darfur Coalition, the perpetuation of colonialism's historical legacies was manifested through the development ethos: the continuation of oppressive institutional and administrative structures, and the dominance of imperial agencies within the nexus of global power relations.

The coalition naturalized the racialized colonial narrative that attempted to rationalize the conflict in primordial terms as a struggle between imperial Arabs and subjugated native Africans (Mamdani 2009). The example of the Save Darfur Coalition demonstrates how African sovereignty can be undermined by the supposedly 'benevolent international community' in the name of protection, justice and rule of law (Mamdani 2009). There are numerous more recent examples of similar kinds of situations, including the French intervention in Cote d'Ivoire in 2011; the No-Fly zone in Libya in 2010 (when US President Barack Obama responded with military force against Ghaddafi, in the name of protecting the people of Libya); the US pressure to remove Nicolas Maduro in Venezuela in 2011, amongst other examples. Feminist scholars, including Chandra Mohanty (1984) and Patricia McFadden (2000, 2008, 2016), critique the kind of Western feminism that endorses military intervention in the name of 'saving' brown women (see also Tilley and Ajl 2022).

In addition to reinforcing and reproducing colonial and racist explanations for the origins of the violence and undermining and subverting any possibilities for African agency and self-determination under the guise of 'protection', Mamdani shows that the popularization of the Save Darfur Coalition in the first decade of the twenty-first century distracted domestic attention away from the 2003 invasion of Iraq by nearly 200,000 US-led troops. This was tremendously significant for the stabilization of American imperialism. In the USA, Mamdani explains, 'Darfur was presented as a moral rather than a political issue'. Comparing Americans' response to Iraq at the same time, he argues that 'those who march for Save Darfur were responding as humans with a moral obligation, not as citizens'. The conflict in Darfur was easier for Americans to campaign around, because doing so was 'an act not of responsibility but of philanthropy – of largeness of heart . . . cause(s) about which they can feel good'. Iraq and Afghanistan, on the other hand, 'make some Americans feel responsible and guilty to come to terms with the limits of American power'. As one of the authors of this book (Amber), who was a university undergraduate at the University of Seattle in 2004, it is hard to overstate the popularity of Save Darfur on American college campuses at the time.

It is also significant to note that the Save Darfur movement was not expressed in explicitly or directly racial terms. Rather, it was underpinned by 'racial thinking', which erased colonial histories, reifies racializing tribal signifiers and ascribes moral integrity and superiority to predominantly college-educated people in the West. The critical race theorist and scholar of queer studies David L. Eng (2008: 1497) notes that since the emergence of racial thinking in the European Enlightenment, 'race has always appeared as disappearing'.

In response to possible questions about the importance of the good intentions of Save Darfur volunteers and activists, which might seem to preclude the possibility of these individuals being racist, it is important to note that even as racism within humanitarian groups can be obscured, racial thinking and racist ideas continue to structure the development ethos. The motivation for the Save Darfur Coalition can be understood as similar to the impetus behind the colonial 'civilizing mission', which was, ultimately, the moral and ethical salvation of the colonizers, who had a God-given duty to help colonial subjects transition into modernity because they were also motivated to save themselves (in the eyes of their lord). In *Humanitarianism and Suffering: The Mobilization of Empathy*, Wilson and Brown (2009) explore the relationship between public sentiments and participation in humanitarian projects. The ability to impact and influence public sentiment regarding people at a distance has long been instrumental in moving people to act.

RACIALIZATION AND COLONIALITY
IN THE #KONY2012 CAMPAIGN

In 'Rescuing African Bodies: Celebrities, Consumerism and Neoliberal Humanitarianism', published in 2013, Patricia Daley contends with the racist and developmentalist framings of intervention. Within the context of global anti-black racism, Daley analyses the ways in which African bodies become sites for the expression of white and Western celebrity agency through individualized, publicly celebrated humanitarian acts. This kind of 'development work', she argues, entrenches racist ideas about African cultures and peoples, precisely in the name of 'saving' them. Daley describes the ways in which these kinds of individualized celebrity action constitute significant, highly publicized events that contribute to the maintenance of global capitalism. 'Celebrities', she maintains:

play an intermediary role, making market relations and its effects acceptable at the core through consumption at the periphery via humanitarian intervention. Central to this process is how humanitarian crises are framed by these Western cultural elites – often in opposition to African agency and progressive social movements. Crises are decontextualized and non-consumerist and radical political agendas are represented as flawed. Celebrities act to steer global mass political engagement away from those that are antagonistic towards capital, therefore, undermining the potential for global cohesion around emancipatory politics. (Daley 2013: 377)

Daley considers the case of #Kony2012, a campaign launched by the American charity Invisible Children that aimed to draw attention to the realities of young people affected by conflict in Uganda, which mirrors many of the themes discussed in relation to the Save Darfur Campaign. The twenty-nine-minute film, launched online in early March 2012, was the first humanitarian video to go viral, garnering more than 26 million views in its first four days on the Internet, while the #StopKony hashtag trended on Twitter and Facebook. The video is a characteristic example of the ways in which white agency and benevolence are celebrated, while being positioned alongside inaccurate and limited explanations of the conflict, which simplify the viewer's understanding, thereby reinforcing racial stereotypes and endorsing Western military intervention. Jason Russell, a white, male, American activist, narrates the video. Describing Joseph Kony to the viewers, he declares that:

His forces are believed to have slaughtered tens of thousands of people and are known for hacking the lips off their victims. Kony has been wanted by the international criminal court since 2005 on charges that include crimes against humanity. He has been living in the bush outside Uganda since that time.

The US designated the LRA a terrorist group after September 11, and in 2008 began actively supporting the Ugandan military. In October, the president deployed 100 combat-equipped troops – mostly special operations forces – to Uganda to advise regional military units in capturing or killing Kony. (Russell, speaking in 2012 film, Kony2012)

The #Kony2012 campaign promoted an action called 'Cover the Night', which called on the public to plaster the phrase '#Kony2012' in as many places as possible by 20 April 2012. This involved encouraging the public to purchase fliers and bumper stickers emblazoned with Joseph Kony's face to stick to laptops and on public walls and pavements; to tweet and re-tweet the image; to 'like' #Kony2012 social media posts; and to purchase T-shirts, plastic bracelets and other items from the #Kony2012 'action kit'.

Daley (2013) argues that this kind of 'performative action does not require solidarity and can be devoid of any critical or radical urge'. The campaign came under considerable international pressure for: (1) spreading misinformation about the location, size and scale of the conflict, including inflating the numbers of children that had been abducted as child soldiers; (2) the misuse of funds, by spending money on the promotion of the informational campaign rather than on any real change on the ground; and (3) endorsing US military support and intervention in the region. In her filmed reaction to the campaign, the Ugandan journalist Rosebell Kagumire (2012) critiqued the video as dated and noted that she could not even determine the purpose of the video for the first five minutes.

The group released a second video, *#Kony2012 Part II: Beyond Famous,* which did not go viral. This video includes Ugandan civil society members, but uses a normative developmentalist ethos that echoes, rather than challenges, the directives of the first film. These are examples of the ways in which social media activism reproduces racially segregated communities while granting its (predominantly white, structurally advantaged) audience the pleasure of imagining themselves as anti-racist. Sara Ahmed (2007: 154) explains that in a sense, 'whiteness is an orientation that puts certain things within reach. By objects we would include not just physical objects, but also styles, capacities, aspirations, techniques, habits'.

It is also important to note that in our supposedly 'post-racial' present (i.e. the contemporaneous Euro-American political climate in which racism is deemed to be archaic and a thing relevant only to our understanding of the past), the more 'positive images' that are being used in humanitarian marketing today are no less demeaning or implicitly racist. In such marketing, the success and accomplishments of the recipient of aid are presented as possible exclusively through the care and material gifts of white benefactors (Daley 2013). The Nigerian-American novelist and political commentator Teju Cole (2012) characterized the #Kony2012 campaign as being part of the 'white-saviour industrial complex'. He writes,

> Africa has provided a space onto which white egos can conveniently be projected . . . the complex conceives of complicated problems of gross material inequality and suffering as merely problems of care. (Cole 2012: n.p.)

The 'white-saviour industrial complex' names the pervasive phenomenon in which Euro-Americans, often white and economically privileged, imagine themselves as saviours, as helpers, for people in the Global South. This kind of action, Cole writes, tends to be 'performative altruism': posturing or public displays of goodness intended to impress, or mislead, and which serve to empower the giver/helper and disempower the receiver (themes we explore in greater length in Chapter 2). Cole (2012: n.p.) argues that '[a]ll the saviour sees is need, and he sees no need to reason out the need for need'. White-saviour behaviours ignore the complex histories of racism, colonialism and capitalism.

BARBIE SAVIOUR AND MUZUNGU COMICS

Humorous and creative critiques have done important work to de-naturalize whiteness and raise awareness of the role of racialization and racism within international development, including the *Barbie Saviour* Instagram account, which provides commentary on white saviourhood. Against the prioritization of Eurocentric epistemological frameworks, and Western paternalistic attitudes towards the targets of development intervention, *Muzungu Comics* also contends with the microaggressions of bourgeois 'good intentions' in development spaces. Such comedic critiques of development can provide a compelling foundation for rich classroom debates and uncomfortable conversations. These materials encourage both novice and advanced learners to become cognisant of and to expose racialized ways of thinking within development practices and development studies.

A 2014 Saturday Night Live (SNL) skit, *39 Cents*, looks back at racialized tropes of the 'African village' as palatable for and receptive to the colonial 'civilizing mission'. In a classroom setting, we show students

47

excerpts of the 1949 British colonial film *Daybreak in Udi*, set in the Nigerian town of the same name. There is a particularly powerful moment in the film when several Nigerians appeal to a British colonial official for his assistance and expertise in bringing modernization and development to the town. The film is an example of colonial filmic propaganda, depicting British colonialism as well-intentioned and beneficial, and the community as divided, yet ultimately sympathetic to and receptive of British intervention.

We follow these excerpts with a screening of *39 Cents*. In the skit, the members of an unnamed village are outraged by the insignificant sums of money being requested by the solemn white, male actor who is visiting their town to film a promotional video for a non-profit organization. Three of the black community members are vocally scornful of the marketing campaign, questioning how the monthly request for donations of '39 cents' was calculated, and ridiculing the sum as insufficient. 'Ask for more!', one calls out to the white man at one point. The white man responds, '39 cents is exactly what these people need', in an attempt to reaffirm his privilege and power as an expert. The skit presents a critique of international aid as an apparatus that perpetuates 'mere survival' for communities of colour.

DEVELOPMENT AND THE COLONIAL MATRIX OF POWER

The Mexican post-development thinker Gustavo Esteva (2010) calls development a 'new colonial episode', amounting to a 'huge and irresponsible experiment' that we need to abandon. Meanwhile, the Uruguayan political ecologist Eduardo Gudynas (2011) describes development as a 'zombie category', because while its looming death has been permanently (re)announced in cyclical fashion since the 1980s, it seems ever-capable of resuscitation. The German sociologist Wolfgang Sachs (1992: n.p.) refers to development as a 'plastic word [and] an empty term' that, 'even at its birth . . . was designed to make the world in the image of the United States of America'. As an organizing framework, development effects a disavowal of other ways of living and of existing. Escobar (1995) thus characterizes the history of development as, 'the history of the loss of an illusion, in which many genuinely believed'. He writes:

> The fact that most people's conditions did not only not improve but deteriorated with the passing of time did not seem to bother most experts. Reality, in sum, had been colonized by the development discourse, and those who were dissatisfied with this state of affairs had to struggle for bits and pieces of freedom within it, in the hope that in the process a different reality could be constructed. (Escobar 1995: 5)

Following Escobar, we might prod our readers to ask whether development has 'colonized reality'. As with other illusions – or, even, delusions – the authenticity of the belief is not important. What we mean by this is that it is unimportant whether individual development practitioners believe in doing good or have good intentions. The material, epistemic and relational outcomes of the development illusion are more significant. (This is a theme that will emerge and re-emerge throughout our conversations here.)

The discursive power of development, as an ethos, functions not merely to inform action, legitimise humanitarian interventions and construct representations of people and places as 'undeveloped'. It also acts as an apparatus of promise and obfuscation that preserves economic inequalities by framing and delegitimizing them as somehow culturally or environmentally specific. The root idea – both in the academy and in popular culture – that societies are *un*-developed because they *lack* something creates the context for a solution-oriented response. The nature of what is lacking has been long debated: from a lack of self-control, to a lack of environmental abundance, work ethic, education, or financial investment. It is this epistemic premise that has fostered the orienting logic that the Global South, and Africa in particular, is a 'problem' (Daley and Murrey 2022a).

Development continues to be central to contemporary geopolitical debates and relations, as well as to subjective experiences of knowing, seeing and being – and to the social worth of different groups. As an illusion, development simultaneously endorses and negates particular ways of being and thinking. Notable possibilities that development forecloses, for instance, are conversations on repair, which has been offered as a terminology and a framework that might offer an alternative to the development ethos: 'Some argue we should talk about "repair" rather than aid, as doing so would make explicit the systematic reparations for the violence imposed by donor countries in their colonial past' (Peace

Direct 2021). To fully understand the imperative of the political project of repair in the wake of international development, we must recognize the harms effected on the ecologies, socio-economies and people of the South in the name of capitalist development in the Global North. This is the subject of our next chapter on the relationship between capitalism, development and active impoverishment.

QUESTIONS FOR FURTHER THOUGHT

We have said that there are many different definitions and understandings of development, however, not all definitions of development are equal or accurate. Explain.

Kamna Patel (2020) asks, '[w]ithin our disciplinary debates and research (with implications for development practice through our teaching of would-be practitioners), why is race largely absent as an analytical lens?' How might you respond to this question?

What is the relationship between intervention and the development ethos?

'Some traditional accounts of development may work to encourage students in wealthy countries to imagine that "development" does not really concern them; it happens in other places (places called the "Third World", the "developing world", the "Global South" or the "non-West").' How and to what extent are we, as Cheryl McEwan (2018) argues, 'all implicated in development'?

Is comedy an effective method for challenging racism and/or whiteness in development discourse? Why, or why not?

REFERENCES

Ahmed, S. (2007) 'A phenomenology of whiteness', *Feminist Theory*, 8(2). https://doi.org/10.1177/1464700107078139.

Balibar, É. (2005) 'The construction of racism', *Actuel Marx*, 38(2), pp. 11–28.

Cole, T. (2012) 'The White-Savior Industrial Complex', *The Atlantic*, 21 March. Available: www.theatlantic.com/international/archive/2012/03/the-white-savior-industrial-complex/254843/.

Daley, P. O. (2007) *Gender and genocide in Burundi: The search for spaces of peace in the Great Lakes Region*. Oxford: James Currey.

Daley, P. O. (2013) 'Rescuing African bodies: Celebrities, consumerism and neoliberal humanitarianism', *Review of African Political Economy*, 40(137), pp. 375–93.

Daley, P. O. (2007) *Gender and genocide in Burundi: The search for spaces of peace in the great lakes region*. Washington, D.C.: Georgetown University Press.

Elliott-Cooper, A. (2021) *Black resistance to British policing*. Manchester: Manchester University Press.

Eng, D. L. (2008) 'The end(s) of race', *PMLA*, 123(5), pp. 1479–93.

Escobar, A. (1995) *Encountering development: The making and unmaking of the Third World* Durham, NC: Duke University Press.

Esteva. G. (2019[2010]) 'What is development?' in *Oxford Research Encyclopedia of International Studies*. Oxford University Press. https://oxfordre.com/internationalstudies/internationalstudies/abstract/10.1093/acrefore/9780190846626.001.0001/acrefore-9780190846626-e-360.

Furnivall, J. S. (2008) 'The background of colonial policy and practice' in *The Development Reader*, edited by Sharad Chari and Stuart Corbridge. London and New York: Routledge.

Grosfoguel, R. (2008a) 'Transmodernity, border thinking and global coloniality: Decolonizing polticial economy and postcolonial studies', *Eurozine*, 4 July. Available: https://bit.ly/2FkCmwk (Accessed 13 April).

Grosfoguel, R. (2008b) 'World-system analysis and postcolonial studies: A call for a dialogue from the "Coloniality of Power" approach', in *The Postcolonial and the Global*, edited by Krishnaswamy Revathi and John C. Hawley, Minneapolis and London: University of Minnesota Press, pp. 94–104.

Hall, S. (1996) 'The West and the rest: Discourse and power' in *Modernity*, edited by Stuart Hall et al., Oxford: Blackwell, pp. 185–227.

Hancock, G. (1989) *Lords of poverty: The free-wheeling lifestyles of power, prestige and corruption of the multi-million dollar aid business*. London: Macmillan.

Hart, G. (2009) 'Development critiques in the 1990s: culs de sac and promising paths', *Progress in Human Geography*, 25(4), pp. 649–58.

Jefferess, D. (2015) 'Introduction: The "white man's burden" and post-racial humanitarianism', *Critical Race and Whiteness Studies*, 11(1), pp. 1–13.

Kothari, U. (2005) 'Introduction' in *A radical history of development studies: Individuals, institutions and ideologies*, Kothari, U. (ed.) London: Zed Books.

Kothari, U. (2006) 'An agenda for thinking about "race" in International Development', *Progress in Development Studies* 6(1), https://doi.org/10.1191/1464993406ps124o.

Li, T. M. (2007) *The will to improve: Governmentality, development and the practice of politics*. Durham, NC: Duke University Press.

Mamdani, M. (2009) *Saviors and survivors: Darfur, politics, and the War on Terror*. New York: Doubleday.

Mawdsley, E. and Taggart, J. (2021) 'Rethinking d/Development', in *Progress in Human Geography*, 46(1), pp. 3–20.

Mamdani, M. (201) *Saviors and survivors: Darfur, politics, and the War on Terror*. New York: Doubleday.

McFadden, P. (2008) "Interrogating Americana: An African feminist critique" in Riley, Mohanty and Pratt (eds.), *Feminism and war: Confronting US Imperialism*. London: Zed Books, pp. 56–67.

Mignolo, W. and Escobar, A. eds. (2013) *Globalization and the decolonial option*. New York and London: Routledge.

Mignolo, W. and Tlostanova, M. V. (2009) 'Global coloniality and the decolonial option', *Kult*, 6, pp. 130–47.

Mohanty, C. T. (1984) 'Under Western eyes: Feminist scholarship and colonial discourses', *Boundary 2*, 12/13(3/1), pp. 333–58.

Ndlovu-Gatsheni, S. (2012) 'Beyond the equator there are no sins: Coloniality of being in Africa', *Journal of Developing Societies*, 28(4), pp. 419–40.

Ndlovu-Gatsheni, S. J. (2023) 'Beyond the coloniser's model of the world: Towards reworlding from the Global South'. *Third World Quarterly*. DOI:10.1080/01436 597.2023.2171389.

Pailey, R. N. (2019) 'De-centring the "white gaze" of development', *Development and Change*, 51(3), pp. 729–45.

Patel, K. (2020) 'Race and a decolonial turn in development studies', *Third World Quarterly* 41(9), pp. 1463–75. DOI: 10.1080/01436597.2020.1784001.

Pierre, J. (2019) 'The racial vernaculars of development: A view from Africa', *American Anthropologist*, 122(1), pp. 86–98.

Quijano, A. (2000a) 'Coloniality of power, Eurocencrism, and Latin America', *Nepantla: Views from South*, 1(3), pp. 533–80.

Quijano, A. (2000b) 'Colonialidad del poder y clasificación social', *Journal of World Systems Research*, 6(2), pp. 342–86.

Rodney, W. (1973) *How Europe underdeveloped Africa*. London and Dar-Es-Salaam: Bogle-L'Ouverture Publications.

Sachs, W. (2019) 'Foreword: The development dictionary revisited', in *Pluriverse: A post-development dictionary*, edited by A. Kothari, A. Salleh, A. Escobar, F. Demaria, and A. Acosta. New Delhi: Tulika Books, xi–xvi.

Shivji, I. G. (2006) 'The silences in the NGO discourse: The role and future of NGOs in Africa', *Africa Development*, 31(4), pp. 22–51.

TallBear K. (2003) 'DNA, blood, and racializing the tribe', *Wicazo Sa Review*, 18, pp. 81–107.

Tuck, E. and Yang, K.W. (2012) 'Decolonization is not a metaphor', *Decolonization: Indigeneity, Education & Society*, 1(1), pp. 1–40.

Tilley, L. and Ajl, M. (2022) 'Eco-socialism will be anti-eugenic or it will be nothing: Towards equal exchange and the end of population', *Politics* (ahead of print), pp. 1–18.

Wariboko, W. E. (2011) '"Race" and the "civilizing mission": Their Implications for the Framing of Blackness and African Personhood, 1800-1960', *African Affairs*, 110(441), pp. 667–69, https://doi.org/10.1093/afraf/adr052.

White, S. C. (2002) 'Thinking race, thinking development', *Third World Quarterly*, 23(3), pp. 407–19.

Wilson, R. A. and Brown, R. D. (eds.) (2009) *Humanitarianism and suffering: The mobilization of empathy*. Cambridge: Cambridge University Press.

Wolfe P. (2006) 'Settler colonialism and the elimination of the native', *Journal of Genocide Research*, 8, pp. 387–409.

FILMS

Film Crown Unit (1949) *Daybreak in Udi*. Directed by Terry Bishop. https://commons.wikimedia.org/wiki/File:Daybreak_in_Udi_(1949).webm

Saturday Night Live (2014) *39 cents*. www.youtube.com/watch?v=MEb_epsuLqA

Kagumire, R. (2012) 'My response to KONY2012'. Available at www.youtube.com/watch?v=KLVY5jBnD-E.

GREY MATERIALS

Bah, O. S. (2018) '1.1.5. Introductions', '1.1.6. The Missions', and '1.3.8. Smiling Mzungu' in *MDGs: Mzungus in Development and Governments: An ethnography of customs, beliefs and why international development goals for nations fail*. PhD thesis, SOAS. Available: https://mdgcomics.com/phdcomic/.

Bheeroo, L. et. al. (2020) 'Time to dismantle racism in international development', *Bond*. Available: www.bond.org.uk/news/2020/06/time-to-dismantle-racism-in-international-development.

Forte, M. (2014) *Good intentions*. Montreal: Alert Press.

Hirsch, A. (2018) 'Oxfam abuse scandal is built on the industry's white saviour mentality', *The Guardian*, 20 February. Available: www.theguardian.com/commentisfree/2018/feb/20/oxfam-abuse-scandal-haiti-colonialism.

Maren, M. (1997) *The road to hell: The ravaging effects of foreign aid and international charity*. New York: Simon & Schuster.

Monga, C. (2020) 'Discrimination and prejudice in development', *Brookings*. Available at www.brookings.edu/blog/futuredevelopment/2020/07/15/discrimination-and-prejudice-in-development/.

Price, S. (2020). Do black lives matter for UK aid? *LSE Blog*. Available: https://blogs.lse.ac.uk/brexit/2020/06/26/do-black-lives-matter-for-uk-aid/.

2

Impoverishment is an *Active* Process: Capitalism and Development

Now we would like to demystify a central paradox of modern day 'progress': the existence of decidedly established and entrenched international development structures, institutions and projects aimed at eradicating poverty (and its related social, environmental and biological ills) alongside extreme levels of national and global income inequality (e.g. Piketty and Goldhammer 2014; Alston 2020). Despite 75-odd years of international development programming, global impoverishment, by many indicators, has only intensified, particularly in the past three decades. Why is this so? Why has international development (writ large) been so unsuccessful?

We resoundingly dismiss the depoliticizing and demobilizing narratives of poverty as a static phenomenon that emerges or exists organically. Seen from the tradition of dependency theory, world systems analysis and political ecology, impoverishment is an *active* process. It is cultivated over time, through historical relations, concrete actions and material processes. To combat impoverishment, we need an active politics that undoes and rethinks these processes and relations. What is the role and place of international development within this project? What *can* be its role, given that its preeminent model – that of the non-profit organization (NGO) – has been resigned to de-politicization from its inception?

In order to better understand more contemporary continuations of the close relationship between capitalism and international development, we critically assess the popularization of the language of leadership and of the entrepreneur/social entrepreneur by looking at curriculum and training in leadership academies and programmes. Why are so many activists and young people compelled to enter the gig economy, tech industries or run consultation side hustles? We ask readers to consider whether the popular celebrations of the new social entrepreneur reproduce neoliberal subjectivities, or in fact offer a bottom-up alternative to hegemonic corporate sectors and mainstream development.

ANTI-COLONIAL AND DECOLONIAL SOUNDTRACK

Seun Kuti's 2011 song 'IMF' (as in the International Monetary Fund) and Yemi Alade's 2019 'Poverty' are more contemporary cultural critiques of the active impoverishment of African societies. Kuti calls out debt as an ongoing mechanism of theft, manipulation and impoverishment.[1] Alade speaks back to the experience of active impoverishment through a Nigerian perspective, illustrating the often wide acceptance of capitalist illusions of progress and prosperity as it is through a neoliberal entrepreneurial spirit that 'poverty no go locate us'.[2]

The song, 'Quelle École?' or 'what school?' by Cameroonian reggae artist Sultan Oshimin[3] and the Ivorian musician Douk Saga's song 'Saga Cité'[4] are examples of commentary on neoliberal capitalism from francophone Central and West African perspectives. Oshimin's song *What School?* describes the hollowing out of the state via what he refers to as 'so-called state education' in Cameroon in the early 2000s. What school, Oshimin asks, if there are no books, no running water and overcrowded classrooms, with students listening to lectures through the windows? On the other hand, Douk Saga's song heralded the highly influential musical and dance phenomena known as *coupé-décalé* (which translates as 'cut and run' – as in, what a scammer does after they've stolen = money). The song showcases and sometimes glamourizes the highly masculine scamming culture of 'feymania' that emerged across West and Central Africa in the context of post-colonial active impoverishment and neoliberal austerity. The song also exposed the phenomenon of 'white poverty' in European cities to West African audiences, in contradiction to the dominant cultural representations of European wealth and modernity.

---

1. www.youtube.com/watch?v=8fGcf3GODKE.
2. www.youtube.com/watch?v=g29DqU5iRVc.
3. www.youtube.com/watch?v=sPcBza7IVI8.
4. www.youtube.com/watch?v=OSls9A5nGRw.

THE RELATIONSHIP BETWEEN CAPITALISM
AND DEVELOPMENT

We here build upon our previous chapter on how forms of colonial persistence – or coloniality in the present – are embedded within and, as some scholars argue, constitutive of international development. Now we turn our attention to the global political economies which structure and inform economic divisions and inequalities across history and geography. In this sense, we are interested in understanding the persistency of impoverishment into the twenty-first century. We frame our analysis within a critical political economic understanding of poverty: To understand impoverishment, we must first understand wealth, capital and exploitation (Gibson-Graham 2006). We must consider the nearly messianic belief in the infallibility of economic growth to contribute to better worlds – to trigger social and economic transformation.

In the face of the ideology of growth at all costs, when we actually look at the material conditions of the majority of the human population, we can see that impoverishment has not been reduced in much of the world. We in fact see that living conditions have worsened for many, even amidst the prevalence of anti-poverty campaigns and the flourishing of non-profit sectors designed to address and reduce poverty (Bond 2006; Bush 2007; Veltmeyer 2020).

To understand these greater levels of impoverishment, we must address labour rights, corporate hegemony and the vast regimes of extraction and accumulation which displace and appropriate land, nature and value from the people and life worlds in the peripheries (Rodney 1973; Wallerstein 1974; Bryant and Bailey 1997). For the Egyptian-Senegalese political economist Samir Amin, the 'underdevelopment' of the Global South is the deliberate consequence of an exploitative economic relationship between the Global North (the 'core') and South ('the periphery') and a Eurocentric world view in institutions and practices that legitimizes these forms of imperial exploitation (1972, 1976, 1989). For Amin and other Marxist and dependency theorists, the remedy to this uneven relationship would be through 'delinking' or breaking from neoliberal global capitalism (Amin 1990). The fostering of delinked economic models will occur through self-reliance, solidarity and collective ownership of resources and the means of production (ibid.).

Some people, including our students, might be resistant to the notion that global impoverishment is increasing. In capitalist and developmentalist states, we have been socialized by media, education and political spheres that share a collective envelopment within the relentless ideological and cultural machine of capitalism. Indeed, you might have attended lectures or events at our own school or university where speakers and lecturers refer off-handily to the accepted notion that poverty is on the decline.

There are complex roots to this persistent faith. Critical scholars have long maintained that education serves as a key mechanism for the production and maintenance of capitalist societies. It does so by preparing a malleable workforce and reinforcing capitalist values and ideologies, like those that encourage individualism, consumerism and competition (Freire 1968). If you were educated in England (or with British curriculum in former colonies), you might have been taught in schools about how the ingenuities of the industrial revolution and British labour and intellectual rigor contributed to the unique soundness of the British economy (Dorling and Tomlinson 2019; Puttick and Murrey 2020). In the United States, you might have been taught about American exceptionalism and the independent and entrepreneurial spirit that permitted early settlers turn away from the monarchy and allowed individuals to 'pull themselves up by their bootstraps' in a society said to recognize and celebrate merit rather than race, class or caste (Apple 1979). In Singapore, you might have been taught about the island's ideal geostrategic location and the country's early acceptance of market logic. These are just a few of the hegemonic explanations for the concentration of wealth and capital that preclude conversations around settler colonialism and entrenched class and racial divisions within societies. They fail to consider the wider globalized political economy, in particular the reliance on the importation of affordable natural resources to bolster domestic industry. Against this model of education as a commodity that reproduces social inequalities, critical pedagogies that foster disobedience to capitalism can contribute to liberation, liveable futures and multispecies flourishing (Freire 1968; hooks 1994).

THE ULTIMATE DEBATE: IS POVERTY INCREASING OR DECREASING?

The pro-capitalist ideas we are often exposed to in schools are bolstered by data from the World Bank and the United Nations Millennium

Campaign that rates of 'extreme poverty' – until very recently – were on the decline. This is a tidy story for capitalists. It has traction because we want to believe it. Unfortunately, poverty is not disappearing in the way that the World Bank and UN has claimed. By some measures, in fact, impoverishment has gotten significantly worse. Yet, the World Bank has an incentive to declare poverty rates to be on the decline given its prominence as both the world's leading development organization as well as the institutional power responsible for rolling out the free market and neoliberal structural adjustment programmes of the 1980s and 1990s in most of the Global South.[5]

The Millennium Declaration of 2000, adopted by the United Nations, declared its main objective as being to reduce global poverty by half by 2015. However, after the signing of the agreement, this goal was rearticulated: the German economic philosopher Thomas Pogge (2010) explains that no longer would the goal line be to halve *global poverty*, but rather to halve the proportion of the world's people living on less than a dollar a day. This shifted the focus to income levels and changed the statistical baseline from absolute numbers to proportional ones. This immediately rendered the target much easier to achieve: it reduced the target number by 167 million people (Pogge 2010: 209–215; Hickel 2017). Nothing in the world concretely changed. All that changed was the scope – or the 'optics' (Hickel 2017) – of the UN's target itself. The absolute numbers of people living in poverty could thereby remain completely unchanged and, because of population growth, less people *proportionally* would be understood as living in 'absolute' or 'extreme' poverty. Thus, with literally no action or change to address impoverishment, poverty can be declared to have been proportionally reduced.

The baseline for the analysis then underwent two further revisions. The goal was resituated so that it was no longer 'halving the proportion of impoverished people in the [entire] world' – rather it was, 'halving the proportion of impoverished people living in developing countries' (Hickel 2017). This strategic decision instrumentalized the faster-growing demo-

---

5. The World Bank's self-declared mission is 'to work with countries towards alleviating extreme poverty and boosting shared prosperity through inclusive, sustainable growth' and is often described in hegemonic development circles as the world's most important poverty allieviating institution.

graphic of countries in the Global South to again create the illusion of effective poverty reduction.

Finally, the timeline for assessment was moved back by a decade. Although the Millennium Campaign against poverty did not begin until 2000, they measured poverty reduction from a decade earlier, beginning in 1990, thus retroactively including all poverty reduction accomplished in China throughout the 1990s (Pogge 2010; Hickel 2017). This was even though these were merely number games that, again, had absolutely nothing to do with the Millennium Campaign.

The South African economic anthropologist Jason Hickel explains that this series of statistical manoeuvres fundamentally narrowed the target figure: from what began as a goal to reduce poverty amongst 836 million people, the campaign eventually settled with a target headcount of 324 million. As he writes, 'Having dramatically redefined the goal, the Millennium Campaign can claim that poverty has been halved when in fact it has not. The triumphalist narrative hailing the death of poverty rests on an illusion of deceitful accounting' (Hickel 2017).

In *The Divide*, Hickel traces the strategic shifting of the goalposts for measuring global poverty by the World Bank. For example, the World Bank asserted that the number of impoverished people had declined by 400 million between 1981 and 2001. However, the way they measured this decline was by arbitrarily calculating poverty according to the value of $1.08 in 1993 rather than the original baseline of $1.02 (according to 1985 purchasing power parity [PPP]), which, because of inflation over time, was lower in real terms. As Hickel writes, 'With this tiny change – a flick of an economist's wrist – the world was magically getting better, and the Bank's PR problem was instantly averted' (2014, n.p.).

The International Poverty Line (IPL) is a monetary threshold that is used by international organizations and institutions to measure extreme poverty on a global scale. In 2022, the IPL was set at $2.15 per day (increased from the previous threshold of $1.90), using what is known as purchasing power parity (PPP), or an economic system for evaluating and measuring the price of certain goods in different geographical regions. PPP is used by governments and agencies to facilitate comparisons of what people can afford to buy. However, the IPL tells us almost nothing about inequality within countries, as it erases impoverishment within wealthier countries and focuses exclusively on consumption rather than on other markers of wellbeing, happiness or health. The IPL has therefore been criticized for its arbitrariness and susceptibility to statistical manipulation. For example, in 2014 the IPL was set at $1.25 per day according to what people could buy in the United States in 2005. Yet, by this time it was clearly impossible to survive in most wealthy countries with that amount. The US government in 2015, for example, performed a bare-needs, mere-survival assessment for people (just to meet minimum nutritional requirements) and declared this amount needed to be at least $4.20 per day (Hickel 2017).

But even modest changes in the International Poverty Line could fundamentally challenge the celebratory narratives (of poverty reduction) of the World Bank and other international agencies. For example, an IPL of just $2.50 in 2015 would have rendered the number of people living in poverty as 3.1 billion people. Yet this is approximately three times the number that the Millennium Campaign declared in 2015. As Hickel explains,

> This marginal increase dramatically shifts the accepted wisdom of global poverty: this would mean it is getting worse rather than better, with nearly 353 million more people impoverished today than in 1981. If we remove the gains of China and calculate how many more people are impoverished today than in 1981, this figure is a staggering 852 million more people living in poverty today than in 1981 (2014, n.p.).

If the IPL was adjusted to $5 or $10 even just a few years ago, 5.1 billion people would have been understood to be living at poverty-levels. This is 80 per cent of the world's population. These metrics are dishonest, and it is important for us to have this shared critical political economic understanding. Once calculated, promoted and publicized, these declarations of poverty reduction are taken as truth, as facts, by people and actors across the world. They thereby become an accepted wisdom that informs action in the present. This 'illusion of deceitful accounting' has been quickly picked-up and absorbed into the narratives of the corporate media. It also filters down into the textbooks and educational activities of schoolchildren around the world.

Despite the reporting of most global media outlets and countless articles and op-eds in the *Washington Post* and the *Financial Times*, as well as seventy-plus years of international development programming, global impoverishment and regional economic inequalities in particular, by many indicators, have only intensified, particularly in the past three decades. In Chapter 1, we discussed the *Saturday Night Live* skit and the arbitrary demarcation of '39 cents' as the sum needed to support people in a fictional village. The humour here at the expense of the financial conclusions drawn by experts finds its echo in the rising hegemony of the 'international poverty line' (IPL), or the threshold for global poverty, which was established by the World Bank in the 1990s and which has since gained widespread acceptance.

The seduction of 'development' persists. We realize some of our students, readers and colleagues will be uncomfortable with a turning away from the idea of development. Jeffrey Sachs, the former director of the Millennium Development Goals and special adviser to the UN Secretary General Ban Ki-moon, is read around the world and has tremendous influence in determining global aid policies. His book, *The End of Poverty*, argues that poverty is neither structural nor historical – it is rather just a natural accident of geography and climate that, with the right amount of social and political engineering, can be overcome (Sachs 2005). So, we arrive at this passive, decontextualized understanding of poverty as a historical accident.

THE IDEA OF PASSIVE 'UNDERDEVELOPMENT'

Part of the reasoning behind these rather superficial explanations of global economic inequality and poverty lies in the malleability of the terms themselves. 'Underdevelopment' and 'development' are passive adjectives – built within them are sets of rhetorical tools to describe and therefore understand the world, specifically economic inequalities and poverty. Many texts on international development trace the modern usage of 'underdeveloped' to the second inaugural address of American president Harry Truman in 1949 (Hickel 2017), and this event has been marked as significant by scholars of international development – referred to as the 'Truman doctrine'.

Interestingly, Truman's focus on underdevelopment in this speech was somewhat random. It appeared as an afterthought after a mid-level functionary in the US State Department pushed forward with an idea to spin the inaugural address and to get it some press by calling for 'development'. Truman thereby announced that his administration would give aid to Third World countries to help them 'develop'.

This was the first inaugural address to ever be broadcast on television, and 10 million people watched it – making it the single most watched event in history at the time. Amidst American nationalism, exceptionalism and anti-communism, Truman said,

> More than half of the people of the world are living in conditions approaching misery . . . their food is inadequate. They are victims of disease. Their economic life is primitive and stagnant . . . [BUT] for the first time in history, humanity possesses the knowledge and skills to relieve the suffering of these people. The United States is pre-eminent among nations in the development of industrial and scientific techniques . . . our imponderable resources in technical knowledge are constantly growing and are inexhaustible . . . We must embark on a bold new program for making the benefits of our scientific advances and industrial progress available for the improvement and growth of underdeveloped areas . . . It must be a worldwide effort for the achievement of peace, plenty and freedom.[6]

There were no actual plans for this 'bold new program', as he called it. But what this speech did was provide a powerful way to think about the emerging international order: after the Second World War, European imperialism was declining and colonized and marginalized people began demanding their rights. Socialism and communism threatened capitalism's dominance, but this ideology of 'development' provided a new framework not only for understanding inequalities but for managing world affairs, particularly those relating to the less economically wealthy countries of the world.

According to Truman, what was needed was support for the conditions necessary to replicate features of American society across the world – high levels of industrialization and urbanization, technologization of agriculture, rapid growth of material production and living standards, and the adoption of Western values. In *Encountering Development* Arturo Escobar explains that 'this dream was not solely the creation of the United States but the result of the specific historical conjuncture at the end of the Second World War. Within a few years, the dream was universally embraced by those in power' (1995: 4). This caveat about the dream for those in power is important.

---

6. Truman's speech is available online at www.youtube.com/watch?v=gytbJo_bmxA. We suggest begining around minute 14:20, where this excerpt is taken from.

Recalling the clip discussed in Chapter 1, from *Daybreak in Udi*, the British colonial administrator referred offhandedly to the resistance of people to certain forms of modernization and progress. If you watch the film in its entirety, you'll note that this dichotomy between traditional and modern is the source for most of the film's dramatic tension. At the time, in the 1950s and 1960s, it was considered accepted knowledge that enormous sacrifices were necessary to roll-out the economic agenda of growth-centric development being advocated by the Truman doctrine.

The United Nations Department of Social and Economic Affairs released a document in 1951 reiterating the Western model of development thinking, informed by US president Harry Truman, of the 1950s:

There is a sense in which rapid economic progress is impossible without painful adjustments. Ancient philosophies have to be scrapped; old social institutions have to disintegrate; bonds of cast, creed and race have to burst; and large numbers of persons who cannot keep up with progress have to have their expectations of a comfortable life frustrated. Very few communities are willing to pay the full price of economic progress. (United Nations Department of Social and Economic Affairs 1951: 15; cited by Escobar 1995: 4).

This recognition of the costs and burdens of the wholescale economic and social re-engineering was not enough to question the entirety of the project, however, which was supposedly conducted through goodwill alone. Embedded within growth-led and abstract economic thinking is the accepted norm of calculated collateral casualties. While this kind of thinking was evident throughout the post-war period, it was also informed by antecedent capitalist and colonial influences regarding the costs of doing business.

What is important for our examination here is that for those Western and non-Western elites who accepted the Truman doctrine, it was not colonialism and enslavement or related plunder and extraction that caused such vast differences in the quality of life between the metropole and the periphery or the North and the South (McFadden 2008), rather it was this abstract thing, 'underdevelopment'. This passive term implies that there is what Hickel calls the 'Great Arrow of progress' – this term is important in exposing the myth of what was standard doctrine within the social sciences through the 50s and 60s and finds its echo in some

63

popular contemporary ideas about the free market and about so-called 'emerging markets', ideas which continue to reflect racialized and colonial roots) (Tilley 2020).[7]

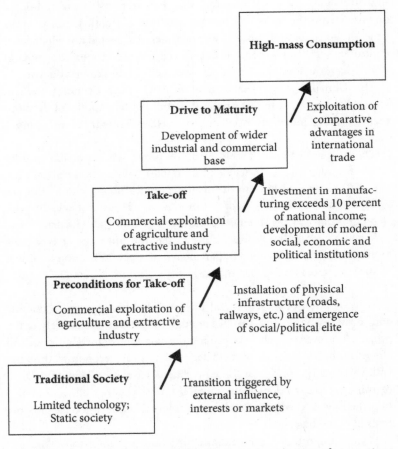

Figure 1   Authors' adaptation of W. W. Rostow's (1960) stages of economic growth, from *The Stages of Economic Growth: A Non-Communist Manifesto.* Cambridge University Press.

---

7.   Theories of modernization did not emerge in isolation. From Darwin's work, Herbert Spencer argued for the adaptive primacy of some races over others – what he called the 'survival of the fittest'. These are a set of ideas known as evolutionary sociology, an inheritance from the pseudoscientific fields of eugenics and craniology, all of which were sets of Eurocentric thinking positing that the so-called 'races' of humans were inherently distinct and that these features could be extrapolated to provide explanatory

In development economics, this was expressed through the theory of 'modernization', promoted prominently by Walt Rostow, which was based upon the theoretical hypothesis that societies evolve along a linear trajectory. In this 'non-communist manifesto', Rostow outlined five stages through which countries transition on their path from being a 'traditional society' to the apex of industrial economies. The theory has been criticized for its inherent Eurocentrism, racism and linearity. The idea is that there is *a traveling model* that can be superimposed from society to society (i.e. that what works here will work there). The point we want to emphasize here is that this model of development erases historical, geographical and cultural context. Colonialism is erased. Slavery is erased. Economic connections between societies are erased. Therefore, we will quickly recognize, culpability for colonialism is erased as a factor contributing to inequalities. The continuation of the political economies of extraction and economic relations into the post-colonial period are erased. Rostow, in an attempt to prevent independent nations being attracted to communist development models, presented the poor economic conditions of those states as a natural consequence of their 'backwardness', and argued that progress was inevitable if they followed the Western model of modernization.

INTELLECTUALS FROM THE GLOBAL SOUTH SPEAK BACK: THE IMPORTANT LEGACY OF DEPENDENCY THEORISTS ON UNEVEN DEVELOPMENT

These ideas did not go unchallenged. Dependency theorists of the 1970s rejected the mainstream hegemony of modernization. Guyanese theorist Walter Rodney's (1972) ground-breaking political economy of Africa, *How Europe Underdeveloped Africa*, was an important text in challenging the myth of modernization and providing an alternative understanding of poverty in Africa as *actively* produced through hundreds of years of exploitation by European companies and countries.

---

value for differences between societies, namely why certain of them were supposedly 'stagnant' while others were 'superior'. Spencer and the other evolutionary thinkers of the nineteenth century were the stewards of the ideological institutions that played a key role in ushering in an era of class and race-based inequality.

Rodney looks at the ways in which intra-African trade was intentionally disrupted by early European explorers beginning as early as the 1490s. He considers the human and material consequences of the deprivation of laborers from the African continent before and then during the transatlantic slave trade. In his examination, he looks at how the enrichment of Europe and the New World was directly dependent upon the extraction of raw materials and humans from across the African continent, but particularly West and Central Africa.

For more than four centuries (from the end of the fifteenth to the nineteenth centuries) somewhere between eleven and twenty million people were captured, enslaved and forcibly transported across the Atlantic Ocean. From a critical political economic and world systems analysis, we see that the uneven geographies of development reveal over-development in some areas and the transferal of labour, capital and resources from the peripheries to the core are more consequential to maintaining poverty. It would, indeed, be more accurate to make underdeveloped into a transitive verb. 'Under-developed': To have had one's development intentionally obstructed, undone or reversed by an external power (Hickel 2017).

Immanuel Wallerstein developed world systems theory to describe the ways in which global capitalism spatially divides the world into three hierarchical zones. The world's most dominant countries of 'the core' pulled resources, goods and people to their gravitational centres through institutionally and financially accumulated privilege and power. In this world system, the semi-periphery countries have a certain amount of economic and social power, but they are not fully integrated into the global economy. Countries in the periphery are the most economically disadvantaged and their economic systems are structured to the betterment of the core (predominantly) and the semi-periphery (to a lesser degree).

In this, we understand the broad relationship between development in one area and underdevelopment in another area. The over-development of North America, for example, has material consequences for the rest of the world. When North America represented 6% of the world's adult population but held 34% of global household wealth in 2006 (according to a UN study on Personal Assests from a Global Perspective; see Davies 2006), resources are not only not being allocated evenly but their allocation is *highly* uneven. In 2021, half of the global population owned a mere 2% of global wealth, while the top 10% owned 76% of total household wealth (at Purchasing Power Parity) and captured 52% of total official

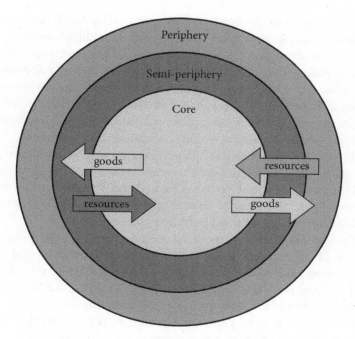

Figure 2   Adaptation of Wallerstein's
World System Theory Model (1974).

income generated during the year (Myers 2021). Of course, enormous inequalities exist within countries. According to the Credit Suisse Global Wealth Report, in 2022, the US also had the largest number of ultra-high-net-worth individuals, with 140,000 people owning wealth more than than 50 million USD (5). Materially, replications of capitalist development in the periphery are impossible; there are simply insufficient resources to allow for such growth. Beyond this, the material progress of the core is dependent upon the continual under-development of the societies in the periphery for its own development.

WHAT IS HIDDEN BY THE STORY OF INTERNATIONAL DEVELOPMENT: CAPITAL FLIGHT, ODIOUS DEBT AND THE IMPERATIVE OF REFUSAL

Capital flight refers to the practice of stashing large sums of money in offshore accounts, often illegally or illicitly, to avoid paying taxes. This practice is facilitated by financial loopholes – or we might more accurately say 'financial black holes' – in other countries, which have financial incentives to store these illicit profits. The Burundian economist Leonce Ndikumana explains that when we look at capital flight from African countries, we see that the gaps in industry and corporate profits between Africa and elsewhere in the world are smaller than officially calculated (meaning more capital is being generated than is officially recorded). He argues that this practice, in addition, underestimates economic inequalities within countries – as the wealth of the elite is not measured, and indeed does not contribute to shared economic wellbeing. Capital flight reduces the available resources for a country's needs, increases debt burdens, undermines public finances and fosters conflict (Boyce and Ndikumana 2012; Ndikumana and Boyce 2021).

We need not think these practices are somehow particular to countries in Africa, of course, as the Panama Papers infamously showed that the offshore fund run by David Cameron's father, Blairmore Holdings Inc., had paid no British tax for three decades because it was registered in the tax haven of the Bahamas. They hired a contingent of residents in the Bahamas to sign the paperwork on their behalf to effect the fraud (*Panama Papers*). The point here is that theft and stashing money abroad to avoid paying taxes are widely practiced by the world's elite, the extent of which is illustrated by the Panama Papers. The complicities between Western and African elites are outlined in further detail in John Perkins' (2004) book *Confessions of an Economic Hitman*. Perkins self-identifies as an 'economic hitman' (an assassin hired to kill slowly, via economic means), working for a consulting firm hired by the US government to convince leaders of countries in the Global South to accept loans for infrastructure projects that directly benefit US corporations.

The British political theorist Timothy Mitchell (2002), in *Rule of Experts*, demonstrates how US corporate agricultural firms profited from food dumping by connecting such practices to narratives of 'development' in Egypt – practices that disrupted local markets, fostered dependency and contributed to food injustice and impoverishment. These policies were supported by international financial institutions like the World Bank and the International Monetary Fund. These kinds of loans benefit US corporations because loan conditionality often requires that those governments agree to privatize public services, including water and electricity, to US corporations. Perkins calls out the pervasive practices of bribery and corruption fostered by US corporations to achieve their objectives of absolute growth and profit-creation. These are mutually beneficial financial structures, which exclude most of the world's population and concentrate wealth in the hands of a few.

In their book *Africa's Odious Debt* Léonce Ndikumana and James K. Boyce (2011) explain that many African countries pay more on debt repayment – or servicing external debt – than on their health care budgets. When a government incurs debt for purposes that do not benefit the people and the banker or granter knows or *should know* (i.e. lenders have a duty to due diligence and also cannot pretend to be innocent to these practices) that these funds would not be used for the benefit of the population, this debt is called 'odious'. Naming such practices in global racial capitalism as invalid and illegitimate is a means of empowering people with the right to refuse repayment. It also exposes the deep-seated complicities between authoritarian states and the international financial system. In the early decades of the post-colonial moment, for example, authoritarian leaders were able to raise significant funds for personal projects and to pacify resistant populations (by using funds to finance military and security forces) in contexts wherein a lack of funds and resources may likely have seen them removed from power. Government leaders can take on sizeable debts to finance large-scale infrastructural projects in order to promote their party as pro-active and 'modernizing'; too often, these have been 'white elephant projects' that do not benefit the country's economy or people. Such projects have been poorly executed or manipulated to facilitate embezzlement in kleptocracies (in which the members of the government actively steals money from the public treasury by setting up limited liability or shell corporations).

A contemporary example is the Kribi Deep Sea Port in Cameroon, which displaced an estimated 30,000 people, and was inaugurated in 2018. This project was funded primarily with loans from the Bank of China (207 billion CFA francs, according to Reuters; this is approximately $334.87 million) and the African Development Bank (which loaned €114.33 million in October 2021 and approved an additional €39.62 million in June 2022, according to an African Development Bank Group Press Release from 23 June 2022; approximately $163.96 million total). Construction was contracted out to Chinese corporations and final planning prepared by the Dutch consultancy firm Royal Haskoning (Nkot and Amougou 2021: 241). Nkot and Amougou have written an informative history of the project, from the initial feasibility studies in the 1970s to the eventual partnerships between the Cameroonian government and key international players at the China-Africa Summit in Beijing in December 2008. The seaport continues to be hugely underutilized because of high operating costs and a lack of transport and infrastructural coordination (Ojuku, Ngouanet and Ngwa 2014); at the same time, the President Paul Biya remains 'the main beneficiary of [the] euphoria raised by the implementation of structural projects' (Nkot and Amougou 2021: 250).

Ultimately, odious debt contributes to the stabilization of authoritarian power and the active impoverishment of people and communities. The important research of Ndikumana, Boyce and their team in *Africa's Odious Debt* (2011) shows that, far from being exceptional, most of the debt incurred by African countries during the twentieth century was odious. These corrupt lending practices have enriched and maintained in power odious leaders as it has profited and benefitted foreign governments, multilateral institutions and private banks. This is a toxic and structural mix that cannot be addressed by singling out 'bad actors'. They painstakingly unpack the human consequences of governments in Africa prioritizing national resources for the repayment of foreign debt. Their 2011 interview with the independent broadcaster, *The Real News Network*, is a useful initial engagement with their work (youtube.com/watch?v=unGLRG-vinw). We suggest attending in particular to minutes 01:00–7:33, in which they argue that infant mortality rates in African countries are tied to this odious debt in the prioritization of debt repayment over the health and wellbeing of their people. The repayment of odious debt has drained resources that should have been used to improve health provisions, including medical services and clean water, by forcing African governments (in their analysis they draw heavily on cases in Nigeria, Angola, Congo-Brazzaville and Gabon) to cut spending on essential services. Cancelling this debt is imperative.

In their work on capital flight (2012, 2013), Ndikumana and Boyce indicate that *half or more* of the money transferred to African countries as foreign loans exited in the same year as capital flight. Again, we see that the normative decontextualized story of development omits and erases these kinds of material subsidizations of Euro-American by the peoples of the Global South.

The mainstream depoliticization of poverty also erases another history that transpired alongside the dominance of the International Development story – the often-violent dismissal of anti-imperial and anti-capitalist experiments for social wellbeing as 'dangerous'. While there are a great many such stories, we will here explore one of great significance. Thomas Sankara (1949–87) was one of the world's most prominent Pan-African socialist revolutionaries. He was a military captain and a president, an unapologetic anti-imperialist, a critic of patriarchy and partner in the 'total emancipation' of women, a formidable and often amusing orator and a humble but resolved human committed to the co-creation of a more just world. In the early 1980s, he undertook a grounded, applied and radical approach for the transformation of the state for the wellbeing of the people of Burkina Faso. Sankara was also distinctive for his revolution's – the August Revolution – successes, including achievements in food self-reliance, the importance given to ecological balance and reforestation, rapid infrastructural achievements and advances in healthcare.

At the time, by the World Bank's published metrics, Burkina Faso was the world's third poorest country. Sankara called for a fundamental break from epistemic and economic dependency on Euro-America. This was a radical paradigm of social, political, economic and ecological justice. In 1987, he spoke at the African Unity Organisation Summit against odious debt, proposing that the countries of Africa stand together and refuse to repay it.[8] Sankara called odious debt a form of 'technical assassination' that engendered 'financial slavery', which is to say 'real slavery'. He insisted that many of the challenges the Burkinabé people faced on a daily basis were rooted in neo-colonial relationships and structures that were perpetuated through an international development paradigm that suppressed local innovation and co-opted sovereignty (Jackson 2018: 133). He demanded that anti-imperial projects be fixed in a meaningful self-sufficiency and self-pride that, as he said, 'refused to accept a state of [mere] survival'.

Sankara situated international development within this matrix of cultural imperialism. This necessitated the complete refashioning of international development aid:

---

8. We recommend watching portions of this speech or screening it in your classrooms, particularly from the beginning to minute 3:55; it is available on YouTube: www.youtube.com/watch?v=DfzoToJEnu8.

Aid must go in the direction of strengthening our sovereignty, not undermining it. Aid should go in the direction of destroying aid. All aid that kills aid is welcome in Burkina Faso. But we will be compelled to abandon all aid that creates a welfare mentality (Sankara, One Color: African Unity, 125).

Sankara worked against the fostering of a 'welfare mentality', toward 'decolonizing our mentality and achieving happiness'. In a global political economy premised on the exploitation and annihilation of entire communities, and an international development regime premised on 'mere survival', the Burkinabé had been disallowed self-worth, pride and consequently – as Sankara argued – happiness. Meaning, pleasure and self-appreciation were derived from working, creating and building together – these were central aspects of his revolutionary pedagogy for humanization.

He emphasized national food sovereignty, argued against over-dependence on foreign aid, and implemented several important pioneering ecological programs. He was the president for only four years before he was assassinated in 1987, but in that short time he managed to make the country self-sufficient in basic foodstuffs. The revolution transformed the health system, improved access to education, dramatically increased literacy and recuperated the pre-colonial practice of planting a tree sapling to mark special occasions and combat desertification of the Sahel.

Sankara was assassinated on 15 October 1987; he predicted his own death beforehand (Murrey 2018). We return again to his speech at the United Nations in 1987, in which Sankara declared:[9]

I want this conference to adopt as a necessity [the stance] that we cannot repay this debt. Not with warlike intentions, but to prevent us from being individually assassinated. If Burkina Faso stands alone in refusing to pay, I will not be here for the next conference. But, with everyone's support – which I need – we would avoid paying. By that, we would devote our small resources to our own development.

In their considerable research following the assassination, Carina Ray, Bruno Jaffré and a number of investigative journalists have looked at Liberia, Cote d'Ivoire, Libya and France's involvement in or implicit

---

9. Listen to minutes 02:00–02:58: www.youtube.com/watch?v=9VZEkURD9oI.

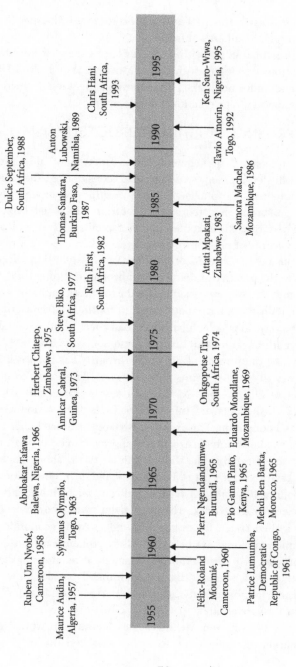

Figure 3 Incomplete timeline of assassinations, executions and 'suspicious' deaths of leaders in Africa from 1955 to 1995.
Source: Timeline by author (Murrey 2019).

support for the assassination plot and support for Blaise Compaoré, who assumed power after Sankara's murder.

Sankara's assassination fits within a larger landscape of the assassinations of dangerous development thinkers (Murrey 2019). Indeed Hickel devotes a chapter in his book *The Divide* to a consideration of the role of political assassination in international development.

EMERGENCE OF PHILANTHROCAPITALISM

We cannot understand the contemporary function of aid, humanitarianism and development without also considering the role of 'philanthrocapitalism' – capitalists or very wealthy people who profess to engage in philanthropic activities that contribute to social, economic or ecological betterment – in contemporary capitalism. If we look at the contemporary forms of philanthrocapitalism, we can observe a marked rise in the scale and explicitness of this form of 'charity'. Philanthrocapitalism refers to the practice of doing philanthropic (not-for-profit) work in ways that emulate corporate practice (in the for-profit capitalist world). Philanthrocapitalism is a term that came into common parlance in 2006 to describe the ways in which philanthropy had become more resemblant to for-profit markets, with their 'investors' and 'social returns'.

The increasing dominance of big philanthropists has been traced by Linsey McGoey in *No Such Thing as a Free Gift: The Gates Foundation and the Price of Philanthropy*. McGoey closely examined the negative consequences of the outsized influence of philanthropic foundations like the Gates Foundation. For example, McGoey estimates that in the first 15 years of the twenty-first century, approximately 45,000 private foundations were created in the United States – this is about 5,000 new foundations each year (2015: 17). Fundamentally, such foundations lack popular accountability and yet have significant platforms to promote their own views and agendas. The vast majority of charitable donations in the United States, for example, do not provide economic relief for low-income individuals, rather, as McGoey explains (2015: 18), they are much more likely to direct funding channels at religious or cultural projects, both of which tend to have predominantly wealthy and white audiences. These foundations also frequently partner with (and promote) profiteering corporate entities.

For example, the Bill and Melinda Gates Foundation works closely with pharmaceutical companies in their advancement of a global health agenda that scholars have likened to 'global health imperialism' (Levich 2015: 704). The American software developer and co-founder of the Microsoft Corporation, Bill Gates, and his former wife Melinda, have become highly influential within policy programming and circles working on global health and poverty reduction, despite neither having formal education in health systems, medicine or the capitalist and colonial economic systems that foster impoverishment. Their foundation had an endowment worth $43.5 billion by 2015, with an annual expenditure of $4 billion towards projects for the reduction of malaria, polio, tuberculosis, HIV and other diseases (Levich 2015: 704). Gate's policy aspirations included 'a public call for [the] ambitious . . . creation of a global, militarized, supranational authority capable of responding decisively to outbreaks of infections disease' (ibid.). In the wake of the Ebola outbreak in Guinea, Liberia and Sierra Leone (December 2013–March 2016), Gates speculated that a 'supranational authority' would need to bypass or suspend various constitutional guarantees to freedom and foster worldwide surveillance networks in the name of tracking and addressing the global spread of disease. In other words, Gates argued that military logistics (including communications and emergency preparedness) should be leveraged to contain epidemics.

Pushing against simplistic and securitized solutions to medical emergencies, the geographer Lioba Assaba Hirsch (2019, 2021), who conducted research in Sierra Leone on the 2014–15 Ebola outbreak, argues that the epidemic was shaped by a complex interplay of colonial-racial, social and environmental dynamics. For Hirsch, the British-led international medical response was shaped by pre-existing racism and colonial injustice, particularly anti-blackness and the underlying structural issues of active impoverishment. She makes a case for further work towards re-humanization in the wake of coloniality, drawing from the scholarship of Christina Sharpe (2016) articulating 'the wake' as a means to speak to the ongoing legacies of slavery, through the metaphor of the turbulent and unpredictable consequences of a ship's passage through water: much like the wake ripples far beyond the passage of the ship, the aftereffects of enslavement persist beyond its abolition. Reading Hirsch and Gates side-by-side we are made aware of the imperial dangers and inadequacies of Gate's call for heightened security and surveillance as a viable response to disease.

The investigative journalist Anand Giridharadas, author of *Winners Take All: The Elite Charade of Changing the World*, argues that plutocratic classes maintain the capitalist status quo through big philanthropy, which provides a strategic illusion that market-based solutions can resolve the problems of economic and ecological destruction. This illusion is strategic because it maintains that the world's most powerful capitalists are contributing in *generative* ways towards socio-ecological betterment, thus promoting their image, establishing their influence on public policy and distracting from the material violence of capitalism and coloniality (that we will discuss in Chapter 3). Giridharadas writes about the seduction of the *idea of doing good*, and how he was himself caught up in this illusion during his time with the Aspen Institute. Philanthrocapitalism reinforces economic inequalities and the concentration of wealth, as he explains in an extended interview produced by VPRO Documentary in 2020.[10]

Giridharadas critiques philanthrocapitalism for positing a 'win-win ideology' that suggests that the very system that generated vast human inequalities – the transfer of value in the form of surplus from natural resources and labour, what David Harvey (2004) calls 'accumulation by dispossession', literally the theft of various forms of value from people and nature – can be redeployed to offer solutions to the problems of wealth inequality. These supposedly kind capitalists come, then, to dominate the imagination of our possible solutions to the very problems created by capitalism. Giridharadas characterizes this system as a kind of religious gospel of entrepreneurship, one that glorifies the 'multi-stake-holder approach' and 'social enterprise' and 'social innovation'. These solutions are superficial precisely because they do not seek to actually address the roots of systemic inequality and racialized and gendered global capitalism.

McGoey (2015: 19) writes that 'philanthropists themselves are often the first to admit that their philanthropy is aimed at preserving rather than redistributing wealth'. She reminds us of the words of the Mexican business magnate and richest person in the world from 2010 to 2013, Carlos Slim, who said 'Wealth is like an orchard. You have to share the fruit, not the trees'. She argues that his candour illustrates something else that is distinctive about the new philanthropists: their forthrightness about the personal advantages of philanthropy. Gift-giving is a useful

---

10. www.youtube.com/watch?v=qcHlNKLQBIM&t=1247s; we particularily recommend watching minutes 06:00–08:47 in the classroom.

vehicle for preserving privilege, something that distinguishes them from earlier donors (ibid).

In her work on TED Heads, McGoey writes about the Skoll World Forum, held annually at our institution, at the University of Oxford's Said Business School to promote and galvanize 'social entrepreneurs'. An event which costs upwards of £6,000 per ticket. As she explains,

> the fact that events such as TED or Skoll, touted as promoting global democracy and increased prosperity for the poor, are far too exorbitantly priced for most of the world's poor – or even most jobbing management scholars at some of the world's oldest universities – is not something that troubles the organisers. If anything, the exclusivity of the events is their strongest appeal. (2015: 65)

She traces the emergence of the dominance of social entrepreneurship – something that is absolutely evident in the funding calls for research and the drive for certain collaborations at our institution, and even the language of our students – writing, of how:

> the continued insistence that new entrepreneurial movements are playing a revolutionary role in global poverty reduction [continues] despite the lack of clear evidence . . . the new social investors believe that business success *is* evidence of social value. There is no longer any whiff of atonement or reparation for past corporate practices (2015: 85).

NEOLIBERAL SUBJECTIVITIES: DISCOURSES OF LEADERSHIP AND ENTREPRENEURSHIP

The World Economic Forum (2022) estimates that 60 per cent of Africa's population is under the age of 25, making it the most youthful region in the world. In some countries, such as South Africa in 2022, the youth unemployment was as high as 63.9 per cent against an official national rate of 34.5 per cent.[11] From elite, neo-imperial and often militarised perspectives, the possibility of youth uprisings is seen as a threat to neoliberal

---

11. Department of Statistics, Republic of South Africa (2022) https://www.statssa.gov.za/?p=15407.

capitalism and therefore the population is deemed as being in need of ideological pacification (Campbell and Murrey 2014). It is little surprise, then, that neoliberal discourse and policies since the 1980s have reasserted the role of the self-actualized, responsible individual in economic development and that a great number of educational initiatives have further entrenched this vision. This involves a discourse that presents problems in the Global South (and particularly in Africa) as essentially the result of 'bad leadership' (see Murrey 2018) and/or the lack of entrepreneurial skills and knowhow. The structural causes of high rates of youth unemployment are therefore ignored, as youth are targeted to become better 'future leaders' and entrepreneurs (Dolan and Ryak 2016). Youth education involves promoting a form of citizenship that is associated with business skills, innovation, risk taking and self-reliance (DeJaeghere and Baxter 2014). De Sá Mello da Costa and Silva Saraiva (2012), for example, examine the entrepreneurship modules being promoted in Brazilian universities that embrace the logic of capitalism. They write that '[i]t is through success that a given entrepreneur is discursively constructed as "master of [their] destiny" and able to minimize the uncertainties of life. [They] then become a hero who is supposed to be imitated' (2012: 609). For youth, role models come from the tech-gig economy, with billionaires such as Mark Zuckerberg, Steve Jobs, Bill Gates, Jack Ma and Elon Musk are held up as exemplars.

At the same time as exceptional figures are celebrated and emulated, as de Sá Mello da Costa and Silva Saraiva explain, there is a 'discourse of failure [that] is produced silently in the form of unproductiveness, sterility, laziness, and professional disqualification' (2012: 609). Yet, the ability of the poor to succeed at entrepreneurship, in the context of neoliberal globalization, depends on a range of structural factors, some of which, as Langevang and Gough (2012) document for young women dressmakers and hairdressers in Ghana, include the uneven effects of trade liberalization leading to either new or cheaper products from abroad and professionalization, excluding those young people learning on the job.

In many societies of the Global South, the impacts of decades of state withdrawal and austerity, neoliberal self-help fads and globalizing YouTube/TikTok capitalist culture have given rise to a celebratory illusion of infinite 'start-up entrepreneurs'. This new economic subject is autonomous, self-motivated and infinitely optimistic, capable of overcoming enormous economic, structural and historical barriers to monetize their personal skills and/or small resources in order to cultivate new wealth and self-sufficiency in the capitalist gig economy. For example, Andrea Pollio (2021) traces the 'evangelical' influence of post-dotcom Silicon Valley (as a language and a model) on emergent entrepreneurs in Cape Town. Pollio, drawing from Richard Barbrook and Andy Cameron, describes the ways in which a 'Californian ideology' travelled to South Africa as a kind of 'market fundamentalism based on a promethean belief in the salvific power of digital technologies' (2021: 48). Ultimately, the mobilization and acceptance of these economic practices, he argues, 'allow[s] global corporations to use market experiments with poverty to deepen their understanding of and, possibly, their domination over markets that are yet to be fully colonized by technocaptialism' (2021: 63). Similarly, Dolan and Ryak's study of a social enterprise targeting poor and marginalized youth in Nairobi, Kenya, note that

> there is an emphasis on training at a practical, psychological and moral level to produce this army of entrepreneurs who are enjoined to relinquish the quest for formal employment and go from "jobseeker" to "job-creator". The entrepreneur emerges as both beneficiary and catalyst, producer and product of this new economy of development (2016: 515).

Such programmes often focus on 'inclusion' through the promotion of consumer goods to impoverished people living in similar conditions.

Thus, people who were once labelled 'informal sector workers' are now represented as micro-entrepreneurs. Mishra and Raju Bathini (2020) discuss how the media discourse in India works to support the global corporation Uber by presenting its drivers as self-reliant citizens contributing to India's economic development, and Uber itself as an emancipatory tool. A great many initiatives promoting youth entrepreneurship are visible on the Internet and can be easily accessed by our students for analysis. In Africa, they have also been aimed at changing the image of the continent as one that is embracing of modernity and simultaneously authentically 'African'.

Using a range of sources, particularly digital ones, in our teaching we examine the range of activities that have been used to target youth to embrace entrepreneurialism. One African example is the 'How we Made it in Africa' campaign.[12] The campaign is promoted on several social media platforms, such as @MadeItInAfrica, and uses straplines such as 'Thinking outside the box: Five innovative business models in Africa' and 'Don't be a jobseeker: [we will] role model how you can create [jobs] for others'. We ask readers or students to consider: What subjectivities are promoted in these discourses and representations, and what do they tell us about the state/society relations that are being promoted? How do those in the Global South differ from those targeting youth in the Global North?

CONCLUSION

Our attention has focused on the actual rather than hoped-for consequences of development projects. Claude Ake (1996: 1) articulated a powerful thesis about the connections between politics, the state in Africa and (under)development:

> [. . .] the assumption so readily made that there has been a failure of development is misleading. The problem is not so much that development has failed as that it was never really on the agenda in the first place. By all indications, political conditions in Africa are the greatest impediment to development . . . *African politics has been constituted to prevent the pursuit of development and the emergence of relevant and effective development paradigms and programs.*

Neo-imperial relations and post-colonial politics foster, sustain and intensify impoverishment. Development has been 'unsuccessful' in eradicating poverty, but it does *do* something. That 'something' will be the focus of the next two chapters on violence, neoliberalism and development without the peoples of the Global South.

In 2020, the World Bank published a report on global poverty, *Poverty and Shared Prosperity 2020: Reversals of Fortune.* The report projected a deepening of global impoverishment in the wake of COVID-19. David Malpass, the then president of the World Bank wrote,

> The report's projections suggest that, in 2020, between 88 million and 115 million people could fall back into extreme poverty as a result of

---

12.   At www.howwemadeitinafrica.com/.

the pandemic, with an additional increase of between 23 million and 35 million in 2021, potentially bringing the total number of new people living in extreme poverty to between 110 million and 150 million. Early evidence also suggests that the crisis is poised to increase inequality in much of the world. The crisis risks large human capital losses among people who are already disadvantaged, making it harder for countries to return to inclusive growth even after acute shocks recede.

Nowhere in the bank's suggestions for reform do we see attention to debt absolution or the financial structures which burden countries in the Global South to the off-loading of negative consequences of crisis. For activists, the 1980s debt restructuring in Latin America is criticized as triggering the loss of a decade of welfare progress, this felt like two decades in much of Africa (Bond 2006).

Writing in the shadow of the 2008 Global Financial Collapse, as she attended the Skoll Forum in Oxford, McGoey shared the closing remarks of the founder of the forum, Jeff Skoll, who said to the audience:

you are keystone species in the social change architecture. Your role is strengthened by the economic crisis. We leave Oxford with a renewed sense of what is possible. Last year we said social entrepreneurs had arrived; now I say they are to take the lead to show the way to the rest of the world. A crisis is a terrible thing to waste (87).

Those familiar with the work of the Canadian political economist Naomi Klein (2008) will be aware of the historical pattern of capitalist and plutocratic classes instrumentalizing various natural and unnatural crises and disasters for even greater levels of profitability and social restructuring. Today, we have only begun to scratch the surface of some of the explanations for global economic inequalities, but we can begin to see why debt justice, the redistribution of wealth, the end to capital flight and greater awareness of and policymaking against the continued extraction of labour and resources from the peripheries, for example, are necessary conditions for an end to the current global economy that causes impoverishment.

QUESTIONS FOR FURTHER THOUGHT

What are the relations between economic structure and individual action? What is the role or function of 'philanthrocapitalism' in contemporary capitalism?

Policy leveraging. Odious debt. Capital flight. Political assassination. These are all phenomena that were central to this chapter's materials. Choose one of these and discuss its relevance for our understanding of the political economies of international development.

Many of the readings and videos considered in this chapter articulate a messianic or missionary-like zeal to the ideologies of development as a 'succour to humanity's woes'. From Teresa Hayter's early work at the World Bank (in the 1960s), to Giridharadas' reading of today's social entrepreneurs, what do you make of this metaphor (development-as-religious belief)? Is it apt? Why or why not?

What are some of the problems associated with the poverty line? Given your response, is the category valuable or meaningful (or might it be)?

Consider whether the narrative of the 'new social entrepreneur' reproduces neoliberal subjectivities or offers a bottom-up alternative to mainstream development. Why are activists and young people compelled to enter the gig/tech industry?

FILMS/VIDEOS

Historical videos

US President Harry Truman's 1949 inaugural address. Available: www.youtube.com/watch?v=fWwcZLNrtAY.

Sankara, Thomas, President of Burkina Faso. Speech on the United Front Against Debt. 1987. www.youtube.com/watch?v=DfzoToJEnu8.

Films

Life and Debt (2001) Documentary. Available: https://urbanareas.net/info/life-debt-documentary/.

Poor us: An animated history of poverty (2012) Animated documentary, directed by Ben Lewis. Available: www.youtube.com/watch?v=TxbmjDngois.

The End of Poverty? (2008) Documentary. Available: www.dailymotion.com/video/x22eynh.

War by Other Means – IMF and the World Bank (1992) Documentary by John Pilger. Available: www.youtube.com/watch?v=79bZ71fUZRU.

Geographies of Racial Capitalism (2021) An Antipodean Short Film with Ruth Wilson Gilmore. Available: www.youtube.com/watch?v=2CS627aKrJI.

Charity: How Effective is giving? (2020) *The Economist*. Available: www.youtube.com/watch?v=QaN6ibm5r-I&feature=share.

Reports & Websites/Grey Materials

Alston, Philip (2020) *The Parlous State of Poverty Eradication, Report of the Special Rapporteur on Extreme Poverty and Human Rights.* 44th Session of Human Rights Council, agenda item 3, 15 June–3 July 2002. Available: https://chrgj.org/wp-content/uploads/2020/07/Alston-Poverty-Report-FINAL.pdf.

Bretton Wood's Project (2020) *The World Bank: What it is and how it works.* Available: www.brettonwoodsproject.org/2020/07/the-world-bank-what-is-it-and-how-it-works/.

Bretton Wood's Project (2019) *What are the Bretton Wood's institutions?* Available: www.brettonwoodsproject.org/2019/01/art-320747/.

Bretton Wood's Project (2019) *What are the main criticisms of the World Bank and the IMF?.* Available: www.brettonwoodsproject.org/2019/06/what-are-the-main-criticisms-of-the-world-bank-and-the-imf/.

Flechtner, S. (2018) 'Think positive, climb out of poverty? It's just not so easy!' *Developing Economics*, 8 September. Available: www.developingeconomics.org/2018/08/09/think-positive-climb-out-of-poverty-its-just-not-so-easy/.

Margonelli, L. (2017) 'Meet the Flexians', *Pacific Standard*, 4 June. Available: www.psmag.com/social-justice/meet-flexians-government-business-media-money-power-wall-street-65029.

Mercatante, E. (2020) 'Uneven development and imperialism today: Engaging with the ideas of David Harvey', *Left Voice*. Available: www.leftvoice.org/uneven-development-and-imperialism-today-engaging-with-the-ideas-of-david-harvey.

Oxfam (2022) 'Inequality Kills: The unparalleled action needed to combat unprecedented inequality in the wake of COVID-19'. Available: https://policy-practice.oxfam.org/resources/inequality-kills-the-unparalleled-action-needed-to-combat-unprecedented-inequal-621341/; 'Ten richest men double their fortunes in pandemic, while incomes of 99 percent of humanity fall'. Available: www.oxfam.org/en/press-releases/ten-richest-men-double-their-fortunes-pandemic-while-incomes-99-percent-humanity.

REFERENCES

Abrahamsen, R. (2016) 'Discourses of democracy, practices of autocracy: Shifting meanings of democracy in the aid-authoritarianism nexus' in *Aid and authoritarianism in Africa*. Uppsala: Nordic Africa Institute.

Ake, C. (1996) *Democracy and development in Africa*. Washington, D.C.: Brookings Institution Press.

Apple, M. W. (1979) *Ideology and curriculum*. London: Routledge.

Amin, S. (1972) 'Underdevelopment and dependence in Black Africa – Origins and Contemporary Forms', *Journal of Modern African Studies*, 10(4), pp. 503–24.

Amin, S. (1976) *Unequal development: An essay on the social formations of peripheral capitalism*. Pierce, B. (trans.). New York: Monthly Review Press.

Amin, S. (1989) *Eurocentrism*. Moore, R. (trans.). New York: New York University Press.

Amin, S. (1990) *Delinking: Towards a polycentric world*. London: Zed Books.

Bond, P. (2006) *Looting Africa: The Economics of Exploitation*. London: Zed Books.

Boyce, J. and Ndikumana, L. (2011) *Africa's Odious Debts: How Foreign Loans and Capital Flight Bled a Continent*. Zed Books.

Boyce, J.K. and Ndikumana, L. (2012) *Capital Flight from Sub-Saharan African Countries: Updated Estimates, 1970 - 2010*. PERI Research Report, October 2012.

Bryant, R. L. and Bailey, S. (1997) *Third world political ecology*. London: Routledge.

Bush, R. (2007) *Poverty and neoliberalism: Persistence and reproduction in the Global South*. London: Pluto.

Campbell, H. and Murrey, A. (2014) 'Culture-centric pre-emptive counterinsurgency and US Africa Command: Assessing the role of the US social sciences in US military engagements in Africa', *Third World Quarterly*, 35(8), pp. 1457–75.

Davis, J. B. (2006) 'The global distribution of household wealth', *United Nations Blog*. Available: www.wider.unu.edu/publication/global-distribution-household-wealth.

Davis, M. (2008) 'The Invention of the Third World' in Chari, Sharad and Stuart Corbridge (eds.), *The Development Reader*. London and New York: Routledge.

DeJaeghere, J., and Baxter, A. (2014). 'Entrepreneurship education for youth in sub-Saharan Africa: A capabilities approach as an alternative framework to neoliberalism's individualizing risks', *Progress in Development Studies*, 14(1), pp. 61–76.

Dolan, C. and Rajak, D. (2016) 'Remaking Africa's informal economies: Youth, entrepreneurship and the promise of inclusion at the bottom of the pyramid', *The Journal of Development Studies*, 52(4), pp. 514–29, DOI: 10.1080/00220388.2015.1126249.

Dorling, D. and Tomlinson, S. (2019) *Rule Britannia: Brexit and the end of empire*. London: Biteback Publishing.

Escobar, A. (1995) *Encountering development: The making and unmaking of the Third World*. Princeton: Princeton University Press.

Escobar, A (1995) 'The problematization of poverty: The tale of three worlds and development' in *Encountering Development: The making and unmaking of the Third World*. Princeton, N. J.: Princeton University Press.

Escobar, A. (2004) 'Development, violence and the new imperial order', *Development*, 47, pp. 15–21.

Escobar, A. (2007) '"Post-development" as concept and social practice' in Aram Ziai (ed.) *Exploring Postdevelopment: Theory and practice, problems and perspectives*. London/ New York: Routledge, pp. 18–33.

Ferguson, J. (1990) *The anti-politics machine: 'Development', depoliticisation, and bureaucratic power in Lesotho.* Cambridge and New York: Cambridge University Press.

Gibson-Graham, J. K. (2006) *The End of Capitalism (as We Knew It): A feminist critique of political economy.* Minneapolis: University of Minnesota Press.

Gibson-Graham J. K., Cameron J. and Healy S. (2013) *Take back the economy: An ethical guide for transforming our communities.* Minneapolis: University of Minnesota Press.

Giridharadas, A. (2018) *Winners take all: The elite charade of changing the world.* New York: Alfred A. Knopf.

Goldman, M. (2001) 'The birth of a discipline: Producing authoritative green knowledge bank-style', *Ethnography*, 2(2), pp. 191–217. https://doi.org/10.1177/14661380122230894

Grech, S. (2008) 'Disability, poverty and development: Critical reflections on majority world debate', *Disability & Society*, 6, pp. 771–84.

Hagmann, T. and Reyntjens, F. (2016) 'Introduction' in *Aid and authoritarianism in Africa.* Uppsala: Nordic Africa Institute.

Harvey, D. (2004) 'The "new" imperialism: Accumulation by dispossession', *Socialist Register*, pp. 63–87.

Hickel, J. (2014) 'Exposing the great "poverty reduction" lie. *Al Jazeera Opinion*, 21 August. www.aljazeera.com/opinions/2014/8/21/exposing-the-great-poverty-reduction-lie/.

Hickel, J. (2017) *The divide: A brief guide to global inequality and its solutions.* London: Penguin Random House.

Hirsch, L. A. (2019) *Antiblackness and global health: Placing the 2014-15 Ebola response in Sierra Leone in the colonial wake.* Doctoral thesis (PhD), UCL (University College London).

Hirsch, L. A. (2021) 'Race and the spatialisation of risk during the 2013-2016 West African Ebola epidemic', *Health Place*, 67(102499). https://doi.org/10.1016/j.healthplace.2020.102499

Jackson, N.A. (2018) '"Incentivised" Self-Adjustment: Reclaiming Sankara's revolutionary austerity from corporate geographies of neoliberal erasure' in Murrey, A. (ed.) *A certain amount of madness: The life, politic, and legacies of Thomas Sankara.* London: Pluto Press, pp. 113–25.

Jerven, M. (2013) *Poor numbers: How we are misled by African development statistics and what to do about it.* Ithaca, NY: Cornell University Press.

Kapoor, I. (2002) 'Capitalism, culture, agency: Dependency versus postcolonial theory', *Third World Quarterly*, 23(4), pp. pp. 647–64.

Kirsch, S. (2014) *Mining capitalism: The relationship between corporations and their critics.* Berkeley, CA: University of California Press.

Klein, N. (2008) *The shock doctrine.* London: Penguin Books.

Levich, J. (2015) 'The Gates Foundation, Ebola, and global health imperialism', *The American Journal of Economics and Sociology*, 74(4), pp. 704–42.

Livingston, J. (2019) *Self-devouring growth: A planetary parable, as told from Southern Africa*. Durham, NC: Duke University Press.

Mawdsley, E. and Taggart, J. (2021) 'Rethinking d/Development', *Progress in Human Geography*, 46(1), pp. 1–18. https://doi.org/10.1177/03091325211053115.

McGoey, L. (2015) *No such thing as a free gift: The Gates Foundation and the price of philanthropy*. London: Verso Books.

Mercer, C. and Mohan, G., Power, M. (2003) 'Towards a critical political geography of African development', *Geoforum*, 34(4), pp. 419–36.

Merry, S. E. (2016) *The seductions of quantification: Measuring human rights, gender violence, and sex trafficking*. Chiago: Chicago University Press.

Mitchell, T. (2002) *Rule of experts: Egypt, techno-politics, modernity*. Berkeley: University of California Press.

Montero, S. (2018) 'Leveraging Bogotá: Sustainable development, global philanthropy and the rise of urban solutionism', *Urban Studies*, 57(11), pp. 2263–81.

Myers, J. (2021) 'These charts show the growing income inequality between the world's richest and poorest'. World Economic Forum. Available: www.weforum.org/agenda/2021/12/global-income-inequality-gap-report-rich-poor/.

Nkot, F. and Amougou, G. (2021) 'Cameroon's Kribi deep seaport construction project: Between state ownership and tendencies of extraversion' in Kaag, M., Khan-Mohammad, G., Schmid, S. (eds), *Destination Africa: Contemporary Africa as a centre of global encounter*. Leiden: Brill, pp. 235–60.

Ndikumana, L. and Boyce, J. (2021) *Capital Flight from Africa, 1970-2018, New Estimates with Updated Trade Misinvoicing Methodology*. PERI Research Report, May 2021.

Ocampo, E. and Neu, D. (2008) *Doing missionary work: The World Bank and the diffusion of financial practices*. Halifax: Fernwood Publishing Co.

Perkins, J. (2004) 'An economic hit man is born' in *Confessions of an economic hit man*. London: Ebury Press.

Piketty, T. and Goldhammer, A. (2014) *Capital in the twenty-first century*. Cambridge, MA: Belknap Press.

Pogge. T. (2010) *Politics as usual: What lies behind the pro-poor rhetoric*. Cambridge: Polity Press.

Pollio, A. (2022) 'Acceleration, development and technocapitalism at the Silicon Cape of Africa', *Economy and Society*, 51(1), pp. 46–70.

Puttick, S. and Murrey, A. (2020) Confronting the silence on race in geography education in England: Learning from anti-racist, decolonial and black geographies', *Geography*, 106(1).

Radcliffe, S. A. (2005) 'Development and geography: Towards a postcolonial development geography?', *Progress in Human Geography*, 29(3), pp. 291–8.

Rahnema, M. and Bawtree, V. (1997) 'Introduction' in Rahnema, Majif and Bawtree, Victoria (eds), *The Post-Development Reader*. London: Zed Books, pp. ix–3.

Rajagopal, B. (2001) 'The violence of development', *The Washington Post*, Editorial, A19.

Rodney, W. (1973) *How Europe underdeveloped Africa*. London and Dar-Es-Salaam: Bogle-L'Ouverture Publications.

Sachs, J. (2005) *The end of poverty: Economic possibilities for our time*. London: Penguin Books.

Sachs, W. (1992) 'Development: A guide to the ruins', *New Internationalist* https://newint.org/features/1992/06/05/keynote.

Sande Lee, J. H. (2015) *Developmentality: An Ethnography of the World Bank-Uganda Partnership*. New York: Berghahn Books.

Selwyn, B. (2017) 'The Big Lie' in *The struggle for development*. Cambridge: Polity Press.

Sharpe, C. (2016) *In the wake: On blackness and being*. Durham, NC: Duke.

Smirl, L. (2015) *Spaces of aid: How cars, compounds and hotels shape humanitarianism*. London: Zed.

Stone, D. (2019) 'Transnational policy entrepreneurs and the cultivation of influence: individuals, organizations and their networks', *Globalizations*, 16(7), pp. 1128–44.

Tandon, Y. (2008) *Ending Aid Dependence*. Nairobi and Dakar: Fahamu.

Tiafack, O., Chrétien, N. and Emmanuel, N. (2014) 'Development polarisation in Limbe and Kribi (Littoral Cameroon): Growth challenges, lessons from Douala and options', *Current Urban Studies*, 2, pp. 361–79.

Truman, H. (1949) Inaugural address. Delivered at the US Capitol in Washington D.C. Transcript available at www.trumanlibrary.gov/library/public-papers/19/inaugural-address.

United Nations (1951) *Measures for the economic development of underdeveloped countries*. New York.

Uvin, P. (1998) *Aiding violence: The development enterprise in Rwanda*. West Hartford, Connecticut: Kumarian Press, Inc.

Veltmeyer, H. (2020) '"Capitalism, development, imperialism, globalization: A tale of four concepts', *Globalizations*, 17(8), pp. 1335–49.

Wallerstein, I. (1974) *The modern World System I: Capitalist agriculture and the origins of the European world-economy in the sixteenth century*. New York: Academic Press.

Watts, M. (2003) 'Development and governmentality', *Singapore Journal of Tropical Geography*, 24(1), pp. 6–34.

Ziai, A. (2007) 'Development discourse and its critics: An introduction to post-development' in *Exploring Postdevelopment*.

3

Development and Violence/
Development as Violence

Violence is fundamental to the ongoing reordering of the social and natural world for capitalist accumulation, just as it was central to the introduction and maintenance of both imperialism and colonialism. This chapter explores how violence has remained embedded within the organizing logics and structures of international development. Our engagement through and with decolonial critique is carried out with a shared dedication to collaborative and targeted anti-colonial, anti-imperial and anti-racist illuminations and unmaskings of the institutions at the forefront of contemporary colonial violence, especially corporate and military entities and the knowledge regimes that empower them.

David Harvey calls the violence of neoliberal capitalism 'accumulation by dispossession', involving 'wholesale dispossessions . . . appropriations and exploitations', because capitalism 'internalizes cannibalistic as well as predatory and fraudulent practices' (2004: 75). We meanwhile argue that the intersection of race, space and place affects the scale and extremity of this violence (Fanon 1963; Mbembe 2019). Historical renditions of violent capitalism in non-European and colonized spaces were masked by the production of imaginative and violent geographies associating these spaces with 'barbarism' (Apter 2008; Jackson 2009). Thus, the West had long viewed the Global South as a place of 'barbaric violence' executed by 'backward' peoples. After their two World Wars, European governments and their allies have perpetrated acts of violence, conflict and wars globally and almost continuously in the Global South, largely in the pursuit of wealth.

In a *Washington Post* article, Balakrishnan Rajagopal (2001) claimed that there is 'international indifference to the violence of development projects', pointing particularly to the dispossession and displacement of people off their land, which pushes them into poverty through what he terms 'development cleansing'. He singles out large infrastructure constructions, such as the Narmada Dam in India, but equally significant are the destruction of livelihoods that occurs through the building of roads, railways and pipelines (Murrey 2015). These forms of violence are presented as necessary side effects of the promise of development and of modernity (Mowforth 2014; also Chapter 2).

Development ideologies that emerged in the 1940s incorporated the colonizers' view of peoples and their alleged capacities for violence. Ashley Noel Mack & Tiara R. Na'puti (2019: 348), writing about gendered violence against Natives Peoples in the settler colonial societies of North America, encourage us to challenge 'colonial unknowing', which 'renders unintelligible the effects of colonial relations of power and mark colonization and dispossession with a finality even though colonial violence is ongoing'. Violence exacted against people racialized as non-white is indeed ignored, downplayed, excused and legitimated. Fanon notes how the settler refers to native people in 'zoological terms' as, like animals, the latter are expected to have tolerance to higher thresholds of pain and suffering.[1] This draws from a civilizational discourse that attributes a racial hierarchy to the valuation of life. Achille Mbembe (2019: 76–77) describes the colonies as spaces of exception, existing juridically outside the law, where 'peace' is more likely to assume the face of 'endless war'. 'In the conqueror's eye, *savage life* is just another form of *animal life*' (76), where the native 'is relegated between "subjecthood and objecthood"' (ibid.: 79). Therefore, in the Global South, these categories of violence interact and are legitimated, normalized and socialized. In a colonial context, capitalist extractive processes required the dehumanization of people racialized as not white so that they could be subjected to the violence of land dispossession, displacement, genocide, forced labour, enslavement, apprenticeships, mutilations, indentureship and scorched earth (Fanon 1963).

Since the beginning of the development era in the 1940s, countries in the Global South have experienced myriad forms of militaristic violence, including proxy Cold Wars, civil wars, genocide and low intensity warfare. Less overt, but of equal significance, is the everyday violence to

---

1. For example, then-chief economist of the World Bank, Larry Summers, stated in a memo that 'the economic logic behind dumping a load of toxic waste in the lowest wage country is impeccable and we should face up to that' (*The Economist*, 15 February 1992). The justification was low life expectancy, plenty of land, and so on.

which people are subjected through forced displacement, chronic hunger, maternal and infant mortality, lack of access to clean water, pollution from extractive activities and heightened levels of personal insecurity – the last of which has impelled self-imprisonment in gated communities or barricaded dwellings. Even though the gaze of development experts has targeted direct violence such as civil wars, they have done so by abstracting violence from the concrete historical conditions that have produced it. We support Simon Springer's (2011) contention that the violence of neoliberalism becomes justified as a cleansing tool within the creation of a new order organized by the market. Extraction for development has become a paradigm. Therefore, violence should be understood as a process – a reflection of the turbulent landscape of capitalism.

ANTI-COLONIAL AND DECOLONIAL SOUNDTRACK

The songs framing this chapter are Blick Bassy's 'Ngwa'[2] and 'Woñi'.[3] Bassy is a Cameroonian singer-songwriter whose 2020 album pays tribute to Cameroonian anti-colonial independence fighters (*les maquisards*) assassinated by French colonialists and their proxy armies in the 1950s and 60s. High-profile Cameroonian leaders assassinated in this period include Ruben Um Nyobè, Dr Félix-Roland Mounié and Ernest Ouandié. It is impossible to ascertain exact numbers of deaths because the colonial archives were destroyed and sabotaged, but an estimated 300,000–600,000 Cameroonians were killed fighting for independence from France in what was called the *guerre cachée* or the 'hidden war', thus named because speaking about it publicly (including saying the names of assassinated leaders) was a criminal offence in post-colonial Cameroon. In the music video for 'Woni', an adolescent girl is shown images of Um Nyobè by her grandmother as Bassy sings:

> our country grew up in fear . . . our people grew up in fear . . . my grandfather grew up in fear . . . Um Nyobe grew up without fear . . . Moumié died without fear . . . our country is dying, dying of fear. Our country is dying, us, we do nothing but drink beer.

---

2. www.youtube.com/watch?v=DJHXlc7Afzk.
3. www.youtube.com/watch?v=sKjo6sWZrSM.

Bassy's songs provide a commentary on colonial violence and its cultural and social persistence in the present.

THE MULTIPLICITY OF VIOLENCE

Even where there is no outright war, militarism contributes to enduring violence. In understanding the conditions of peace, Johan Galtung (1969) developed a tripartite classification of violence: direct, structural and cultural. Direct violence refers to physical violence against the person, as in warfare or assault. Cultural violence includes the gender-based violence associated with patriarchy; for example restricting a person's ability to pursue education or certain forms of labour on the basis of their gender identity, or the stigmatization of people with mental health problems, or the marginalisation experienced by elderly women. While such practices may be accepted in particular cultural settings, they are nevertheless dynamic and linked to particular historical and structural contexts. Structural violence is often less visible than direct violence, as it is embedded within social, political and economic structures and institutions, and frequently it is not recognised as a form of violence. Galtung (1969: 171) explains that 'if people are starving when this is objectively avoidable, then violence is committed, regardless of whether there is a clear subject-action-object relation'. Structural violence can lead to interpersonal violence. The concept was later expanded to include the violence arising from the deliberate maintenance of a global system of capitalist economic inequity.

The South African scholar of environmental humanities Rob Nixon (2011) further elaborates a concept of 'slow violence' to address the violence of climate change, toxic waste, deforestation, mega dam construction, oil spills and their environmental aftermath, which often take place gradually or invisibly. As the term suggests, these forms of violence unfold incrementally and thus with little of the fanfare reserved for episodic and spectacularized episodes of direct and physical violence (Nixon 2011). This violence is insidious and frequently overlooked, deeply entangled as it is within social, economic and ecological forms of injustice. Drawing from a decade of work in two communities along the Chad-Cameroon Oil Pipeline, one of the co-authors of this book (Amber) writes about the potentials for forms of 'slow dissent' – that is, intergenerational struggle manifested through stories, song, building anger and fluctuating forms of direct dissent – in communities subjected to authoritarian-sponsored slow violence (Murrey 2015, 2016). The material and concrete dispossessions, appropriations and pollutions of extractive capitalism (and their uneven racial, sexual and gendered impacts) are at the forefront of resistance for those with a commitment to decolonizing international development, which has for too long offered ideological cover and displaced angst with seductive fantasies of betterment via capitalism. We have had enough of the violent system in which development is embedded.

In the Global South, all forms of violence were aggravated following the introduction of neoliberal polices in the 1980s onwards. Still, civil warfare is often interpreted by liberal scholars and policymakers as arising from internal factors, such as ethnicity or the 'resource curse'. Following Springer (2011), we argue that violence has its own spatiality and temporality: it is historically rooted and spatially expressed and relational. In the Global South, the colonial legacies of state formation and militarism support violent resolutions at different spatial scales, ranging from the national to the domestic, and from the exceptional to the everyday.

MILITARISM AND DEVELOPMENT

'Militarism' refers to the ideology that sees a society's security as depending on the constant preparation for war against external or internal enemies. It is a demonstration of the coercive power of the state as it seeks to dominate and secure its territory. 'Militarization', meanwhile, refers to the processes through which the ideology of militarism penetrates society. Economic, cultural and social life are mobilized to see violence as the means through which disputes can be resolved. Militaries are therefore seen as essential to the building of the nation-state and to the defence of the nation (Abrahamsen 2018). Norbert Elias (1987), meanwhile, claimed that, by monopolizing the means of violence for itself, the state removes violence from everyday life, whether by consent or force. Theories of the modern state formation in Europe contend that consent is accordingly obtained through the development of a 'social contract' between state and society – that is people abrogating individual right and liberty to the state who maintains social order.[4] However, the Polish sociologist Zygmunt

---

4. Seventeenth & eighteenth century European political philosophers, such as Thomas Hobbes (17th. c), John Locke (17th. c) and Jean-Jacques Rousseau (18th. c) developed the concept of 'the social contract'.

Bauman (1995: 91) challenged the view that the modern nation-state has removed violence from everyday life. Referring to the Jewish Holocaust, he saw 'modern genocide [as] an element of social engineering, meant to bring about a social order conforming to the design of the perfect society'. Violence remains an integral part of the modern nation-state: genocide and other extreme forms of can be perceived as legitimate violence when at the core of the civilizing process.

One of us (Patricia) (2008: 9) coined the term 'the genocidal state' to define states where the 'politics of exploitation, exclusivism, racism, eugenics, militarism, extremism and patriarchy' comes together in a society, and where the politics of competition means the elimination of the other and results in acts of genocide, war and embedded militarism. A genocidal state has a military expenditure that outstrips social expenditure along with 'the training of the security services for the domestic control of citizens, the penetration of militarism into societal institutions, and the regional expansion of warfare, through the transferal of genocidal ideas relating to the conduct of war' (ibid.). Militarism has led to genocide and warfare in colonial and post-colonial states and continues to be expanded through international trade in weapons of war, the primacy of the Global North's security concerns (e.g. the 'war on terror'), and peace-building interventions aimed at stabilization and securitization.

A question that is often posed with respect to militaries from the Global South is whether their role is to defend the state and its citizens from foreign incursions or to protect the state and state elites from internal demands of the citizens. Military regimes in Africa, for example, have continued the colonial authoritarian approach to governance. To answer this question, one needs to consider the histories of the military's relationship to both the state and extractive capitalism. Post-colonial societies, in which violence is normalized and militarism is pervasive, have histories of subjection to extraction that produced forms of accumulation destructive of life. These forms have intensified under neoliberalism.

COLONIAL VIOLENCE OR 'BULA MATARISME'[5]

Given the European colonial origins of many contemporary states in the Global South, an examination of the colonial state's modes of imposition

---

5.   Bula Matarisme is a Congolese term meaning 'to break stones, break everything, to destroy any resistance' (Dia Wamba 2000: 1).

and the changes it has effected in the relationship between the people and the military can enable a greater understanding of violence in the postcolonial nation-state, and in the processes of extraction known as 'international development'.

In states formed by force and dominated by authoritarian rule, the 'social contract' does not exist. The colonial state was formed by and through violence. The intensity of its violence depended on the relationship between the civilian population and the security institutions. Colonial armies and police were recruited from outside the territories within which they operated, or from specific ethnic groups labelled by Europeans as martial races or 'tribes' to denote their physical build and supposed propensity for warfare (e.g. Kamba in Kenya, mainly northerners in Ghana and Nigeria).

The Southern African feminist scholar Patricia McFadden (2008) critiques the liberal scholarship on the African state that seeks to view these places through the lens of historical European state formation. We must instead understand the state that Europeans built in Africa: 'Africans inherited a colonial state that represented and performed all that colonialism meant for subjugated, exploited, and disposed people. It was a fundamentally undemocratic, racist, exclusionary institutional and ideological system, constituted of deeply racist, misogynistic relationships of power and suppression' (ibid., 138). She notes how, 'fashioned after the systems of the colonizing society in class and racial terms, [colonial military structures] operated on behalf of the state'. What was initially exceptional violence became routinized and banal during the colonial period, as people were socialized into accepting their treatment and material conditions.

A well-documented example of colonial violence was exacted against the Congolese people in the Congo Free State, which was claimed by King Leopold of Belgian as his private property. Leopold gave concessions to rubber and other extractive companies, who then exercised necropolitical control by extracting wealth from forced labour and natural resources. The American historian Adam Hochschild (1998) describes how villagers existed in a slave labour system where each adult male had a quota of rubber to collect. Those who failed were beaten or had their hands and feet amputated. Armed resistance to conquest and constant rebellions from local people led to military campaigns and massacres. Hochschild (1998:163) reports how 'the entire system was militarized, with each con-

94

cession or rubber company having its own militia'. The state military (*Force Publique*) had garrisons everywhere and often supplied 'their fire-power to the companies under contract' – together they took hostages and subdued rebellious villages (ibid.: 163). Some 10 million people were killed and maimed during Leopold's ownership of the territory. Ongoing violence in the Democratic Republic of Congo (DRC) is the outcome of historical political economic relations, competition over land and strategic resources that involves the elimination of competitors. Such violence is evident at every spatial scale from the national to the everyday practices at the local level.

Mbembe (2019) introduced the concept of 'necropolitical governance' to explain the colony as a space of exception. Racism meant that 'colonies could be ruled in absolute lawlessness', as they were not 'organized as a state form and do not create a human world'. In the colonial paradigm, 'the sovereign [retains the right to] kill at any time and in any manner' (ibid.: 78). He goes on to discuss the social and spatial reorganization of society into the colonial order alongside the violence that underpins the late modern colonial regimes, where the people 'experience a permanent condition of "being in pain"' (ibid.: 91) – where '*death-worlds*' are created, in which 'vast populations are subjected to living conditions that confer upon them the status of the *living dead*' (ibid.: 92, emphasis original).

Colonial necropolitical violence was also visible in Germany's genocide in Namibia (1904–1908) (Melber 2005; Sarkin 2011); Britain's brutal suppression of rebellion, as with the Mau Mau in 1950s Kenya (Elkins 2005; 2022); the wars of liberations from Portuguese colonial rule in Angola, Mozambique and Guinea Bissau; from French rule in Algeria;[6] and, in southern Africa, from white supremacist states in Zimbabwe, South Africa and Namibia. These forms of liberatory wars enacted what Frantz Fanon would term 'revolutionary violence'.

A number of films have depicted the historical violence that accompanied European colonization, including *White King, Red Rubber, Black Death* (2003); *Concerning Violence* (2014); and *Exterminate all the Brutes* (2021). Examples, meanwhile, of the postcolonial continuation of violence and the centring of the white gaze in cinema include *The Constant Gardener* (2005), *Blood Diamonds* (2006), *Blood Coltan* (2010)

---

6. For details, see the 1966 film *The Battle of Algiers*.

and *Machine Gun Preacher* (2011). Readers may be familiar with Joseph Conrad's *The Heart of Darkness* (1899), which reinforced the stereotype of the 'dark continent'. You might also have read Barbara Kingsolver's *The Poisonwood Bible* (1998), set in the Congo at the time of independence, or Ngũgĩ wa Thiong'o's *Weep not, Child* (1964) set in Kenya during the Mau Mau war of independence (1950s).

Independence did not result in changes to the extractive modes of accumulation. Liberal development theorists and policymakers ignored historical specificities, especially the violent components of European economic ascendancy and the exogenous dimensions of the ongoing violence of accumulation by dispossession. African scholars, including Claude Ake and Patricia McFadden, have documented how African political elites were co-opted into the system of extraction either through greed or by adopting ideologies of development based on the anti-communist 'stages of economic growth' trajectory put forward by Rostow in 1960 (as discussed in Chapter 2). Leaders who aspired to a model of development that addressed social and racial injustices found themselves vulnerable to assassinations by the West or internal forces aligned with external interests.

NEOLIBERAL VIOLENCE

The neoliberal phase of capitalism undermined state-centred approaches to development, heralding a return to the conditions that prevailed in much of the Global South countries under colonialism. As we will discuss in Chapter 4, neoliberal capitalism centres paradigms of extraction and extractivism, removes the welfarist contract between state and citizens and pushes responsibilities for the social reproduction of life purely on to the individual. Under neoliberalism, militaristic violence has intensified and has been used to sustain extractive activities across the globe (Akiwumi 2012). Springer (2012: 138) argues that 'the relationship between neoliberalism and violence is directly related to the system of rule that neoliberalism constructs, justifies, and defends in advancing its hegemonies of ideology, of policy and program, of state form, of governmentality, and ultimately of discourse'. Neoliberalism provides the context for the establishment, maintenance and extension of hierarchical orderings of social relations. These orderings are re-created, sustained and intensified, often through racialized processes of 'Othering'. Neoliberalism has been integral to contemporary violence through the generation of social divisions.

The social inequalities that deepened after the introduction of neoliberalism in Africa in the 1980s led to conflicts, some of which transformed into civil wars in the 1990s when about sixteen African countries were engulfed in warfare and, in some cases, genocidal violence.[7] Large numbers of civilian deaths and crimes against humanity occurred, with estimates of one million deaths in the 1994 genocide in Rwanda; 300,000 in Burundi between 1996 and 2000; and over two million in the DRC (Daley 2008).

While explanations for these wars varied, popular interpretations in the Global North reflected the colonial lens through which the West sees African crises, drawing on racist tropes. Wars were attributed to the resurgence of atavistic, age-old hatreds. These wars were said to be irrational, brutal, inhumane, given the use of rape as a weapon of war and rudimentary technology (e.g. the machete). But assault rifles, such as the Soviet Kalashnikov Model 1947 (AK-47), were clearly visible and widely available after the collapse of the Soviet Union and the liberalization of the arms trade. Using what became known as the 'new barbarism thesis', development policymakers ignored the devastating outcomes of the economic policies promoted by the international financial institutions and Western governments, and instead treated the violence as having local origins and the effects of violence as economic externalities, thus avoiding any responsibility.

While hegemonic Euro-American powers have sought to use the International Criminal Court to pursue justice for victims of neoliberal wars in Africa, Kamari Clarke (2019: 12)[8] argues that:

Through the systematic elision of the root causes propelling violence, international criminal law finds a concrete "Other": a singular perpetrator – a commander directing mass violence, a warlord – whose agency can be severed only through external judiciaries, and whose acts of violence are recontextualized within a new political and moral economy based on victims' justice, diverting focus away from "the enabling cycles of production and consumption that sustain war in the first place".

---

7.   Protracted warfare occurred in Sudan, Somalia, Uganda, Sierra Leone, Liberia, Ivory Coast, Rwanda, Burundi, Angola, Eritrea, Ethiopia, Zaire/DRC, Eastern Nigeria, Chad and Senegal.
8.   See also Ba (2020).

Gnaka Lagoke's (2023) work on the ICC's prosecution and eventual acquittal of former Ivoirian President Koudou Laurent Gbagbo and his close political ally Charles Blé Goudé further demonstrates the neo-imperial potentials of this uneven instrument of global power. In 2011, Gbagbo was arrested in the wake of a contested presidential election with Alassane Ouattara, the former deputy managing director of the International Monetary Fund. As the 2011 revolutions rocked Tunisia, Egypt and Libya, and global attention was directed elsewhere, French-backed NATO troops quietly expanded their ongoing 'Opération Licorne' (active since September 2002). Under the guise of 'peace keeping', French military troops provided logistics and transport to pro-Ouattara/anti-Gbagbo forces. After several sustained nights of bombing at the Presidential Palace, Gbagbo was arrested and transferred to the Hague, where he was charged with four counts of crimes against humanity. A complex and contested trial ensued, in which episodes of violence on both sides of the conflict were heard. Strikingly, the bulk of material evidence demonstrated violence *against* pro-Gbagbo political supporters, including what became known as the 'massacre at Duékoué', a neighbourhood of Abidjan where hundreds of people were killed, burned and buried in mass graves as anti-Gbagbo, French-backed militias swept the country on their way to the capital, Abidjan (as initially documented by the Red Cross and later by Human Rights Watch 2012). After eight years, Gbagbo was ultimately acquitted on all counts. Following the ruling, however, he was prohibited from returning to his country and pressured to agree to never run for political office, despite being found not guilty (Lagoke 2023). While he has since been able to return, such contemporary political arrangements demonstrate the weaknesses within formations of the oft-evoked 'international community', which presume an impartial community rather than a network of various state and institutional actors motivated by economic tensions often based on imperial debris.

The post-Cold War conflicts were the outcome of the intersection of multiple forces that included competition between corrupt and authoritarian state elites and the deteriorating living conditions caused by structural adjustment programmes. However, as these wars were no longer considered to be proxy ideological wars for the Cold War superpowers, Western scholars and development policymakers looked beyond populist explanations to more sophisticated causal factors (Kaldor 2001). Focusing on endogenous and criminalized explanations, these scholars gave primacy to the affective desire of 'greed' over grievance or structural factors, and discounted the question as to why ordinary people, especially the youth, might choose to join rebel movements. What is known in the development literature as 'the greed versus grievance debate', occurred between those scholars advocating a neo-classical economic approach based on econometric modelling to explain wars (Collier and Hoeffler 2002), and those adopting a political economy approach (Keen 2012). The former argued that war is caused by greed rather than by the grievance of the poor, the disenfranchized and the unemployed. Greed is seen as intrinsic to states labelled 'failed' owing to their own internal pathologies and dysfunctionalities. Attributing violence to greed contributed to the popularity of the 'resource curse' as an explanation for civil warfare. Simply put, development economists contended that countries with a high percentage of non-renewable primary commodity resources are more prone to conflict (Collier and Hoeffler, 2002). They focused specifically on revenues from primary commodities – high-value mineral-rich resources such as oil, diamonds and gold – that can finance conflict. Some who embraced the greed thesis, such as Collier, were working with the World Bank, whose structural adjustment policies contributed to poverty (Chapter 2). The simplistic formulation of the 'greed' and resource curse theses have been challenged by critical development and peace scholars as well as economists from the World Institute for Development Economics Research.[9]

On the other hand, critical scholars have pursued a political economy interpretation with a focus on multiple factors, of which grievance was but one. They argue that ahistorical and endogenous interpretations produce only partial accounts of the palimpsest of violence occurring in places of extraction and intensifying under neoliberalism (Carmer 2003; Keen 2012). In short, war is caused by multiple internal and external factors including repression, intra-elite competition, violent extraction and invasions. War is linked to histories of accumulation in Africa and can be profitable for certain actors. But, exogenous factors, such as resource extraction and global resource demand, are not given weight by neoliberal policymakers.

The American political ecologist Michael Watts (2003) discusses how oil extraction produces and reproduces violence in the Niger Delta of

---

9. See for example, see Murrey and Jackson (2019) as well as Indra De Soysa (2002).

Nigeria. Oil has been extracted from the region since the 1960s. Between 2015 and 2020, Nigeria earned USD 206 billion from oil exports,[10] without adequately addressing the poverty or the environmental destruction in the oil-producing areas. In the Niger Delta, the normalized violence of extraction takes various forms: oil spills, gas flares and extensive damage done to fisheries and water sources. The Delta area has remained poor with minimal health and education facilities. Protests by indigenous groups have been either violently suppressed, as with the killing of Ken Saro Wiwa in 1995,[11] or co-opted and included in state legitimated violence. Watts (2004: 201) has argued that oil revenues 'ushered in a miserable, undisciplined, decrepit and corrupt form of "petro-capitalism" in Nigeria'. The resource curse thesis excludes the role of transnational capital and Western governments' interest in the oil. Instead, Watts shows that 'petro-capitalism operates through a particular configuration of firm, state, and community', in what he terms an 'oil complex'. This complex is strongly territorial and generates new forms of 'governable spaces' (the oil community, the ethnic community and the nation) that challenge community authority and the nation-state project. Watts uses the concept of the oil complex to recognize the existence of relational spaces, where multiple interacting hierarchies of governance exist in different places, and at a range of scales, making it difficult to reach resolutions that are satisfactory for all, therefore producing and maintaining 'economies of violence' (ibid.).

The neoliberal wars of the 1990s and 2000s reinforced the ideology of militarism and increased militarization despite the UN-led promotion of peace. To explore militarization, readers might investigate the level of state military expenditures using data compiled by the Stockholm International Peace Research Institute (SIPRI). From a social welfare perspective, it is worth noting that the larger the proportion of GDP spent on military expenditure, the fewer the resources for social welfare provision-

---

10. Data compiled from *OPEC 2020 Annual Report*.
11. Leader of the Movement for the Survival of the Ogoni People (MOSOP), a resistance movement formed in 1992 to protest environmental destruction occurring in the region. In 1995, Saro-Wiwa was executed along with eight other activists by the military regime. The UN Environment Programme published a report in 2011 stating that it would take thirty years and USD 1 billion to clean up Ogoniland; see www. unep.org/explore-topics/disasters-conflicts/where-we-work/nigeria/environmental-assessment-ogoniland-report.

ing. This is more acute in African countries such as Namibia, Mali and Uganda, where data for 2020 indicate that 2.5 per cent and above of gross domestic income is used for weapons (SIPRI 2022).[12] In such countries, social welfare provision is poor and guided by neoliberal doctrines; the state has either withdrawn or provides inadequate services.

The continued militarization of African countries even as they experience economic austerity is a reflection of the necropolitical governance that persists at a global scale and its links to ongoing coloniality. Since the terrorist attacks of 9/11, attempts in the US to seek retribution through the 'war on terror' to secure its supply of oil and other strategic minerals have led to the expansion of the US and other Western militaries in Africa, sometimes under the rhetoric of securing aid, helping women and girls, and supporting other externally funded development projects. The US Africa Command (Africom), a special military unit targeting Africa, was established in 2007. Under the Presidency of Barack Obama (2009–17), AFRICOM expanded its military presence across the continent, even in countries where there had been opposition under the previous president, George W. Bush. The Sahel Initiative, a Western military operation which involved French, US and UK presence in the Sahel region was portrayed as a mission to counter militant Islamist groups (Al Shabaab – Somalia; Boko Haram – Nigeria; Ansar Dine and Movement of Oneness and Jihad in West Africa – Mali).

Western governments' alliances with Islamic Jihadists have also been used to promote Western interests in Africa. This is exemplified in the Benghazi region of Libya as part of the effort to overthrow the Libyan President Muammar Gaddafi. In 2011, the US, France, and the UK invaded Libya under the pretext of supporting the uprising against Gaddafi. The invasion secured the West's control over Libya's oil, but left the country itself plunged into a chaos which remains unresolved in 2023. The Jamaican-American peace scholar Horace Campbell (2013) documents 'the colossal failure' of the intervention: despite resulting in the execution of Gaddafi by his own people, the intervention led to thousands of Libyan deaths and failed to achieve democracy. Meanwhile in north-eastern Nigeria and Chad, the presence of Islamic militants among

---

12. See SIPRI, 'SIPRI Update April 2022: New military expenditure data, Stockholm Forum registration, impact of war in Ukraine on food security, and more' at www.sipri. org/media/newsletter/2022-april.

repressive militarized states has only increased people's vulnerability to physical and structural violence (Mustapha and Ehrhardt, 2018).

AFRICOM is used to maintain US global hegemony in the face of China's investments in Africa (Chapter 7). The link between finance and the military industrial complex is represented by the 2017 opening of a Chinese military base in Djibouti in close proximity to a US military base, increasing the likelihood of the African continent becoming a theatre for war between global superpowers.

PRIVATIZING WARFARE

With Western powers pursuing perpetual war to ensure their economic hegemony, the use of conventional militaries has become less attractive in democratic contexts. The outsourcing of military interventions has expanded the ways in which accumulation can occur in a military-industrial complex. One development under neoliberalism has been the expansion of private security firms and the formalization of mercenaries into private military contractors (PMCs). These include Western-based companies such as G4S, SERCO, Xe, Dyncorp and Blackwater, as well as the Russian company Wagner. Their activities vary from protecting Global South elites to the operations of multi-national companies (particularly for mineral extraction) and UN agencies; they include fighting in wars in lieu of Western militaries or in support of host states. In May 2013, a US government's Congressional Research Service report stated that there were 18,000 private security contractors employed in Afghanistan by the US Department of Defence in addition to 65,700 military personnel (Schwartz and Church 2013). The ongoing war across the Sahel in Africa has seen the proliferation of PMCs on the continent. One report states that

> The UN's peacekeeping mission in Mali . . . and French *Operation Barkhane* forces operating in the Sahel are notably supported by British, French, American and Ukrainian companies that provide supplies, weapons, security, and logistical support. At least 21 American companies are listed as military service providers in North Africa and the Sahel for AFRICOM alone and if the CIA and other US organizations were included the number would be higher. Russian contractors are

also involved and range from assisting Khalifa Haftar in Libya to intervening in the Sahel and Central Africa.[13]

Two important problems caused by PMCs are their lack of public accountability and their desire to increase profits for shareholders. Atrocities committed by conventional troops can potentially be officially investigated and addressed through national or international courts.[14] but there is no mechanism for documenting and reporting those carried out by PMCs. Furthermore, a business model dependent on warfare prevents the revelation of crimes that could negatively affect operations and gives a concrete meaning to the idea of perpetual warfare as a means of accumulation.

The human cost of perpetual warfare is immense. One consequence of militarization and warfare is displacement, whereby people are forced to flee their homes, either becoming internally displaced within their countries or in another country as refugees. In mid-2022, the UN estimated that 103 million people were forcibly displaced globally, of whom 53.3 million were internally displaced. As conflicts become intractable, many refugees remain in protracted exile or are recycled (moving back and forth across a border after each episode of violence), becoming reliant on international humanitarian aid. The United Nations defines a protracted refugee situation as 'one in which refugees find themselves in a long-lasting and intractable state of limbo. Their lives may not be at risk, but their basic rights and essential economic, social and psychological needs remain unfulfilled after years in exile' (UNHCR 2004). Those internally displaced may find themselves unable to return to their homes for years, if at all.

Host states around the world have increasingly perceived refugees as the 'dangerous Other'. Indeed the act of flight from fear of persecution and death can result in long-term detention and criminalization (Mountz 2020; Loyd et al. 2016). In some African countries, refugee camps have become carceral spaces for containment before repatriation (Brankamp 2021) while, in a minority of cases, resettlement to a third country typ-

---

13. See *Sahara Focus*, MENA Intelligence Report (27 June 2019) "Business of war: private security companies in the Sahel", https://menas.co.uk/blog/private-security-companies-sahel.
14. This is a possibility despite Western governments deliberately trying to prevent their troops from being tried for war crimes at the International Criminal Court.

ically in the Global North. Brankamp and Gluck (2022) observe how refugees are governed by counterterrorism, in the 'war on terror' context. Under such circumstances, the humane political response is to advocate for camp abolition (Brankamp 2021: 106) to ensure 'more viable, safe, and humane futures for people on the move'.

Since the first decade of the twenty-first century, the level of outright warfare has decreased in Africa. In some regions of the DRC, Burundi and Rwanda, Nigeria, Mali, Cameroon, Ethiopia, Niger and Burkina Faso, 'low intensity warfare' is ongoing, where rebel groups still pose a threat to people's security. These states are conducting warfare in parts of their territories, without formal declarations of war. In states where peace agreements have been signed between warring factions (a process overseen by international actors), UN peacekeeping missions are normally deployed. These missions proliferated in the 1990s and early 2000s. In 2022, the UN's peacekeeping budget, which is on the decline, was US $6.5 billion for twelve peace-keeping missions (UNHCR 2022). Along with international and regional agencies, governmental and financial institutions, such as the African Union or ECOWAS, the World Bank and NGOs, the UN establishes what scholars term 'the liberal peace' (Richmond 2006; Daley 2007). This peace refers to the policies pursued in states undergoing reconstruction (after wars in the 1990s and early 2000s) that involve an almost universally applied, formulaic 'peace package' of power sharing, security sector reform and the reintroduction of harmful economic liberalization policies. It is very much an externally managed process, involving the United Nations and various Western governments who provide their funding. Western and UN troops oversee the demobilization of government troops and rebel armies before integrating both into one new army, which normally involves reducing its size and retraining. Since the early 1990s, the liberal peace has been implemented in Rwanda, Burundi, DRC, Liberia, Sierra Leone, Cote d'Ivoire, South Sudan and Somalia.

In the mid-1990s, the UN sought to diversify the origins and genders of its peacekeepers. This led to a biopolitical selection from the Global South, especially to places considered highly dangerous, such as Somalia. This shift in personnel followed a public outcry when US soldiers were killed in Somalia after the 1992 failure of an invasion to protect the humanitarian mission (Amar 2012; Henry 2019). It was no longer considered politically feasible to lose Western military members in peacekeeping missions. National armies and police forces in the Global

South are thus trained (by Western militaries and police) and equipped for external peace keeping. Through this process, Global South states have been able to strengthen their security services and gain what has become a lucrative form of revenue. Payments to peacekeepers are made directly to states, and, in most cases, their personnel salaries may surpass their normal income in the regular army and police.

Critics of the liberal peace argue that it reinforces state authority and does not address deep structural violence, maintaining a significant potential for further outbreaks of war. The demobilization of government troops and rebel armies tends to leave most military personnel disaffected, unless they are recruited into UN peacekeeping missions. In post-conflict countries, the UN and Western governments carry out what they define as stabilization. According to the UK government's Stabilization Unit (2014), 'stabilization is . . . an activity undertaken as an initial response to violence or the immediate threat of violence . . . when undertaking stabilization interventions, the UK seeks to protect the means of survival and restore basic security, promote and support a political process to reduce violence as well as prepare a foundation for longer term stability'.[15]

In Africa, stabilization involved military interventions, such as those in Mali, the Democratic Republic of Congo (DRC) and Niger. Marta Iñiguez de Heredia (2019: 627) contends that stabilization reproduces colonial tropes and relations of racialization, coercion and oppression, arguing that the UN stabilization framework in the DRC 'not only dehistoricises and blames the DRC for the situation it is in, [but also] simultaneously frees historical structures co-created by international actors from responsibility for the DRC's economic, political and social challenges'. She adds that 'stabilisation has also strengthened the capacity of national elites and foreign investors to control sizeable portions of [the] Congolese economy around a neo-liberal logic' (ibid.: 636).

'Stabilization' further strengthens the state's authority at the expense of local democratic groups. It prioritizes state investment in military and security activities over the rebuilding of vulnerable post-war communities. Grievances beyond those of the rebel elites remain unaddressed, and impunity remains prevalent as the internationally sponsored Truth and Reconciliation Commissions have no judicial powers. Justice is

---

15. See 'UK Government's Approach to Stabilisation', http://sclr.stabilisationunit.gov.uk/ publications/stabilisation-series/487-uk-approach-to-stabilisation-2014/file.

contracted-out to the ICC, where the trials of individual high-profile cases occur far away from the arena of conflict and address too few of the architects of violence (Clarke 2011 and 2019). Stabilization maintains the processes of militarization and systemic insecurity, normalizing militaristic violence as a condition of peace.

Stabilization also provides a justification for African countries to invade others, such as Rwanda's invasion of the Democratic Republic of Congo in 1996 and Kenya's invasion of Somalia in 2011. Samar Al-Bulushi (2019) uses the term 'cosmopolitan militarism' to describe how Kenya, the scene of ethnic violence during the 2007 elections, was able to deploy a discourse that rebranded the country as a bastion of peace in the region. It thus justified the 2011 invasion of Southern Somalia as an attempt to chase down the Islamic terrorist group Al-Shabaab. With Kenya acting as the West's regional champion in the War on Terror, Al- Bulushi concludes that 'the project of cosmopolitan militarism is central to this endeavor, cultivating new imaginative geographies, militarized masculinities, and religiously inflected attachments to war' (ibid.: 338).

MILITARISM AND VIOLENT MASCULINITIES

Daley (2008: 31) contends that 'state legitimation of violence in the public sphere leads to its extension into the private and the personal'. Until recently, military institutions were the domains of men and involved the promotion of a hegemonic, violent masculinity that strengthened patriarchal systems through the domination of women (Fanon 2008). Amina Mama and Patricia McFadden have enriched our understanding of the role of the gendered dimensions of militarism in Africa, especially its relationship to patriarchy, racism and violent masculinities. Mama and Okazawa-Rey (2014) and Mama (2014) have examined how the effects of continued militarization on West African societies have 'undermine[d] the prospect for democratization, social justice and genuine security, especially for women' (Mama and Okazawa-Rey 2014: 41). McFadden (2008: 149) considers the history of militarism in Africa and explains how the 'notions of rampancy (as violent masculinist impunity) and plunder (as the process of primitive accumulation necessary for the ensconce-ment of a class to be able to rule) acquire a specifically feminist and radical appeal'. She argues that working class and peasant African men use militarism often with impunity to capture wealth from the state and to 'exercise or facilitate the violation of women's bodily and sexual integrity as an expression of "reclaimed" African masculinity' (2008: 149). For McFadden (2008), Africans can understand and also transform the state if they adopt a critical feminist discourse that sees 'militarism as central – conceptually and empirically – to the deployment of the state as a site of accumulation by various ruling classes throughout history, as well as a vehicle of repression, surveillance, and exclusion of the majority of people, particularly women, the young, and the elderly in working communities' (152).

Sexual violence is a major feature of interpersonal violence in militarized societies. Since the 1990s, international policy discourse and interventions on sexual and gender-based violence (SGBV) has tended to focus on sexual violence in war. In international criminal law, rape has been made a war crime.[16] This has generated much needed attention on a problem that was ignored in earlier wars and have led to justice for some women survivors. Yet, at the national and local level, even where laws have been changed, women have difficulties bringing charges against men and face degrading treatment by the police (Eriksson Baaz and Stern 2013).

Western media have sensationalized wartime rape in African countries with misleading headlines, such as 'Why the eastern DRC is the "rape capital of the world"'. This not only leads to generalizations and reproduction of colonial stereotypes about African men as rapists, but may have also intensified militarized masculinity and violence against women and girls.[17] These violent narratives can be compelling for activists and NGOs seeking to raise funds. However, they reduce the survivors to agen-

---

16. Rape was recognized as a war crime in 1998 at the International Criminal Tribunal for Rwanda in the Jean-Paul Akayesu case. See *The Prosecutor v. Jean-Paul Akayesu (Trial Judgment)*, 1998, ICTR-96-4-T, International Criminal Tribunal for Rwanda (ICTR), www.refworld.org/cases,ICTR,40278fbb4.html. The UN Security Council passed Resolution 1820 in 2008, which states 'rape and other forms of sexual violence can constitute war crimes, crimes against humanity, or a constitutive act with respect to genocide' (3). See http://unscr.com/en/resolutions/1820.

17. See Fiona Lloyd-Davies, 'Why Eastern DR Congo is "Rape Capital of the World"', *CNN*, 25 November 2011, https://edition.cnn.com/2011/11/24/world/africa/democratic-congo-rape/index.html. In response, see Justine Masika Bihamba, 'The "Rape Capital of the World"? We Women in Congo Don't See it That Way', *The Guardian*, 9 November 2017, www.theguardian.com/global-development/2017/oct/09/the-rape-capital-of-the-world-we-women-in-democratic-republic-congo-dont-see-it-that-way.

tless victims and ignore local mobilization against violence and solidarity. Furthermore, they obscure evidence that international peacekeepers are themselves implicated in sexual violence (Daigle et al 2020). Mack and Na' puti (2019: 347), remind us that:

> gendered violence is historically and presently a colonial tool that wields power over and against Indigenous peoples, attempting to destroy or erase their sovereignty and lives . . .[it] is a complex social problem that (often in seemingly contradictory ways and at various intersections) reinforces White supremacy, patriarchy, heteronorma-tivity, binary Western epistemologies of gender, and capitalist logics. (2019: 350)

WOMEN'S RESISTANCE TO GENDERED VIOLENCE: #BRINGBACKOURGIRLS

In April 2014, the Islamist militant group, Boko Haram, kidnapped 276 girls from the Government Girls Secondary School in the town of Chibok, Borno State, Nigeria, sparking a national and international outcry and producing a discourse that perpetuated racialized imaginaries of African and Islamic masculinities. Amid calls for more militarization and international interventions from local NGOs, the Twitter hashtag 'Bring Back Our Girls' went viral. The hashtag was mobilized to bring attention to the kidnapping and to emphasize how violence against women of colour is overlooked by the global media. Celebrities from the Global North, including Michelle Obama, the wife of the then US president, tweeted and retweeted in support of the campaign. Yet, the case of #BringBack-OurGirls demonstrates how international supporters can take up local women's activism against violence, leading to ineffective interventions that do not address the core problems.[18]

While the focus on international institutions, Western governments and celebrities has fallen on addressing sexual violence in warfare, research shows that it can intensify even in the post-war period and is

---

18. To fully consider this, readers and educators may wish to access the website of https://bringbackourgirls.ng/, set up by Nigerian activists to consider how the activists represent the girls compared with international media such as the *New York Times*. Readers can also consider the different strategies of resistance deployed by other women's movements such as: https://idlenomore.ca/ (an Indigenous Movement in Canada) or the #MeToo Movement (metoomvmt.org).

a consequence of violent masculinities, demobilization, poverty and destitution (Daley 2015). Despite periodic attention to the kidnapping through the hashtag campaign, the underlying problems that created the environment through which the violence occurred (including active impoverishment, labour exploitation, economic abandonment and state withdrawal) have remained.

The presence of peacekeepers is associated with militarized masculinity, and reports of peacekeepers' sexual exploitation of women have led to calls for the UN to take action to protect women (Simić 2010; Daigle et al 2020). The UN's diversity programmes now include more female peacekeepers, but, while this might have reduced reported cases of sexual violence, Henry (2012) shows how racial ideology continues to play out in the peacekeeping process, with Indian female peacekeepers seeing themselves as superior to black female Liberians, for example. The Nigerian military response has been criticized for exacerbating conflict in the region, triggering further displacements. Addressing the intertwined root causes of gender violence requires a holistic, comprehensive and long-term approach that simultaneously accounts for complex and changing socio-economic and political features.

CONCLUSION

Violence is constitutive of development. It is historically and spatially constructed. Violence is rooted in colonial experiences and has remained pervasive in many societies in the Global South. In spaces of development intervention, postcolonial states were largely conceived through militarized violence legitimated by security fears amidst the intersection of racialization, violent accumulation and the normalization of colonial spaces of exception, operating outside legal norms with impunity. Consequently, direct, structural and slow violence predominate where conflict are marked by histories of extractivism, biopolitical governance and imaginative geographies of the 'Other'.

Neoliberalism has reproduced historically violent economies. Neoliberal policies contribute to the persistence of inequalities and violence, which are compounded in post-war societies, and where not just colonial unknowing but development unknowing persists, even as development scholars and policymakers make very little attempt to see the relationality of causes. Societies in the Global South continue to be militarized through the 'global war on terror' and UN peacekeeping or stabilization missions – with the dehumanizing consequences that result from the continued normalization of warfare, such as the humanitarian incarceration of millions of people on the move, sustained gender-based violence, the perpetuation of patriarchal regimes of domination and the inability of the affected peoples to live fully as human beings.

QUESTIONS FOR FURTHER THOUGHT

Discuss colonial violence. How is violence theorized by scholars from the South, and what contributions do they make to new conceptual geographies of violence?

Examine Martin Mowforth's (2014) claim that violence is needed to ensure the 'success' of development projects.

Longer thinking activity: you may wish to craft short biographies of Patrice Lumumba (De Witte 2002) or Thomas Sankara (Murrey 2018) as a way of understanding the history and violence of the US's global and ongoing crusade against communism and racial justice (including, for example, the FBI surveillance of activists during COINTELPRO (1956–71), within Black Lives Matter and #NoDAPL at Standing Rock; Bevins 2021).

Longer activity: you may wish to read Frantz Fanon's essay entitled 'Concerning Violence' (Chapter 1 of The Wretched of the Earth) and watch the 2014 film Concerning Violence, directed by Goran Hugo Olsson and narrated by Lauryn Hill. Is there potential for revolutionary and emancipatory violence within decolonial options?

FILMS ON THE PHYSICAL AND STRUCTURAL VIOLENCE OF EXTRACTION IN AFRICA

Blood Coltan. Documentary film. Available: www.youtube.com/watch?v=cM23 HXtPPRk.
AFRICA Episode 5: The Bible and the Gun. Available: www.youtube.com/ watch?v=MNWA2cOS7sg.

LECTURES

Achille Mbembe: Frantz Fanon and the Politics of Viscerality. Duke Franklin Humanities Institute. Available: www.youtube.com/watch?v=lg_BEodNaEA.
Dictionary of Now #6 | Achille Mbembe – VIOLENCE. Haus der Kulturen der Welt, Berlin. Available: www.youtube.com/watch?v=4-K9ojIAQ2E.

REFERENCES

Abrahamsen, R. (2018) (ed.) *Conflict and security in Africa.* Suffolk & Rochester, NY: James Currey.

Al Bulushi, S. (2019) '#SomeoneTellCNN: Cosmopolitan militarism in the East African warscape', *Cultural Dynamics*, 31(4), pp. 323–49.

Akiwumi, Fenda A. (2012) 'Global Incorporation and Local Conflict: Sierra Leonean Mining Regions', *Antipode*, 44(3), pp. 581–600.

Alvares, C. (1992) *Science, development and violence: The revolt against modernity.* Delhi: OUP.

Amar, P. (ed.) (2013) *Global South to the rescue: Emerging humanitarian superpowers and globalizing rescue industries.* London: Routledge.

Apter, A. (2008) *The pan-african nation: Oil and the spectacle of culture in Nigeria.* Chicago: University of Chicago Press.

Ba, O. (2020) *States of justice: The politics of the international criminal court.* Cambridge: Cambridge University Press.

Bauman, Z. (1995) *Modernity and the Holocaust.* Cambridge: Polity Press.

Bevins, V. (2020) *The Jakarta method: Washington's anticommunist crusade and the mass murder program that shaped the world.* New York: Public Affairs.

Brankamp, H. (2021) 'Camp abolition: Ending carceral humanitarianism in Kenya (and beyond)', *Antipode*, 54(1), pp. 106–25.

Brankamp, H. and Gluck, Z. (2022) 'Camps and counterterrorism: Security and the remaking of refuge in Kenya', *EPD: Society and Space*, 40(3), pp. 528–48.

Campbell, H. (2013) *Global NATO and the catastrophic failure in Libya.* New York: Monthly Review Press.

Clarke, K. M. (2011) 'The rule of law through its economies of appearances: The making of the African warlord', *Indiana Journal of Global Legal Studies*, 18(1), pp. 7–40.

Clarke, K. M. (2019) *Affective justice: The International Criminal Court and the Pan-Africanist pushback.* Durham, NC: Duke University Press.

Collier, P. and Hoeffler, A. (2002) 'On the incidence of civil war', *Journal of Conflict Resolution*, 46(1), pp. 13–28.

Cramer, C. (2003) 'Does inequality cause conflict?', *Journal of International Development*, Special issue: Explaining violent conflict: going beyond greed versus grievance, 15(4), p. 39.

Daigle, M., Martin, S. and Myrttinen, H. (2020) '"Stranger danger" and the gendered/racialised construction of threats in humanitarianism', *Journal of Humanitarian Affairs*, 2(3), pp. 4–13. https://doi.org/10.7227/JHA.047.

Daley, P. (2007) 'The Burundi Peace Negotiations: An African experience of peace-making', *Review of African Political Economy*, 34(112), pp. 333–52, DOI: 10.1080/03056240701449729.

Daley, P. (2008) *Gender and genocide: The search for spaces of peace in the Great Lakes region of Africa.* Oxford: James Currey.

De Soysa, I (2001) *Paradise is a bazaar? Greed, creed, grievance and governance*, UN WIDER no. 42.

De Witte, L. (2002) *The assassination of Lumumba*. London: Verso Books.

Deeberdt, R and P. Le Billion (2021) 'Conflict minerals and battery materials supply chains: A mapping review of responsible sourcing initiatives', *Extractive Industries and Society*, 8(4). DOI: 10.1016/j.exis.2021.100935.

Elias, N. (1987) 'The state monopoly of physical violence and its infringement', in John Keane (ed.), *Civil society and the State*. London: Verso Books.

Elkins, C. (2005) *Imperial reckoning: The Untold Story of Britain's Gulag in Kenya*. New York: Henry Holt.

Elkins, C. (2022) *Legacy of violence: A history of the British empire*. New York: Knopf.

Eriksson Baaz, M. and Stern, M. (2013) *Sexual violence as a weapon of war?: Perceptions, prescriptions, problems in the Congo and beyond*. London: The Nordic Africa Institute and Zed Press.

Escobar, A. (2004) 'Thematic section: Development, violence and the new imperial order', *Development*, 47(1), pp. 15–21.

Evans, B. (2017) 'Franz Fanon' in *Portraits of Violence: An Illustrated History of Radical Critique*. Ontario: Between The Lines Press. [graphic novel]

Fanon, F. (2008) *Black skin, white masks*. London: Pluto Press. First published in 1952 by Grove Press inc. New York.

Fanon, F. (1990) *The wretched of the earth*. London: Penguin Books. First published in 1963 by Presence Africaine.

Foucault, M. (2000) *Power*. New York: The New Press.

Galtung, J. (1969) 'Violence, peace and peace research', *Journal of Peace Research*, 6, pp. 167–91.

Harcourt, W. (2022) 'Reflection on the violence of development', *Development*, 65, pp. 116–19, https://doi.org/10.1057/s41301-022-00344-1.

Harvey, D. (2004) 'The "new" imperialism: Accumulation by dispossession', *The Socialist Register*, 40, 63–83.

Henry, M. (2012) 'Peacexploitation? Interrogating labor hierarchies and global sisterhood among Indian and Uruguayan female peacekeepers?', in Paul Amar (ed.) *Global South to the rescue*. London: Routledge, pp. 15–35.

Henry, M. (2019) 'Keeping the peace: Gender, geopolitics and global governance interventions', *Conflict, Security & Development*, 19(3), pp. 263–68, DOI:10.10 80/14678802.2019.1608021.

Hudson, H. (2016) 'Decolonising gender and peacebuilding: Feminist frontiers and border thinking in Africa', *Peacebuilding*, 4(2), pp. 194–209.

Hochschild, A. (1998) *King Leopold's ghost: A story of greed, terror and heroism in colonial Africa*. Boston: Houghton Mifflin. Available: www.discardstudies. com/2018/11/01/waste-colonialism/.

Jackson, N.A. (2009) *The spectacle of neoclassical economics: The Chad-Cameroon Petroleum Development Project and exploitation in the Niger delta and the Chad basin*. PhD dissertation, University of Denver.

Iñiguez de Heredia, M. (2019) 'Militarism, states and resistance in Africa: Exploring colonial patterns in stabilisation missions', *Conflict, Security & Development*, 19(6), pp. 623–44.

Kaldor, M. (2001) *New and old wars: Organized violence in a global era*. Cambridge: Polity Press.

Kapadia, K. (ed.) *The violence of development: The political economy of gender*. London: Palgrave Macmillan, 2002.

Keen, David (2012) 'Greed and grievance in civil war', *International Affairs*, 88(4), pp. 757–77, https://doi.org/10.1111/j.1468-2346.2012.01100.x.

Kothari, S. and Harcout, W. (2022) 'Introduction: The violence of development', *Development* 65, pp. 120–23. https://doi.org/10.1057/s41301-022-00346-z.

Lagoke, G. (2023) *Laurent Gbagbo's trial and the indictment of the international criminal court: A Pan-African victory*. Wilmington, DE: Vernon Press.

Liboiron, M. (2018) 'Waste colonialism', *Discard Studies* [Preprint]. Available: www.discardstudies.com/2018/11/01/waste-colonialism/.

Loyd, J., Mitchell-Eaton, E. and Mountz, A. (2016) 'The militarization of islands and migration: Tracing human mobility through US bases in the Caribbean and the Pacific', *Political Geography*, 53, pp. 65–75.

Mack, A. N. and. Na'puti, T. R. (2019) '"Our bodies are not *terra nullius*": Building a decolonial feminist resistance to gendered violence', *Women's Studies in Communication*, 42(3), pp. 347–70, DOI: 10.1080/07491409.2019.1637803.

Mama, A. (2014) 'Beyond survival: Militarism, equity and women's security', in *Development and equity*. Leiden: Brill. https://doi.org/10.1163/978900426 9729_005.

Mama, A. and Okazawa-Rey, M. (2014) 'Militarism, conflict and women's activism in the global era: Challenges and prospects for women in three West African contexts', *feminist review*, 101, pp. 97–123.

Mcfadden, P. (2008) 'Plunder as statecraft: Militarism and resistance in neocolonial Africa', in Sutton, B. Morgen, S. and. Novkov. J. (eds), *Security disarmed: Critical perspectives on gender, race, and militarization*, New Brunswick, NJ: Rutgers University Press, pp. pp. 136–56.

McIlwaine, C. (1999) 'Geography and development: Violence and crime as development issues', *Progress in Human Geography*, 23(3), pp. 453–63.

Melber, H. (2005) 'How to come to terms with the past: Re-Visiting the German colonial genocide in Namibia', *Africa Spectrum*, 40(1), pp.139–48.

Mountz, A. (2020) *The death of asylum: Hidden geographies of the enforcement archipelago*. Minneapolis: University of Minnesota Press.

Mowforth, M. (2014) *The violence of development: Resource depletion, environmental crises, and human rights abuses in central America*. London: Pluto Press.

Murrey, A. (2015) 'Narratives of life and violence along the Chad-Cameroon oil pipeline', *Human Geography*, 8(1), pp. 15–39.

Murrey, A. (2018) (ed.) *A certain amount of madness: The life, politics and legacies of Thomas Sankara*. London: Pluto Press.

Murrey, A. and Jackson, N. (2019) 'Africa and the resource curse idea' in *Encyclopaedia of African Studies*, London: Routledge.

Mustapha, A. R. and Ehrhardt, D. (2018) *Creed & grievance: Muslim–Christain relations & conflict resolution in Northern Nigeria*. Woodbridge, Suffolk: James Currey/ an imprint of Boydell & Brewer.

Nixon, R. (2011) *Slow violence and the environmentalism of the poor*. Cambridge, MA: Harvard University Press.

Okafor-Yarwood, I. and Adewumi, I. J. (2020) 'Toxic waste dumping in the Global South as a form of environmental racism: Evidence from the Gulf of Guinea', *African Studies*, 79(3), pp. 285–304, https://doi.org/10.1080/00020184.2020.1 827947.

Rajagopal, B. (2001) 'The violence of development'. *The Washington Post*, Editorial, A19. www.washingtonpost.com/archive/opinions/2001/08/09/the-violence-of-development/1b169574-3992-44ec-bff9-a1e42857f192/.

Richmond, O. W. (2006) 'The problem of peace: Understanding the "liberal peace"', *Conflict, Security & Development*, 6(3), pp. 291–314.

Rostow, W. W. (1960) *The stages of economic growth: A non-communist manifesto*. Cambridge: Cambridge University Press. pp. 4–16.

Sarkin, J. (2011) *Germany's Genocide of the Herero: Kaiser Wilhelm II, his general, his settlers, his soldiers*, Cape Town, UCT Press.

Schwartz, M., and Church, J (2013) *Department of defense's use of contractors to support military operations: Background, analysis, and issues for congress*. 17 May. Congressional Research Service.

Simić, O. (2010) 'Does the presence of women really matter? Towards combating male sexual violence in peacekeeping operations', *International Peacekeeping*, 17(2), pp. 188–99, DOI: 10.1080/13533311003625084.

Sovacool, B. K. (2019) 'Toxic transitions in the lifecycle externalities of a digital society: The complex afterlives of electronic waste in Ghana', *Resources Policy*, 64. DOI: 10.1016/j.resourpol.2019.101459.

Springer, S. (2012) 'Neo-liberalizing violence: Of the exceptional and the exemplary in coalescing moments', *Area*, 44 (2), pp. 136–43.

Springer, S. (2011) 'Violence sits in places? Cultural practice, neoliberal rationalism, and virulent imaginative geographies', *Political Geography*, 30(2), pp. 90–98. DOI: 10.1016/j.polgeo.2011.01.004.

UNHCR (2022) www.unhcr.org/refugee-statistics.

UNHCR, Executive Committee of the High Commissioner's Programme, Standing Committee, 30th meeting (10 June 2004) 'Protracted Refugee Situations', EC/54/SC/CRP.14.

Uvin, P. (199?) *Aiding Violence: The Development Enterprise in Rwanda*. Boulder, CA: Kumarian Press.

Vann, Michael G. (2010) 'Of Pirates, postcards, and public beheadings: The pedagogic execution in French Colonial Indochina', *Historical Reflections/Réflexions Historiques* 36(2). DOI: https://doi.org/10.3167/hrrh.2010.360204.

Wamba dia Wamba, E, (2000) *Project for the New Congo: The RCD/K political programme*. RCD/Kisangani: Dar es Salaam. Tanzania.

Watts, M. (2004, 2nd edition) 'Violent environments: Petroleum conflict and the political ecology of rule in the Niger Delta, Nigeria', in Peet, R. and Watts, M. (eds.) *Liberation ecologies: Environment, development and social movements*. London: Routledge, pp. 250–72.

Watts, M. (2004) 'Antinomies of community: Some thoughts on geography, resources and empire', *Transactions of the Institute of British Geographers*, 29(2), pp. 195–216.

Watts, M. J. (2003) 'Economies of violence: More oil, more blood', *Economic and Political Weekly*, 38(48), pp. 5089–99.

Zeilig, L. (2015) *Lumumba: Africa's lost leader (life & times)*. London: Haus Publishing.

4

Development Without the Peoples of the Global South

Here we examine the role that the peoples of the Global South are *expected* to play in development, according to hegemonic agendas. Building upon our consideration in Chapter 2 of the instrumentalization of the narrative of poverty, we consider the wider implications for this way of thinking within international development practice. Efforts to decolonize development studies should address state–society relations, especially how the people of the Global South (the Global Majority) have been conceptualized in development discourse and practice. We are interested in prodding our readers to consider what terms have been used to describe people; what roles are assigned to them and their expected contributions to development, and how these have changed with different philosophies of state-society relations, from the colonial period to the era of neoliberalism. Claude Ake (1996: 141), in an analysis of the lack of material improvement after three decades of development, argues that what was happening was 'an attempt to develop against the people' as exogenous agendas dispossessed and alienated the people from their epistemes, social relations and wellbeing. We look at how the role of the people in a social formation depends on the nature of state–society relations that exist and how resources are managed to ensure the common good. It is important to first acknowledge the shifts that arose with colonial rule and their continued legacy. In Chapter 4, we will explore how people resisted and found spaces for maintaining their humanity and freedom of association even amidst colonial oppression.

We emphasize the post-1980s period of the Washington Consensus on development because this has led to profound changes in state–society relations. The shift from democracy as the prima facie method of political accountability to 'good governance', where the state is just one actor among a group of stakeholders, means that the people, framed as another

'stakeholder' in the development enterprise, have been effectively dis-
enfranchised politically. Of particular importance are the imagined
geographies of 'the public' in post-colonial development discourse,
including how and why the language and terminologies of people's
involvement in development changed over time; from population, to civil
society, to stakeholders, to entrepreneurs, to partners and more. A disobedient pedagogy pays attention to this changing language, allowing us to
trace people's shifting relationships to the state and international governments and institutions and imagine different relational futures.

ANTICOLONIAL AND DECOLONIAL PLAYLIST

In Fela Kuti's song 'Teacher Don't Teach Me Nonsense' he criticizes African
governments for their corruption. Kuti (1938–97) was a powerhouse
musician, composer and Pan-African political activist. In the lyrics of the
song, democratic elections in Nigeria and elsewhere on the continent are
described as 'democracy, crazy demo, demonstration of craze, crazy demonstration', a lyric which resonated with the experiences and frustrations of
everyday people. We recommend watching his live performance of 'Teacher
Don't Teach Me Nonsense' at Glastonbury in 1984.[1]

In Belgian-Congolese hip-hop artist Baloji's 2011 song, 'Le Jour d'Après/
Siku Ya Baadaye' or 'independence cha-cha', he revises what is a traditional
and celebratory independence hymn to a lamentation on the troubles experienced in the post-independence moment. Singing in French and Lingala, he
mocks the 'promises of tomorrow . . . of a sovereign state where the ground
slips away between militias and rebels, looting and concealment . . . [as]
people . . . are moved like cattle from plot to plot . . . from governance to
supervision'.[2]

THE GLOBAL MAJORITY IN DEVELOPMENT DISCOURSE

Development thought and practices are permeated with assumptions
as to who the principal actors are, who is ascribed agency at any time
and the role beneficiaries are expected to play. Places of development
knowledge generation and their experts are characterized as active, and
places of development interventions and their recipients as passive, and
as victims in the context of humanitarian interventions. As shown in

---

1. www.youtube.com/watch?v=Ts9y5-nfoQ8.
2. www.youtube.com/watch?v=C4vc25TcIeo.

Chapter 1, these representations, though simple, are the legacy of colonial racial ideologies. Under racial capitalism, people positioned lower down the racial hierarchy gain value only through their categorization as exploitable labour (Robinson 2021). The most extreme form of exploitation was enslavement, where the worker had no rights, where violence was used to maintain production and order (Fanon 1963; Mbembe 2019). In Euro-modernity, racial, ethnic and gendered hierarchies were significant in determining who were considered to have the cognitive abilities to make rational decisions that affect themselves and the wider society. Only those deemed superior could be allowed to participate in governance. In modern European societies, the struggles of the masses for universal enfranchisement are indicative of the power differentials and inequalities that shaped societal development in the West and were foundational to the policies carried into the colonized world (Robinson 2021). Colonized people were infantilized as needing guidance through European (white) paternalism, moral obligations, and tutelage – a process described as the 'civilizing mission' (see Chapter 1).

By the late 1940s, the civilizing mission had transitioned into the development mission, and colonial civil servants into development experts. Racist Euro-American views of the Global Majority were tempered by the global abhorrence of the racial violence of the Holocaust and the rising demands for economic and political freedom from colonized peoples. Development experts shifted the blame for impoverishment onto the colonized and abrogated a trusteeship role for former colonized powers claiming that their historical experience of capitalism and Western modernity provided a universal blueprint and knowledge system to enable development worldwide. As we have explored in Chapter 2, the active cultivation of 'poverty' as a static and naturally-existing (rather than actively cultivated) phenomenon played a central role in this displacement of blame for material inequalities.

The Global Majority was perceived as lacking the attributes and disposition needed to bring about development. Ethnopsychology, a racist science, was deployed to show that Global South peoples would require total transformation in all aspects of life. Richard Peet and Elaine Hartwick (2009:126) state that 'development meant "changing the typical personality"'. They illustrated the perceived psycho-cultural differences between traditional and modern man in development discourse. 'Traditional man' was considered backward-looking, uninterested in new information, different opinions and suspicious of technology, religious and fatalistic, and particularistic. In contrast, modern man was open to new experiences, keen on new information, the outside world, new technical skills, valued science, punctual, universalistic and optimistic. There were no redeeming aspects of 'traditional' man's behaviour and cultures that could be taken into modern society – all their institutions had to be transformed, from extended family to nuclear family and from tribe/ethnic group to nation. Consequently, colonial authorities and later development experts abrogated the responsibility to transform material conditions to people. Again, we might remind our readers of a meaningful scene depicting a common colonial fantasy in the colonial film *Daybreak in Udi* (mentioned in Chapter 1), during which the Nigerian community members turn to the colonial administrator, pleading with him for assistance and guidance in village development projects.

Africans were represented as having contributed very little to their own development, or even as being hindered by local cultural, linguistic and environmental dynamics. Sophisticated structures (e.g. Great Zimbabwe) or complex social formations that Europeans found in Africa were attributed to outsiders. Peter Ekeh (1975: 97) writes that an 'ideological weapon employed by the colonial administrators in emphasizing the necessity of their rule in Africa consisted of downgrading the contribution by Africans to the building of African nations and to history generally'. Meanwhile Claude Ake (1996: 15) discusses how in development discourse, 'Africans, particularly the rural people, are by virtue of being themselves, enemies of progress, including their own progress, for it is their own peculiar characteristics that sustains their underdevelopment'. These views are not peculiar to Africa. Tania Murray Li (2007: 24) found similar sentiments in Indonesia, where in development discourse and practice, since the colonial period, governments, external agencies and indigenous activists have regarded villagers and indigenous people as deficient, as people whose 'conduct is to be conducted'.

Our understanding of how people reacted to the denigration of their agency is complex and varies spatially and temporally. Claude Ake (1980: 16) claims that:

Africans internalized the [development] paradigm's negative image of themselves as well as notions of the superiority of developed societies. It is often assumed in these circles that foreign-made goods are better, that foreign experts know better, and the major business of Africa, indeed the only business, is catching up with industrialized nations.

James Ferguson (1999) shows how people in the Zambian copper belt uncritically internalized beliefs about their deficiencies and the promotion of Northern values. This was achieved not by coercion but by educating desires and configuring aspirations and beliefs whilst excluding the rich insights that could be gained from local people.

Some postcolonial governments adopted socialist discourses that sought to centre people in development. For example, the first president of independent Tanzania, Julius Nyerere, and his political party, Tanganyika African Union (TANU), envisaged a form of development that drew on African communalism. He introduced the concept of *Ujamaa* (familyhood) to mobilize popular participation in the development effort. However, Nyerere did not give people real autonomy to make decisions about their development and violently squashed local initiatives that did not go through the local branch of the political party (Von Freyhold 1980; see also Zeilig 2022: 263ff on the disagreements between Walter Rodney and Nyerere). From the 1980s onwards, development institutions promoted a rationalistic, elitist, and technological governance framework that, according to Raufu Mustapha (2012: 37),

undermines social deliberation and consensus building and promotes the cult of allegedly objective 'neutral expertise'. This emphasis on 'rationalism' has tended to shut out the bulk of the citizenry from the determination of crucial public policies. Instead, policy determination is monopolized by a narrow band of local and foreign elites engaged in self-referential discourses.

It is with this historical context and through a recognition of the asymmetrical power dynamics that exist in development that we ask what roles the people of the Global South are expected to play in the development project. How is the Global Majority represented in development discourse, and what agency is afforded to them to determine their futures?

Are the people considered as 'obstacles' to their own development, in the way they have been represented in colonial and neoliberal discourses that look for the 'progressive farmer' (Li 2007), 'the educated girl' (see Chapter 6; Koffman and Gill 2013; Hickel 2014) or the 'entrepreneur'

(Dolan and Ryak 2016)? Importantly, as our readers will recognise, all of these suggest that the people of the Global South have to undergo transformation along prescribed routes in order to acquire the capacity to become agents of their own development.

We veer away from assumptions that the people lack agency. In our classroom discussions, we seek to cultivate an awareness of Richard Ballard's (2015: 1) argument that people are 'neither passive recipients of development nor passive victims of processes that have caused their marginalization', and still strive to create 'alternative futures'. Working within black and indigenous geographical thought, we encourage ourselves and our readers to reflect on the nuanced realities of life in the Global South, including differences and distinctions across years, borders and oceans (Daley 2020). We ask readers to explore how people imagine and create alternative and anticipatory futures. Focusing on the historical period of twenty-first century neoliberalism, how do people express discontent and contest development, and how is dissent received and acted on by Global South states and by international development agencies?

COMMUNAL LIFEWORLDS IN NON-WESTERN PERSPECTIVES

The relationship between the state and the people affects the sort of social transformation that can take place in a society. Eurocentric development, informed by racial ideologies and taxonomies, has failed to recognize the capacity of indigenous peoples to improve their social condition, as if their survival before conquest was capricious rather than ensured through their own endeavours. Walter Rodney (1972) affirms that work to improve the conditions of life is intrinsic to all human groups. He writes,

> Every people have shown a capacity for independently increasing their ability to live a more satisfactory life through exploiting the resources of nature. Every continent independently participated in the early epochs of the extension of man's control over the environment – which means every continent can point to a period of economic development. (Rodney 1972: 11)

People's capacity for change and for self-governance had required a conceptualization of community that was appropriate to the environmental, political and social challenges they faced. Rodney (1972: 11) continues, 'as human beings battled with the material environment, they created forms of social relations, forms of government, patterns of behaviour and systems of belief – that were never the same in any two societies'.

Prior to European subjugation, multiple forms of social formations existed in the Global South, including feudalism, communalism and both patrilineal and matrilineal kinship systems (Amadiume 1987), as well as some that were nascently capitalist (Rodney 1972; Gunder Frank 1998; Robinson 2021). In the twentieth and twenty-first century, however, the concept of communalism has often been equated with socialism and communism, even though ideas of co-working and communal care for the benefit of all were always essential for human survival and have longer histories that predate either of these ideas. If we adopt the Marxian concept of different social relations being specific to modes of production, then it follows that different forms of sociality and political life existed across the world prior to the global spread of capitalism. Remnants of these remain, but in development discourse they are relegated to the realm of the cultural and the 'traditional'.

In the Global South, social formations were diverse, with empires, centralized states and state-less kinship-based societies. States had different conceptions of territory, land proprietary, boundaries and belonging. Scholars have documented the range and specificities of states in Asia and Africa (Rodney 1972 and 1980; Amin 1979; Diop 1987; Mafeje 1991; Frank 1978 and 2007). Some states were run by dynastic rulers, such as the Qing Dynasty in China (1648 to 1912); the Mughal Empires (1530–1701) in South Asia; the ancient empires of Ghana (tenth and eleventh centuries), Mali (fourteenth century), and Songhai (sixteenth century) in West Africa (Diop 1987). Their geographical size varied. States that maintained unproductive elites had relations with their people that enabled the accumulation of surpluses. In the West African region, Abdoulaye Bathily (1994: 41) refers to the existence of different types of social formations; Some were agrarian, pastoral and military-merchant, especially those on the Trans-Saharan trade routes. States involved in the Transatlantic slave trade were predatory.

These West African states were multicultural and monocultural and had complex and dynamic social structures, some stratified with caste systems. Cheik Anta Diop (1987), in *Precolonial Black Africa*, refers to the constitutional as opposed to absolute monarchies and the prevalence of matrilineal succession. Islamization that began in the eighth century after the establishment of Muslim traders along the trans Saharan trade routes did not change the socio-political arrangements, only the elites were replaced. Diop concludes that pre-colonial African societies were not republics but monarchic democracies, where there were checks on monarchic authority and power. In contrast, Bathily (1994) and Rodney (1980) saw communal decline coming about as the parasitic ruling classes arising from the slave trade intensified their militarization for accumulative purposes; hence, they fell easily to European colonial rule which, in turn, destroyed the remnants of African social formations.

Levels of territorial control over their frontiers varied from one political community to another, were flexible, and were not indicative of state weakness (Asiwaju 1983; Kopytoff 1987; Cormack 2016). Jeffrey Herbst (2000) contrasts the relationship between state power and control over territory in precolonial Africa and in early modern Europe. He argues that precolonial states had fundamentally different conceptions of the relationship between power and space. Prior to colonialism, African states were less focused on territorial acquisition, as land was plentiful. Demographic decline caused by the slave trade and new diseases meant that rights over people were more important since 'it was easier to escape from rulers than to fight them' (Herbst 2000: 39). Although some states sought to exert control over land, Herbst claims that there was a significant difference between the control over the political centre of a state and that over outlying areas. He concludes that the merging of the European and African traditions of 'broadcasting of power' affected how post-colonial states interacted with their people and affected migration patterns within states.

Ownership of the resources, such as land, necessary for the reproduction of both human and non-human life, was not exclusively controlled in the same way as when they became private property under capitalism. Colonial domination introduced the Western concept of land as private property – its exclusive ownership, the demarcation and control of its boundaries and control over the resources therein, and its commodification (Bhandar 2015 and 2018; Jones 2019). As the purpose of the colonial state was to extract wealth for the countries in the metropolitan core, the colonial imperative was to dispossess and expropriate land they labelled as a *terra nullius*.

In many societies of the Global South, the imposition of European land tenure systems through colonialism led to the legalized dispossession of people from their land. Land dispossession and rural (semi-)proletarianization – that is to say, the market-enforced separation of people from their land and means of production and reproduction – have been simultaneously gendered and racialized (Tsikata 2016). The late Zimbabwean political and agrarian theorist Sam Moyo was a leading figure in the development of an active scholarship on the inter-relationships between rural land and labour transitions and struggles in neo-imperial Southern Africa. His invaluable work, including *The Land Question in Zimbabwe* (1995), demonstrated the ways in which European land tenure systems reified gender and racial differences in colonial and post-colonial Zimbabwe. The commodification of resources remains critical to the capitalist system and expanded globally with the spread of European land-ownership practices and European markets. Land in the world beyond Europe, settled by the global majority, was ideologically declared *terra nullius* (empty land) and unowned (even when historically occupied), and could be 'discovered' and claimed by Europeans who would 'improve' the land and be benevolent to the indigenous people by civilizing and converting them to Christianity.

Land dispossession for extraction involved forced displacement, extermination, capture, and commodification (Cole Harris 2004; Li 2014 a and b; Burow et al 2018). In settler colonies, indigenous people were labelled backward and lazy, herded into reserves and their ontologies of land deemed primitive and heathen. Jeffrey Herbst (2000) studied state-making in Africa, and whilst his use of sources by African scholars was limited, he made one important observation that low population densities (a consequence of the slave trade and imported diseases) and land abundance meant that many pre-colonial African states did not use territorial control as the basis of their power. Political authority was maintained at the core of the state, leaving hinterland communities in flux. Social life in pre-colonial non-Western societies – which is to say the forms of relationships people make in order to live in a society – has traditionally been given less attention by scholars due to the perception of its having been pre-modern, primitive, affective and in need of civilizing. Linguistic and cultural practices, however, demonstrate that how the individual was conceived in relation to the wider society was not always transactional. Francis Nyamnjoh (2018) abhors the ways in which

European colonial epistemologies silenced African traditions of being and living in the world. Traditions that eschew the binaries and dualisms of colonial modernity which created divisions of outsiders/insiders and natives/foreigners. For Nyamnjoh, Africans are frontier beings,

> who contest taken for-granted and often institutionalized and bounded ideas and practices of being, becoming, belonging, places and spaces . . . they straddle myriad identity margins and constantly seek to bridge various divides in the interest of the imperatives of living interconnections, nuances and complexities made possible or exacerbated by the evidence of mobilities and encounters. (Nyamnjoh 2018: 258)

Nyamnjoh challenges the imposition of walls and boundaries, as well as the xenophobia and conflict that arises from mobility in post-colonial Africa and evokes conviviality as a form of sociality that recognizes 'incompleteness . . . an attitude towards identities and identification as open-ended pursuits' (ibid.). For example, in many parts of east-central and southern Africa, the concept of *Ubuntu* is used to describe the co-dependence and relationality of human beings (see Chapter 8). It signals the existence of principles that enable communal cohesion and progression that ran counter to ideas on sociality imported by European colonialism and extractive economies. Lesley Le Grange (2019: 324) notes that this is counter to Western traditions of the atomized individual, as the human being is seen as being 'embedded in social and biophysical relations'. We explore the radical ruptures of capitalist neoliberalism offered by *Ubuntu* in Chapter 8.

Societies with participatory governance systems had public/communitarian spaces, where people could debate and settle their disputes. These spaces for public discourse and conflict resolution were especially important in state-less societies and were organized around kin relations. In Central and Eastern Africa, for example, the Kiswahili term *baraza* is used to describe the place and the activity where public debates take place. In Central and West Africa, the term *palaver*, from the Portuguese 'palavra', is used to describe the negotiations and discussions that occur to settle disputes (Teklu 2021). Wamba dia Wamba (1985[2019]), in a discussion of the 'lineage of palaver' in the Congo, describes it as 'an appropriate community method and practice to resolve contradictions among the people, to strengthen organic mutual links of solidarity among all the members of the community (clan, lineage, village, etc.), to completely isolate divisive tendencies and forces from each member of the community as well as from the entire community'. Palaver, he continues,

assumed diverse forms, depending on the time, the place and the type of the dominant political regime prevailing in society. The class which rules society determines positively or negatively the real content of the palaver: either the entire community participates in and organizes itself into a palaver or certain social strata of privileged and ruling groups only do palaver. (Wamba dia Wamba (1985 [2019] n.p.)

The purpose of the palaver is to resolve 'intra-communal tensions' and 'the unity of the community is reinforced after the palaver'. As a system of external domination, colonialism was perpetrated through the introduction of new (often violent) authoritarian modes of control. The imposition of racial and ethnic (tribal) hierarchies during colonial rule destroyed opportunities for participatory (democratic) decision-making. Communal spaces, where people congregated, were often viewed as threatening to colonial authority and were brought under control (e.g. formalized as village councils) or outlawed. In some places, there was a limit to the number of 'natives' that could meet without permission.

Communal life under European colonialism was expected to be non-political, often based on tribal or kinship lines and, thus, was considered pre-modern. Ethnic associations, both formal and informal, were established as Africans moved to work in urban centres and areas of extractive activities. Religious communities, Islamic or Christian, were overseen by clerics and missionaries approved by the colonial administration. Concepts such as citizenship and civil society were considered modern forms of belonging and democratic participation that came with European civilization and had to be learned, and which we will show later on in this chapter, excluded most people.

EUROCENTRIC VISIONS OF STATE–SOCIETY RELATIONS

How do we explain state–society relations in Global South countries under continuing conditions of coloniality? To do so, we turn historically and briefly to the philosophical debates in Europe during the rise of modernity. Here, the collective of the people (the masses) was viewed as having the potential to become the instruments of radical political change, as a propelling revolutionary force to overthrow injustices, as in the Haitian (1789–1804) and later French Revolution (1789–90). Collectivism was understood as a danger to the extant social hierarchy and capital accumulation. It had to be either crushed or managed. Collectivism in the post Second World War period, when articulated as socialism and communism and drawing on the Soviet experience, was considered a danger to capitalism.

For European liberal philosophers, national and societal wealth results from the actions of the individual, *homo economicus* or rational economic man, who, acting in *his* own self-interest, becomes the generator of wealth (as for instance in Adam Smith's *The Wealth of Nations*). They explored how a social formation could emerge whereby competition between individuals is mediated by the law and allowed for the continuing generation of capital, and defined what they saw as separate spheres, that of the state, the family or kinship relations, and that of the wider civic society. From the period of the Enlightenment (seventeenth century onward) concepts such as civil society, citizen and publics emerged to represent Europeans' attempts to interpret the changing and potential relationships between the state and the people that were not, as previously, reliant on 'the natural social order' of kinship or divine ordination. Civil society was conceptualized as a modern sphere, separate from the government, in which individuals, seeking to protect their freedom, cooperate, and contrasted with the pre-modern, affective one determined by kinship. European philosophers also sought to clarify the relationship (obligations and rights) between the state and the individual, and the state and the wider society. For example, Jean Jacques Rousseau (1762) saw the need for a social contract between state and society. The content of these relationships was considered important for the production of capital and later democratic societies.

Later Karl Marx and the Italian Marxist philosopher Antonio Gramsci (2007) conceived civil society as a product of the capitalist system and integral to the state – a sphere of the bourgeois who establish hegemony in order to rule through ideology and consent. In the 1960s, with the expansion of the media, German philosopher and sociologist Jürgen Habermas (1974) postulated that the existence of this bourgeois public sphere (free media and places where public opinion can be formed) or 'publics' was vital to the maintenance of a vibrant democracy. After the fall of the Berlin wall in 1989, civil society was seen as having the potential to nurture democracy and to enable neoliberal capitalism (Putnam 1993).

Within this tradition, 'citizenship' refers to the rights and responsibilities that govern the relationship between a state and its people within a given territory/nation-state (Marshall 1950; Ehrkamp and Jacobsen 2015). Citizenship can be used to determine participation in certain activities of the state, such as the right to vote, stand as an elected representative, join the military, and become a member of numerous democratic organizations. Citizenship has always been conditional and differentiated along axes of social difference, such as race, ethnicity and gender, and differently applied in territories governed by the same state. European philosophers have accordingly tended to exclude or marginalize the experience of racialized and colonized peoples in their theorizations about modern society.

The concepts of civil society, publics and citizenship are products of the ethnocentric experiences of the modern European nation-states as they underwent societal transformation in the context of capitalism. Could they therefore be applied to explain post-colonial societies in territories and, in some cases, social groupings, that were forcibly constructed under colonialism? Epistemologically, these concepts became the frame through which post-colonial Global South scholars sought to understand the complex state–society relations in their post-colonial states. For example, the Indian political theorist and anthropologist Partha Chatterjee (2001: 62), drawing from Gramsci, uses civil society to describe those

institutions of modern associational life set up by nationalist elites in the era of colonial modernity, though often as part of their anticolonial struggle. These institutions embody the desire of the [native] elite to replicate in its own society the forms as well as the substance of Western modernity. It is a desire for a new ethical life in society, one that conforms to the virtues of the Enlightenment and of bourgeois freedom and whose known cultural forms are those of secularized Western Christianity.

Chatterjee claims that civil society, with its links to colonial modernity, excludes the masses; and that a 'political society' comprising political parties and non-party political formations (*panchayat* in rural areas, subaltern movements) mediate between the people and the state.

The Nigerian sociologist Peter P. Ekeh (1975) argues that colonialism has left African societies with two publics instead of the one found in Western societies. The two publics consist of a primordial realm (moral and made up of indigenous authorities and hometown associations) and a civic public one (amoral and produced through colonial interventions and comprised of Western educated elites, the military, the civil service and the police). The civic public operates independently of the private realm even though the actors are the same. Ekeh uses the dialectical relationship between these spheres to explain the nature of postcolonial politics in Africa. Meanwhile, Western-educated Africans gained legitimacy from European institutions and educators and 'were sharply differentiated from the "natives" on the principle that the former were those of the "Europeanized" present and the natives belonged to the backward past' (97). Ekeh blames the political failure that have engulfed post-independence Africa on the absorption of Western ideology about Africa by the African bourgeois who took over the state and their lack of morality. Scholars have challenged Ekeh's division of the two public realms because of the degree of interconnections between them.

Osaghae (2006), building on Ekeh's thesis, attributes the ineffectualness of civil society in postcolonial Africa to the importance of ethnic formations in the development of civil society during the colonial era; in addition, the safety-net the primordial realm provides 'for individuals in the desperate struggle for diminishing resources, but also the resilience of the self-help traditions of the primordial public, and the haven it provides for those exiting from the state and the civic public' (241). Raufu Mustapha (2012), drawing on Habermas, contends that there are multiple publics and 'counter-publics' in African states due to their cultural and ethnic heterogeneity.

Citizenship implies participation and belonging. In Africa, formal definitions of citizenship are still shaped by European modernity and are colonially-derived, as most states are inherited colonial constructs (See Chapter 6 for a fuller discussion). Did the people have access to citizenship rights within the European colonial empires and were those rights expanded or redefined after independence in the new state formations? Mahmood Mamdani (1996: 16) writes of what he terms the 'bifurcated state' produced by colonialism, especially in settler colonies in Africa. In such states, Europeans and 'civilized' urban-dwelling Africans were citizens and had access to rights, whilst the majority of people (rural dwellers/ peasants) were subjects, ruled indirectly through traditional leaders many of whom were appointed by the colonial state. In such contexts, even following independence when states embarked on nation-building, postcolonial authorities had difficulty extending the rights of citizenship to the masses. Poor and rural communities are still perceived as backward, 'bush' people, who cannot understand the workings of the modern world and depend on affective (ethnic/kinship) ties as they progress through life. While the term 'differentiated citizenship' is used to explore the unequal access of social groups to rights within a modern state, we argue that, under coloniality, human rights are not simply benevolently offered to people considered not fully human – they must be wrest.

During the colonial era, the modern media (newspapers, pamphlets and radio in particular) were predominantly urban-based and published in European languages. The official media of the time was produced by colonizers and aimed at white settlers and elite Africans. Religious institutions, Pan-Africanists and nationalist African elites started to produce newspapers distributed largely in urban centres and taken to rural areas by returning migrant workers. These African media were central to the process of anti-colonial mobilization. With ethnic associations predominating in rural areas and among urban based elites, it was only after the end of colonial rule and the rise of dictatorial regimes in the 1970s that scholars sought to explain what constitutes the public sphere in Africa. With the reintroduction of democratic elections and the liberalization of the media, in most states, in the 1990s and the rise of digital and social media, debates on what constitutes the public sphere were once more reignited (e.g. Nyamnjoh 2010). Were there now spaces free from the state in which Africans could freely criticize, debate, and articulate their visions of development without fear of state oppression? In the next chapter, we discuss the use of digital media by social movements and state reactions.

CONCLUSION

In this chapter, we have continued our argument that ordinary, everyday folks have been alienated from development, which has been top-down and imbued with assumptions about people's capacities for change and what is best for them. We argue that development is occurring without the people as active participants in transforming their social worlds. This practice has its roots in colonial ideologies of race and has been perpetuated by the universalization of Western modernity. The Eurocentric mission of finding a classic liberal civil society in Africa has been problematic due to Africa's histories of authoritarianism and ethnic division. Under neoliberalism, the concept of civil society has been further corrupted by development experts. Rather than an organically developed formal civil society of the bourgeois, it is imposed through funding mechanisms from outside. It contains a racialized hierarchy reminiscent of the colonial state, and its relationship to the state, whether international or national, cannot be seen as representative of the people (Shivji 2007).

Marxists have long described capitalism as a shapeshifter, always finding ways to appeal to people's desires, whilst eschewing people-centred change, even in the face of capitalist-driven crises. Neoliberalism has ushered in new languages to centre the rational economic man as the agent of development. Under neoliberalism, the people have become individuated. We recognize the limitations of the entrepreneur (see Chapter 2) as an inclusive and meaningful category that can fulfil the desires of youth, especially when the violence of development has to be overcome in order to succeed. As we work towards decolonial futures, our task is to adopt methodologies that will enable us to learn from the peoples of the Global South about their visions of social worlds that foster human well-being.

QUESTIONS FOR FURTHER THOUGHT

How is coloniality implicated in discourses of agency in development?

What can we learn from African scholars about the changes that have taken place in the social worlds of African peoples under coloniality?

To what extent is it possible to understand the social worlds in contemporary African societies without resorting to concepts that arise from European political modernity?

What are the contradictions of participation according to the doctrine of neoliberalism?

How might an attention to dignity and redistribution change development practice?

REFERENCES

Abdul-Raheem, T. 'Western NGOs in Africa: Bodyguards of the advancing recolonization'. *NGO Monitor: NGOs in Africa: Agents of Change or Change of Agents*, 1(1), pp. 4–6. Kampala, Uganda: The Pan-African Movement Secretariat, 1996.

Amin, S. (1979) *Unequal development: An essay on the social formations of peripheral capitalism*. Translated by Brian Pearce. East Sussex: The Harvester Press.

Ajl, M. and Sharma, D. (2022) 'The Green Revolution and transversal countermovements: recovering alternative agronomic imaginaries in Tunisia and India', *Canadian Journal of Development Studies / Revue canadienne d'études du développement* 43(3), pp. 418–38, DOI: 10.1080/02255189.2022.2052028.

Ballard, R. (2015) 'Geographies of development III: Militancy, insurgency, encroachment and development by the poor', *Progress in Human Geography*, 39(2), pp. 214–24.

Bhandar, B. (2015) 'Title by registration: Instituting modern property law and creating racial value in the settler colony', *Journal of Law and Society*, 42(2), pp. 173–327.

Bhandar, B. (2018) *Colonial lives of property: Law, land, and racial regimes of ownership*. Durham, NC: Duke University Press.

Bathily, A. (1994) 'The West African State in historical perspective', in Egosha E. Osaghae (ed.), *Between State and Civil Society in Africa*. Dakar, Senegal: CODESRIA, pp. 41–74.

Boone, C. (2019) 'Land-related conflict and electoral politics in Africa unlocked', *Oxford Research Encyclopedia of Politics*, online at https://doi.org/10.1093/acre fore/9780190228637.013.758.

Burow, P. B., Brock, S. and Dove, M. R. (2018) 'Unsettling the land: Indigeneity, ontology, and hybridity in settler colonialism', *Environment and Society: Advances in Research*, 9, pp. 57–74 . DOI:10.3167/ares.2018.090105.

Chatterjee, P. (2001) 'On Civil and political society in postcolonial democracies', in Sudipta Kavirj and Sunil Khilnani (eds.), *Civil society: Histories and possibilities*. Cambridge: Cambridge University Press, pp. 165–78.

Daley, P. (2020) 'Lives lived differently: Geography and the Study of Black Women', *Area*, 52(4), pp. 794–800.

Diop, C. A. (1987) *Precolonial Black Africa*. Translated from the French by Harold Salemson. Brooklyn: Lawrence Hill Books.

Ehrkamp, P. and Jacobsen, M. H. (2015) 'Citizenship' in John A. Agnew, et al (eds), *Key Concepts in Political Geography*, London: Wiley-Blackwell.

Ekeh, P. P. (1975) 'Colonialism and the two publics in Africa: A theoretical statement', *Comparative Studies in Society and History*, 17(1), pp. 91–112.

Elkins, C. (2005) *Britain's gulag: The brutal end of empire in Kenya*. London: Pimlico.

Fanon, F. (1990) *The wretched of the earth*. London: Penguin Books. First published in 1963 by Presence Africaine.

Ferguson, J. (1999) *Expectations of Modernity:Myths and meanings of urban life on the Zambian copperbelt*. Berkeley: University of California Press.

Frank, A. G. (1978) *World accumulation, 1492-1789*. London: Palgrave Macmillan.

Frank, A. G. (2007) *Reorient: The global economy in the Asian age*. Berkeley and Los Angeles: University of California Press.

Gramsci, A. (2007) *Selections from The Prison Notebooks of Antonio Gramsci*. London: Lawrence & Wishart Ltd. Edited and translated by Quintin Hoare and Geoffrey Nowell Smith. First printed 1971; Reprinted 2007.

Gunder Frank, A. (1998) *ReORIENT: Global Economy in the Asian Age*. Berkeley: University of California Press.

Habermas, J. (1974) 'The public sphere: An encyclopedia article (1964)', *New German Critique*, 3, 49–55. Translated by Sara Lennox and Frank Lennox.

Hammett, D. & Jackson, L. (2018) 'Developing a "civil" society in partial democracies: In/civility and a critical public sphere in Uganda and Singapore'. *Political Geography*, 67, pp. 145–55.

Harris, C. (2004) 'How did colonialism dispossess? Comments from an edge of empire' *Annals of the Association of American Geographers*, 94(1), pp. 165–82. DOI: 10.1111/.

Herbst, J. (2000) *States and power in Africa: Comparative lessons in authority and control*. Princeton: Princeton University Press.

Hickel, J. (2014) 'The "girl effect": Liberalism, empowerment and the contradictions of development', *Third World Quarterly*, 35(8), pp. 1355–73. DOI: https://doi.org/10.1080/01436597.2014.946250.

Hutchful, E. (1996) 'The civil society debate in Africa', International Journal: Canada's Journal of Global Policy Analysis, 51(1). DOI: j.1467-8306.2004.09401009.x.

Koffman, O. and Gill, R. (2013) 'The revolution will be led by a 12-year-old girl': Girl power and global biopolitics', *Feminist Review*, 105(1), pp. 83–102. DOI:https://doi.org/10.1057/fr.2013.16.

Langevang, T. and Gough (2012) 'Diverging pathways: young female employment and entrepreneurship in sub-Saharan Africa', *The Geographical Journal*, 178(3), pp. 242–52, DOI: 10.1111/j.1475-4959.2011.00457.x.

Le Grange, L. (2019) 'Ubuntu', In Kothari, A. et al. (eds.) *Pluriverse: A post-development dictionary*. Tulika Books, authors UPFRONT, pp. 323–29.

Li, T. M. (2007) *The Will to Improve: Governmentality, Development, and the Practice of Politics*. Duke University Press.

Li, T. M. (2014a) *Land's end: Capitalist relations on an indigenous frontier*. Durham, NC: Duke University Press.

Li, T. M. (2014b) 'What is land? Assembling a resource for global investment', *Transactions of the Institute of British Geographers*, 39(4), pp. 589–602.

Luongo, K. (2014) 'If you can't beat them, join them: Government cleansings of witches and Mau Mau in 1950s Kenya', *History in Africa*, 33, pp. 451–71. DOI: https://doi.org/10.1353/hia.2006.0017

Mafege, A. (1991) *The Theory and Ethnography of African Social Formations: The Case of the Interlacustrine Kingdoms*. Dakar: CODESRIA Book Series.

Mafeje, A. (1998) 'Democracy, Civil Society and Governance in Africa'. Paper presented at the Second DPMF Annual Conference on Democracy, Civil Society and Governance in Africa, United Nations Economic Commission for Africa, Addis Ababa (Ethiopia), 7–10 December.

Mamdani, M. (1990) 'State and Civil Society in Contemporary Africa: Reconceptualizing the Birth of State Nationalism and the Defeat of Popular Movements', *Africa Development / Afrique et Développement*, 15(3/4), pp. 47–70.

Mamdani, M. (1995) 'A critique of the state and civil society paradigm in Africanist studies', in M. Mamdani, and E. Wamba-dia-Wamba (eds.), *African Studies in Social Movements and Democracy*. Dakar: CODESRIA, pp. 602–16.

Mamdani, M. (1996) *Citizen and subject: Contemporary Africa and the legacy of late colonialism*. Princetont: Princeton University Press.

Manji, A. (2021) *The struggle for land and justice in Kenya*. James Currey/ Brewer & Boydell.

Manji, A. (2022) 'The struggles of the Ngorongoro Maasai', *ROAPE*, 11 February. Available: https://roape.net/2022/02/11/the-struggles-of-the-ngorongoro-maasai/.

Marshall, T. H. (1950) *Citizenship and social class: And other essays*. Cambridge: Cambridge University Press.

Mbembe, A. (2019) *Necropolitics*. Durham, NC: Duke University Press.

Mercer, C. (2003) 'Performing partnership: Civil society and the illusions of good governance in Tanzania', *Political Geography*, 22 (2003), pp. 741–63.

Mishra, S. and Dharma, R. B. (2020) 'Uber's entrepreneurship discourse and its neoliberal appeal: Analysis of coverage in English-language dailies in India', *Critical Discourse Studies*, 17(4), pp. 394–411.

Mkandawire, T. (1999) 'Crisis management and the making of "Choiceless Democracies", in Richard Joseph (ed.) *State, conflict and democracy in Africa*. Boulder, London: Lynn Rienner, pp. 119–36.

Mkandawire, T. (2010) 'Aid, accountability, and democracy in Africa', *Social Research: An International Quarterly*, 77(4), pp. 1149–82.

Mustapha, R. (2012) 'The public sphere in 21st century Africa: Broadening the horizons of democratisation', *Africa Development*, 37(1), pp. 27–41.

Nyamnjoh, F. B. (2010) 'Racism, ethnicity and the media in Africa: Reflections inspired by studies of xenophobia in Cameroon and South Africa', *Africa Spectrum*, 45(1), pp. 57–93.

Osaghae, E. E. (2006) 'Colonialism and civil society in Africa: The Perspective of Ekeh's two publics', *Voluntas*, 17, pp. 233–45. DOI: 10.1007/s11266-006-9014-4/.

Peet, R. and Hartwick, E. (2013) *Theories of development: Contentions, arguments, alternatives*. The Guilford Press, New York.

Putnam, R. D. (1993) 'What Makes Democracy Work?', *National Civic Review*, 82(2), pp. 101–7. DOI: https://doi.org/10.1002/ncr.4100820204.

Robinson, C. (2021) *Black Marxism: The making of the Black radical tradition.* London: Penguin Books. First Published 1983. London: Zed Press Ltd.

Rodney, W. (1972) *How Europe underdeveloped Africa.* London: Bogle L' Overture Publications.

Rodney, W. (1980) *A history of the Upper Guinea Coast. 1548-1800.* London: Monthly Review Press.

Sande Lie, J. H. (2015) 'Developmentality: Indirect governance in the World Bank–Uganda partnership', *Third World Quarterly,* 36(4), pp. 723–40.

Sankara, T. (1983) 'Oser inventer l'avenir', *Afrique-Asie.* 15 August, pp. 38–39.

Shivji, I. (2007) *Silences in Ngo discourse: The role and future of Ngos in Africa.* Oxford: Pambazuka Books.

Simpson, A. (2014) *Mohawk interruptus: Political life across the borders of settler states.* Durham, NC: Duke University Press.

Sunseri, T. (2022) 'The Maji-Maji War, 1905–1907'. *Oxford Research Encyclopedia of African History,* 24 February. https://doi.org/10.1093/acrefore/9780190277734.013.15

Teklu, T. A. (2021) 'African Palaver as a model of multiethnic recognition', in Theodros A. T. (ed.) *Moral pedagogies for Africa: From ethnic enmity to responsible cohabitation.* London: Routledge.

Tönnies, F. (2001) (ed. Jose Harris), *Community and civil society.* Cambridge: Cambridge University Press.

Toupin, S. (2022) 'Fugitive infrastructure in the fight against South African apartheid', *Third World Thematics: A TWQ Journal.* DOI: https://doi.org/10.1080/2 3802014.2022.2140190.

Tsakata, D. (2016) 'Gender, land tenure and agrarian production systems in Sub-Saharan Africa', *Agrarian South: Journal of Political Economy,* 5(1), pp. 1–19.

Von Freyhold, M. (1980) *Ujamaa Villages: Analysis of a Social Experiment.* London: Monthly Review Press.

Wamba dia Wamba, E. (1985[2019]) 'Experiences of democracy in Africa: Reflections on practices of communalist palaver as a method of resolving contradictions', *Philosophy and Social Action* 11(3), pp. 1–17. Re-edited & reproduced in 2019 by Libcom.org and available at https://libcom.org/article/experiences-democracy-africa-reflections-practices-communalist-palaver-method-resolving.

World Bank Governance and development (English) (1992) Washington, D.C.: World Bank Group. http://documents.worldbank.org/curated/en/604951468739447676/Governance-and-development

Wright, W. J. (2020) 'The Morphology of Marronage', *Annals of the American Association of Geographers,* 110(4), pp. 1134–49. DOI: 10.1080/24694452.2019.1664890.

Ya'u, Yunusa Z. (2012) 'Ambivalence and activism: Netizens, social transformation and african virtual publics', *Africa Development,* 37(1), pp. 85–102.

Zeilig, L. (2022) *A revolutionary for our time: The Walter Rodney story.* London: Haymarket Books.

5

Resistance and Autonomous Spaces Beyond the NGO: Marronage, Social Movements and Hashtag Dissent

People have not been passive in the face of colonialism or dominant international development paradigms. They desire material well-being and aspire for societal transformation that will improve their lifeworlds and provide dignified futures for their children and communities. In the face of oppression, communities have practiced fugitivity and marronage to produce nurturing spaces beyond the colonial world. They have fought and negotiated alternative paths that sustain life and assert their humanity. Too often, these important histories have been sidelined in development studies curricula. What does it mean to learn and unlearn development alongside resistance to colonial and capitalist worldviews?

Expanding upon disobedient pedagogies (as we explored in our Introduction), we give concrete examples of shifting state's regulatory control of populations through Non-Governmental Organization (NGO) legislation, post-conflict security mechanisms and criminal libel – the latter used to prevent the digital space from becoming a democratic emancipatory space. Students will consider how autonomous communities that foster spaces for people's agency can exist in proximity to spaces of domination, historically and in the present. People have created and nurtured spaces of protest, debate and sociality, which, in recent years, have been aided by social media. The internet has increased the speed and potential for mass mobilization; yet, it has been subjected to policing, surveillance, shutdowns and throttling, and has sometimes facilitated the state's infiltration of movements. Students will examine the use of social media for mobilization and protests, such as Nigeria's 2020 #EndSars campaign and

Cameroon's 2015–2017 #Anglophone struggle, as well as African states' reactions.

DECOLONIAL AND ANTICOLONIAL PLAYLIST

We are invited into a powerful cultural commentary on forms of contemporary frontier-making in the Nigerian rapper Falz's 2018 song, 'This Is Nigeria', which is a cover of Childish Gambino's 'This Is America'.[1] In the song, Falz calls out the criminality, violent dispossession and abandonment fostered by post-colonial petro-capitalism. 'This is Nigeria/ Never ending recession o/ When looters and killers and stealers are still contesting election o/ Police station dey close by 6/ Security reason o'. The song resonates powerfully with the #EndSars protest movement against police brutality in Nigeria, which we consider in our engagement with hashtag dissent (in this chapter).

On the colonial continuities of state violence, we also invite you to listen to Burna Boy's 'Another Story'. Burna sings, 'To understand Nigeria, you need to appreciate where it came from/ In 1900, Britain officially assumed responsibility for the/ Administration of the whole of what we now know as Nigeria from the Niger Company/ They wanna tell you o, tell you o/ Another story o/ Since 1960 them dey play us, why o?'.[2]

RESISTANCE AND MARRONAGE

Colonialism was imposed through conquest, and resistance by local peoples took many forms, from open warfare to everyday forms of struggle (see Chapter 5 on the violent suppression of opposition). Within some colonial-dominated territories, where the terrain was considered inhospitable to white colonialists, communities fleeing enslavement, forced labour and other forms of dehumanization were established. These communities were termed maroon communities and practiced self-government and self-sufficiency (Price 1973; Thompson 2006; Bledsoe 2017).

We introduce here the concept of 'marronage': the quest for freedom from slavery and the autonomous and spatially isolated communities that African enslaved populations have constructed within what Wright (2020) describes as 'unruly environments'. Studies of Maroon communities have tended to focus on those in the Caribbean islands, especially Jamaica and

---

1. www.youtube.com/watch?list=RDVYOjWnS4cMY&v=UW_xEqCWrmo.
2. www.youtube.com/watch?v=JXbWwR4rSmY.

Haiti (Price 1973; Thompson 2006; Bledsoe 2017; Moulton & Salo 2022; Wright 2020). Other communities existed in Northern South America (Suriname, Guyana and Brazil) and the USA, and in parts of Africa, in particular Mauritius (Allen 2004) and Angola (Krug 2018) during the colonial period (Toupin 2022). Students can learn about maroon communities using examples from Nanny Town (Jamaica), Pilaklikaha (Florida), Palmares (Brazil) and Kumako (Suriname) and examine how they sought to generate and foster alternative lifeworlds in colonial settings.

Maroon communities were sites of resistance, militarily, through guerrilla warfare, and epistemically, through cultural retention and innovation. Marronage includes building invisible codes and languages with which oppressed people communicate and form solidarity. Colonial authorities feared oath-taking amongst colonized people and labelled it as 'witchcraft', especially when it involved the supernatural and secrecy and when it was aimed at protecting the colonized. Most uprisings against colonial rule involved a blending of the spiritual with the political or some form of oath-taking. Well known examples in Africa were the Mau Mau war of independence in British colonial Kenya (Elkins 2005; Luongo 2014), and the Maji Maji war in German colonial Tanganyika (Sunseri 2022). Similarly, the Cameroonian anti-colonial movement (1957–71) spearheaded by the Union des Populations du Cameroun (UPC) – or 'les maquisards' – mobilized versions of politico-spiritual self/community relations and sovereignty that pre-dated European arrival (Terretta 2005).

Colonized communities constructed self-governing and self-sufficient communities outside the realm of the state and beyond Eurocentric conceptions of the nation. These spaces provided physical and ontological security from the violence and anxieties that came from operating in a White supremacist European world. Drawing from evidence amongst black and indigenous communities in Belize, Melissa Johnson (2021: 1220) points to the erasure or invisibilization of the practice of commoning in modern European histories of the colonial world and argues that 'these erasures have also contributed to a collective inability to see other-than-capitalist economic activity and organization in the world'. She asks, 'what kind of person, what subjectivity generates and is generated by a collective relationship to resources, or what is a "commoning" subjectivity?' (Johnson 2021: 1220). This is a question that she seeks to answer through empirical evidence, focusing on a communal work ethic, and awareness of power and agency, freedom and love. Johnson's question could be explored when students think about alternatives to capitalism.

RESISTANCE TO NEOLIBERALISM

Discontent with exploitation, government exactions, economic prescriptions, patriarchy, gender-based violence and poor living conditions have long genealogies in the Global South. These intersecting oppressions led to the mobilization of women and the formation of feminist movements. African feminists have a long history of resistance against colonialism and development, dating back to the time of conquest, most of which has been well documented by Pat McFadden (2008), Ifi Amadiume (2000), Oyeronke Oyewumi (2003), Molara Ogundipe-Leslie (1994), Sylvia Tamale (2011, 2020), Philomena Steady (2006), Nkiru Nzegwu (2006), Amina Mama (2020), Wangari Maathai (2008), Ousseima Alidou (2005), Rama Salla Dieng (2022) and others. Feminists have documented how development served first to domesticate women, and later to incorporate them as unpaid labour. Discourses of Western modernity and development policies in Africa have ignored the histories of women's cultural and economic autonomy (Amadiume 2000; Nzegwu 2006; Browdy de Hernandez et al 2010), and, instead, have promoted interventionist policies that represent them as victims and serve to empower them only within a liberal women's right's agenda (see Chapter 6).

The development models promoted by the Global North have not allowed for liberation through political and cultural autonomy or social, ecological and climate justice. We therefore agree with Thomas Sankara (1987) and Claude Ake's (1996) idea that the figuring of a people or their culture and social institutions as an 'obstacle' to their own development is a major failure of any project that aims to materially improve people's lives. As Sankara explained,

> Most important, I think, is to give people confidence in themselves, to understand that ultimately [they] can sit down and write about [their] development, [they] can sit down and write about [their] happiness, [they] can say what [they] want . . . and, at the same time, understand what price must be paid for this happiness. (qtd. in Dembélé 2013; see also Murrey 2020).

He further described his idea of political unity thus,

We should . . . guard against making unity into a dry, paralyzing, sterilizing, monochromatic thing. On the contrary, we would rather see a manifold, varied, and enriching expression of many different ideas and diverse activities, ideas and activities that are rich with a thousand nuances, all submitted courageously and sincerely, accepting differences, respecting criticism and self-criticism – all directed toward the same radical goal . . . the happiness of our people. (4 August 1987, available in Sankara 2007: 387–401).

Flag independence did not change the economic model. Even states that declared themselves 'socialist' found it difficult to shift the patterns of global trade and their unequal position within it. Political competition between elites manifested in ethnic violence, much of which was aggravated by Cold War proxy wars, and the rise of military dictatorships. Many of the new African leaders that emerged, as Ake (1996: 5) notes, 'manipulated ethnic and communal loyalties as a way to deradicalize their followers and contain the emerging class division of political society, which could isolate and destroy them'. Movements for democracy emerged in Africa in the 1980s in reaction to the prevalence of military dictatorships, one-party rule and an abrupt decline in living standards caused by the introduction of the structural adjustment programmes originating from the World Bank, the International Monetary Fund (IMF) and Western governments.

From the mid-1980s widespread protests against austerity measures culminated in pro-democracy movements aimed at changing the economic model. However, in order not to destabilize the extractive processes, Western institutions attached 'political conditionalities' to loans, pressuring governments to introduce multi-party elections. They also popularized the concept of 'good governance' – a technocratic, managerial approach to democracy – which became part of the development discourse (World Bank 1992). Mafege (1998: 9) described 'good governance' as the 'ultimate illusion'. He proceeds: 'indeed, the conditionality of the World Bank and IMF favored more authoritarian regimes than populist ones and in practice proved to be extremely anti-social. Therefore, in their hands the concept of "good governance" should be regarded as an invitation to authoritarianism and a negation of prospects for social democracy'.

Externally sponsored multi-party elections produced what scholars termed 'electocracy' – whereby people vote but are unable to participate in or otherwise influence government (Thomas Sankara, for example, rejected the Western electoral system, critiquing the ways in which it had been instrumentalized as a 'political shell for capitalism'; Sankara 1983). Thandika Mkandawire (1999: 133) uses the term 'choice-less democracies' to describe the lack of freedom in economic policy-making and 'public choices for parties to compete over'. When economic policy is determined externally and there is a lack of local policy formulation and decision-making, questions of sovereignty come to the fore.

To appease critics, international 'aid donors' started processes of localization, and concepts of 'local participation' and 'development partners' thus entered the discourse. While economic reforms under neoliberalism were centred on reducing the role of the state in economy and society, Western governments and human rights organizations became fixated on finding 'civil society stakeholders' in Africa (Mamdani 1990; Hutchful 1997) (see Chapter 4), as a mechanism for mainstreaming resistance. They searched for Western-style autonomous organizations that were independent from the state, assuming that such organizations maintained liberal principles of accountability, transparency, pluralism and the rule of law. Thus, NGOs came to represent civil society and were viewed as vehicles for promoting democracy, accountability and efficiency in service provision, as well as women's empowerment. Western governments directed development funds through their national NGOs, but given the Western scaffolding of the NGO, such organizations professed to be apolitical and relied on 'donor' funds to carry out development projects (Shivji 2007: 22). Issa G. Shivji describes the NGO form in Africa as 'non-political, non-partisan, non-ideological, non-academic, [and] non-theoretical'. Nevertheless, such was the scale of financial transfers to NGOs and the fear of their potential, especially local ones, to mobilize people, governments introduced legislation that centralized registration and monitored NGO activities. In 2019, the Ugandan government reduced the list of registered NGOs from 14,027 to 2119 (*Daily Monitor* 2019).

The process of NGOization neutralized resistance by incorporating activists and transforming their grievances into the language of human rights. International NGOs used the policy of localization to gain insider credibility. Yet they were still criticized for their lack of local accountability to the people they claimed to represent, being internally undemocratic, for stifling local capacity, and for perpetuating a repackaged colonialism. In response to sustained pressure to attend to demands for change more appropriate to the grassroots, development institutions and corporate actors moved in the 1990s to develop more locally-centric programming, at least outwardly. This is a dynamic that Murrey and Jackson (2020: 924) term 'localwashing', whereby corporations 'adopt perception management frameworks characterized by fluctuating processes of evoking, naming, and claiming the racialized local'. Localwashing is done to create a corporate public profile that would present itself as locally-friendly; it can also channel anti-development resistance and deflect blame and historical culpability.

In the late twentieth century, the racial ideologies that informed NGO presence in Africa were even more visible, provoking Abdul-Raheem (1996: 6) to write:

> The racial imbalance is played out every day. Every white person is perceived and received as a boss with an obeisance that will nauseate any conscientious person. . . . The colonial mentality and its lifestyle are back. Most expatriates have their huge houses with all the conveniences, house boys, house girls and a string of people to do their bidding, most of them at the cost of less than a week's travelling ticket on any underground in Europe. Anybody who ever wondered how the colonial staff lived should just visit Kampala, Kigali or Nairobi and hang around the expatriates. Colonial plunderers and marauding pirates like Christopher Columbus, Cecil Rhodes, Lord Lugard were eulogized as adventurers and nation-builders. Their heirs of today are consultants, experts and the NGO community.

Under neoliberalism the collective is seen as a problem if it is not controlled in the form of an NGO that is reliant on external funding for its existence, Yet, for the political elites, even this liberal, mainstream, space poses a threat to their power.

EXPRESSING DISCONTENT WITH DEVELOPMENT IN THE TWENTY-FIRST CENTURY

What avenues exist through which people can voice their oppositional views to the neoliberal project? If formal civil societies are compromised by alliances with states and 'donors', how can people express discontent?

People in the Global South have joined conventional social movements, such as the anti-globalization movements *La Via Campesina*
(https://viacampesina.org/en/),[3] an international peasant movement that
campaigns for rural people and food sovereignty; and the Chipko and the
Adivasis movements in South Asia,[4] who are campaigning for intellectual
and property rights for local and indigenous peoples. Mustapha (2012:
40) contends that in the twenty-first century, 'Africa must move beyond
[European] rationality and its associated concepts of good governance,
"participation", and stylized civil society', and that multiethnic Africa
must have 'multiple publics' that are, in their interaction, 'contestatory'
and 'consensus building'. While the ideal civic public might be co-opted
by the state, other publics exist, especially in the age of globalization
and the Internet. Mustapha joins others in arguing for 'a cultural public
sphere in which politics, personal and public, is transmitted through aes-
thetic and emotional modes of communication' (33), such as through
television soap operas, popular music, and 'infotainment' which reflects
'Africa's orality and musical traditions' (33). Even under military dictatorships, public opinion has been expressed in the cultural sphere through
artists, such as the Jamaican Bob Marley and the Nigerian Fela Kuti, and
the author Ken Saro-Wiwa.

DIGITAL PUBLICS AND CONTEMPORARY SPACES
OF RESISTANCE

Yunusa Z. Ya'u (2012) and Kudakwashe Manganga (2012) have noted
the significance of the Internet for the expansion of the public sphere
in Africa, especially where the established or analogue media tend to
be highly censored, offering few spaces for critique of the state's development policy (Ekine 2010). In fact, to critique is sometimes seen
as not being a 'good citizen', as we have seen in the previous chapter.
Social media and new technologies have provided an alternative public
sphere that engages young people and does not necessitate formal civil
society organization. Social media can be used to mobilize youth pro-
testing against the economic conditions they encounter and against state
violence. Examples include The Arab Spring (Tunisia and neighbour-

---

3. www.viacampesina.org/en/.
4. www.youtube.com/watch?v=qBuOoYZ-U4A.

ing North African countries), Nigeria's #End Sars campaign, Ethiopia's #Oromo movement and the #AnglophoneStruggle in Cameroon (Murrey 2022).

The 'Arab Spring' was a classic example of how social media was used to protest against impoverishment (Al Sayyad and Guvenc 2015; Jackson 2018). On 10 January 2011, Mohamed Bouazizi, a Tunisian street vendor who had been harassed by a police officer that attempted to shut down his business, committed suicide by self-immolation in front of his city's municipal office. The nature of his death galvanized Tunisian protesters against unemployment, low wages and general frustration with the economic state of the country (Bayat 2017). The uprising soon spread throughout Tunisia and to North Africa and the Middle East. Commentators, such as El Haddad (2020) saw the uprisings as the result of a breakdown of an 'authoritarian social contract between state and society, within which the unemployed youth were crucial. The uprising was not primarily a result of organized institutional activity, but rather of informal networks, facilitated in part by new technologies. Social media enabled a strong international dimension with ideas and tactics flowing across national boundaries (Al Sayyad and Guvenc 2015).

Social media is often used for political satire. One such example was the Twitter campaign: #WhatwouldMagafulido?.[5] This was a comedic commentary on Eastern African politics that started in 2016 after the election of Tanzania's authoritarian and anti-corruption President John Magafuli. Social media users in Kenya and Uganda started the conversation on how Magafuli would react to corruption in their countries. Beyond mobilization for in-place protests, social media can provide spaces for intense social commentary. Terms such as 'Kenyan Twitter' or the Nigerian, 'Naija Twitter', are used for specific national debates that take place in the digital space. Nanjala (2018) discusses how digital technology has been used by Kenyan citizens to participate in governance (see also Omanga 2019) and by the state in terms of election technology. Yet, she argues that, despite the initial promises, the digital has not transformed Kenyan politics. Nevertheless it has been significant in terms of raising awareness, such as about the horrific conditions then faced by Kenyan domestic workers in the Middle East (Njoroge 2022).

---

5. www.instagram.com/explore/tags/whatwouldmagafulido/.

In our classrooms, we encourage students to collaborate to deliver presentations that critically examine contemporary movements that engage creatively with social media, often in the face of corporate and state backlash and repression. Many governments have become intoler-ant of social media criticism and its potential for youth mobilization and enforce digital shutdowns. They have enacted restrictive laws and reg-ulations to curb social media use by opposition, block criticism of the government, and to prevent single issue mobilization (Murrey 2022). Tanzania's 2015 Cybercrime Act and 2018 Online Content Regulations mean that criminal charges can be brought against people who are critical of the government online. We ask students to think about how 'netizens' (Internet-citizens) use the digital space to protest.

MATERIALS AND RESOURCES ON TECHNOLOGY

Social Movement Technologies is an organization that collaborates with campaigners and activists around the world to build people power for justice in the digital age. It provides organizing strategy, training and campaign support.[6]

THE #END SARS CAMPAIGN – VOICE OF THE 'SORO SOKE' ('SPEAK UP' IN YORUBA) GENERATION

The #End Sars campaign took place in Nigeria in October 2020 and was a reaction to the violence meted out on civilians by the government's Special Anti-Robbery Squad (SARS). Youth protest was triggered by a video of police officers violently arresting two young men and shooting one of them. The hashtag #EndSars protests started on Twitter, before moving to protests on the streets of Lagos. Amnesty International reported that on '20 October 2020, the Nigerian army violently repressed a peaceful protest at the Lekki toll gate, shooting at the protesters and killing at least 12 people. Since that day, the Nigerian authorities have tried to cover up the events of the Lekki Toll Gate Shooting. They froze protests leaders' bank accounts and fined news agencies who diffused videos of the shooting' (Amnesty 2020), and shut down Twitter in Nigeria.

---

6. www.socialmovementtechnologies.org/about/mission.

THE #OROMO (QEERROO/QARREE) RESISTANCE STRUGGLE IN ETHIOPIA (2015–19)

Another instructive movement that can be integrated into activist and student engagement with social and political change is the Qeerroo/ Qarree movement in Ethiopia. Shared grievances across the Oromia Region gained momentum in 2015, partially in response to the planned administrative expansion of Addis Ababa, which would integrate 1.1 million hectares of land then being administered, under Ethiopia's federalized system of governance by the Oromia National Regional State (ONRS). For Oromo youth protestors (known as Qeerroo/Qarree), the now defunct Addis Ababa Master Plan was a 'Master Killer' (Wayessa 2019) that would bring 40–100 km of ONRS land under the governance of Addis Ababa. As a result, millions of Oromo farmers would be evicted and the governing and schooling language would shift from Afaan Oromo/Oromiffa to Amharic, a politically inflammatory change given a historical context of linguistic marginalization. (In 1941, Haile Selassie banned the Oromo language in governing procedures and schools, and this ban remained in place until 1991.) In February 2016, *Open Democracy* reported that the masterplan:

> possessed all the deficiencies of large development operations in Ethiopia: opacity and confusion, with documents of uncertain status released in dribs and drabs, thus a lack of clarity even about the respective roles of Addis Ababa municipality and the Oromia authorities in the area concerned; a centralising, top-down approach, with no consultation of the people. (see also Cochrane and Mandefro 2019)

Thousands of young people, students, working and unemployed people protested the plan across hundreds of towns and cities throughout Oromia, blocking roads and shutting down businesses.

The state's reaction was both brutal and swift. In response to student- and youth-led peaceful candlelight vigils, police and plain clothed men armed with wooden batons stormed the campus of Jimma University (JU), where one of us (Amber) then worked as a visiting assistant professor from 2015 to 2016. One day in December 2015, hundreds of nonviolent student organizers, as well as those randomly caught in the fray, were chased down on campus, cornered and arrested. Some managed to flee through the back gates into the streets, where military troops were waiting. Unmarked black vans circled the vicinity of the main campus to scoop up and disappear protestors (author fieldnotes, Jimma, December 2015). The protests of 2015/2016 exemplified the long history of state violence in response to nonviolent direct action and political resistance. In 2014, for example, an estimated 500 protestors were killed by security forces in Oromia (Amnesty International 2014). The Ethiopian state responded by cyclically suspending the Internet to the region.

Throughout this period, the Ethiopian government periodically suspended access to the Internet and cut electricity in the Oromo Region. While these tactics were designed to suppress the struggle and deflate collective mobilization, reflections from activists themselves show that digital repression was ineffective, as activists adopted work-around measures and the movement was never dependent upon social media technologies in the first place (Murrey 2022).

THE #ANGLOPHONESTRUGGLE IN CAMEROON, 2016–19

Another important and understudied contemporary movement is the Anglophone struggle in Cameroon. Much like the movement in Ethiopia (which occurred at approximately the same time), the Cameroonian government suspended internet connection in response to the social movement.

In October 2016, in the towns of Bamenda, Buea, Limbe and others in the Anglophone regions of Southwest and Northwest Cameroon, a trade union of teachers and lawyers (the Cameroon Anglophone Civil Society Consortium) staged peaceful protests demanding salary increases and a discontinuation of the requirement that education and legal processes in the predominantly English-speaking region be conducted in French. United by 'the deep perception that they have been purposely marginalized over the years' (Pommerolle and Heungoup 2017: 528), they were soon joined *en masse* by students, Bendskiners (motorbike taxi drivers), transport workers, and others in a long-established form of Cameroonian protest: massive boycotts that effectively turn entire cities into ghost towns, or *les villes mortes*. This style of protest – ghost-towning – has been prevalent in Cameroon since the early 1990s (Amin 2013).

When the ruling party, Paul Biya's RDPC/CPDM (Cameroon People's Democratic Movement), announced it would hold a 'peace parade' in

Bamenda on 8 December 2016 – a blatant attempt to stifle and appropriate the months-long series of protests – people responded by blocking roadways and heckling RDPC supporters. As with previous, predominantly peaceful demonstrations, the government retaliated with extreme force. This time, they used tear gas, water cannons, bully clubs, and live ammunition against protestors. Several dozen were arrested, and movement leaders were disappeared, including the digital activist Jean-Claude Agbortem. Biya's forces killed five people, two of whom were shot in the back. No charges were brought for these deaths (Walla 2017).

Subsequent protests grew in size, and people were outraged about arbitrary detainments, beatings, and both targeted and indiscriminate killings of protestors and bystanders. On 13 January 2017, soldiers opened fire on a crowd of peaceful protestors, injuring three. Ongoing negotiations were halted, and protestors demanded that the government free all political prisoners. In retaliation, the government suspended the Internet for the five million people living in the two English-speaking regions for three consecutive months, or 93 days, from January to April 2017. The stoppage did not cease the deluge of video footage of state violence from circulating online.

Indeed, security personnel filmed their own heavily armed patrols and circulated the videos on Facebook and Twitter, deliberately showcasing grim-faced and heavily armed troops shooting indiscriminately into buildings from the rears of 4x4s, in broad daylight. Calculated to demonstrate the state's might, these videos instilled fear and rage, triggering avalanches of outrage-laden commentary online. Instances of serious violence by security forces were captured on video by onlookers and circulated widely via YouTube, Facebook and Twitter under hashtags including #AnglophoneStruggle, #Ambazonia, #FreeAllArrested, #JusticeInCameroon, #CameroonGenocide and more. Security forces were shown intimidating, disrobing, whipping, beating and hosing groups of people with high-volume water cannons. Anglophone Cameroonians took to Twitter to proclaim, 'the occupier shall have no peace in our territory', and to urge people to 'rise up and resist #France and the colonial army of #Cameroon in our land' (tweet from 24 August 2018), condemning the synergy between the majority-francophone ruling party and French neocolonial corporate and state interests.

In addition to curtailing communications within and between the regions of Cameroon, the government's suspension of the Internet was likely an attempt to block communications between activists and the Cameroonian Diaspora, and to stifle the proliferation of publications critical of President Paul Biya, the RDPC and Biya's entourage (interviews with activists, Yaoundé 2018). Any public gathering that was not orientated toward 'praising the president [was] suppressed by security forces under the pretext of breach of public order, attempt to break the peace of the land, terrorism, unlawful gathering, or threat to state security' (Tapuka 2017: 111). The state's repressive and violent tactics – including pervasive digital infrastructural harm – in response to popular and nonviolent mobilizations in Southwest and Northwest Cameroon triggered the movement's violent transformation (Orock 2021). What began in 2016 as a popular, nonviolent movement for expanded judicial and educational rights and federalism morphed into a splintered and violent separatist insurgency for an independent country of Ambazonia. The resulting Ambazonian conflict has caused the displacement of 768,000 people (Konings and Nyamnjoh 2019; Human Rights Watch 2020) and the killing of an estimated 4,000–12,000 people (Annan et al., 2021: 698).

CONCLUSION

Resistance against oppression has been continuous and has taken many forms. In this chapter we began with the form of struggle that involved autonomous communities existing on the margins of, or within, spaces of oppression. These spaces of marronage are important to demonstrate the potential for creating emancipatory spaces of hope even where they may seem impossible. We realize that academic research on these spaces is increasing and encourage our readers to think about how the concept of marronage may be applied to people resisting development in their everyday spaces in the Global South.

Knowing that resistance to colonial rule is well-documented, we will now turn our attention to resistance against neoliberal authoritarianism. We argue that the radical transformation that should have arisen from the social and political fallout of anti-austerity and structural adgjustment programs (SAP) as well as pro-democracy movements was highjacked by development institutions to suppress criticism of the economic philosophy being promoted across Africa. Organized resistance was mainstreamed and controlled through NGOs that took on the discourse of human rights organizations from the Global North to articulate their grievances. Consequently, the people, especially the youth, found the space to challenge development restricted and did not reflect how they conceptualize their oppression. We argue that the digital space provides an alternative organizational space in which people can voice discontent in their own language and mobilize resistance, even though its limitation as an externally corporate-owned sphere makes it vulnerable to state surveillance and closure. It is worth exploring further the multiple spaces that resistance groups utilize and move between.

QUESTIONS FOR FURTHER THOUGHT

How has social media enabled the development of new publics (civic engagement or activism) in Africa? What are their characteristics and goals? How do they relate to development ideologies/projects and how have states responded?

What sort of narratives are/were we told through social media and how do activists, comedians, journalists and citizen journalists work around infrastructural repression, surveillance, throttling and more?

GREY MATERIALS

Mampilly, Z. Ted talk on *How protest is redefining democracy around the world*. Available: www.ted.com/talks/zachariah_mampilly_how_protest_is_ redefining_democracy_around_the_world.

Scenes from #EndSARS Protest in Lagos, Nigeria, 9 October 2020. Available: www.youtube.com/watch?v=anGQ4sC3FFk.

Anti-police brutality protest in Nigeria. Available: https://qz.com/africa/1915472/ endsars-young-nigerian-protest-rogue-police-unit/.

Whether Africans are seen as part of the global public. Available: www. aljazeera.com/news/2020/01/anger-ugandan-activist-cropped-photo-white-peers-200125083141104.html.

REFERENCES

Alidou, O. D. (2005) *Engaging modernity: Muslim women and the politics of agency in postcolonial Niger*. Madison: University of Wisconsin Press.

Al Sayyad, N. and Guvenc, M. (2015) 'Virtual uprisings: On the interaction of new social media, traditional media coverage and urban space during the "Arab Spring"', *Urban Studies*, 52(11), pp. 2018–34.

Allen, R. B. (2005) 'A Serious and alarming daily evil: Marronage and its legacy in Mauritius and the colonial plantation world', in Alpers, E.; G. Campbell and M. Saloman (eds.), *Slavery and Resistance in Africa and Asia*. London: Routledge.

Amadiume, I. (2000) *Daughters of the goddess: Daughters of imperialism*. London: Zed Books.

Amin, J. A. (2013) 'Cameroonian youths and the protest of February 2008', *Cahiers d'études Africaines*, 3(211), pp. 677–97.

Amnesty International (2020) #ENDSARS MOVEMENT: FROM TWITTER TO NIGERIAN STREETS. Available: www.amnesty.org/en/latest/campaigns/2021/02/nigeria-end-impunity-for-police-violence-by-sars-endsars/.

Anderson, R. N. (2009) 'The quilombo of Palmares: A new overview of a maroon state in seventeenth-century Brazil', *Journal of Latin American Studies*, 28(3), pp. 545–66.

Angel, G. Q-R. (1994) 'The camouflaged drum – melodization of rhythms and marronage and ethnicity in Caribbean peasant music', *Caribbean Quarterly*, 40(1), pp. 27–37. DOI: 10.1080/00086495.1994.116718.

Bayat, A. (2017) *Revolution and revolutionaries: Making sense of the Arab Spring*. Redwood City: Stanford University Press.

Bledsoe, A. (2017) 'Marronage as a past and present geography in the Americas', *Southeastern Geographer*, 57(1), Special Issue: Black Geographies in and of the United States South (Spring 2017), pp. 30–50.

Browdy de Hernandez, J., Douglas, P., Jolaosho, O. and Serafin, A. (2010) *African women writing resistance: Contemporary voices*. Madison: University of Wisconsin Press.

Cochrane, L. and Mandefro, H. (2019) 'Discussing the 2018/19 Changes in Ethiopia: Hone Mandefro', *NokokoPod*, 2, pp. 1–24.

de Sá Mello da Costa, A. and Saraiva, L. A. S. (2012) 'Hegemonic discourses on entrepreneurship as an ideological mechanism for the reproduction of capital', *Organization*, 19(5), pp. 587–614.

Dieng, R. S. (2021) 'From Yewwu Yewwi to# FreeSenegal: Class, Gender and Generational Dynamics of Radical Feminist Activism in Senegal', *Politics & Gender* 12(6), pp. 1–7.

Dunnavant, J. P. (2021) 'Have confidence in the sea: Maritime maroons and fugitive geographies', *Antipode*, 53(3), pp. 884–905.

Ekine, S. (ed.) (2010) *SMS uprising: Mobile activism in Africa*. Senegal: Pambazuka Press.

Elkins, C. (2005) *Britain's Gulag: The Brutal End of Empire in Kenya*. London: Pimlico.

El-Haddad, A. (2020) 'Redefining the social contract in the wake of the Arab Spring: The experiences of Egypt, Morocco and Tunisia', *World Development*, 127. https://doi.org/10.1016/j.worlddev.2019.104774.

Hutchful, E. (1996) 'The civil society debate in Africa', *International Journal: Canada's Journal of Global Policy Analysis*, 51(1). DOI: j.1467-8306.2004.09401009.x.

Jackson, N. (2018) 'Justin Zongo and the place of the "Arab Spring": Repression, resistance, and revolution in Egypt and Burkina Faso', in Wahlrab, A. and McNeal, M. J. (eds) *US approaches to the Arab uprisings*. London: Bloomsbury, pp. 141–62.

Johnson, M. (2021) 'Creole becoming and the commons: Black freedom in Belize', *Environment & Planning E: Nature and Space*, 4(4), pp. 1217–31. DOI: 10.1177/251484861989116.

Konings, P. and Nyamnjoh, F. B. (2019) 'Anglophone secessionist movements in Cameroon', in L. de Vries, P. Englebert, and M. Schomerus (eds.), *Palgrave series in African borderland studies*, London: Palgrave MacMillian, pp. 59–90.

Krug, J. (2018) *Fugitive modernities: Kisama and the politics of freedom*. Durham, NC: Duke University Press.

Luongo, K. (2014) 'If you can't beat them, join them: government cleansings of witches and Mau Mau in 1950s Kenya', *History in Africa*, pp. 451–71. DOI: https://doi.org/10.1353/hia.2006.0017.

Maathai, W. (2008) *Unbowed: An autobiography*. London: Arrow Books.

Mafeje, A. (1998) 'Democracy, civil society and governance in Africa'. Paper presented at the Second DPMF Annual Conference on Democracy, Civil Society and Governance in Africa, United Nations Economic Commission for Africa, Addis Ababa (Ethiopia), 7–10 December.

Mama, A. (2020) '"We will not be pacified": From freedom fighters to feminists', *European Journal of Women's Studies*, 27(4), pp. 362–80.

McFadden, P. (2008) 'Plunder as statecraft: Militarism and resistance in neocolonial Africa', In Sutton, B; Morgen, S. and J. Novkov (eds), *Security disarmed: Critical perspectives on gender, race, and militarization*. New Brunswick, NJ: Rutgers University Press, pp. 136–56.

Mkandawire, T. (1999) "Crisis management and the making of "Choiceless Democracies", in Richard Joseph (ed.) *State, Conflict and democracy in Africa*. Boulder, London: Lynn Rienner: pp.119–136.

Moulton, A. A. and Salo, I. (2022) 'Black Geographies and Black Ecologies as Insurgent Ecocriticism', *Environment and Society*, 13(1), pp. 156–74.

Mutua, M. (2001) 'Savages, victims, and saviors: The metaphor of human rights', *Harvard International Law Journal*, 42(1), pp. 201–46.

Mutua, M. (2009) 'The transformation of Africa: A critique of the rights discourse', *Buffalo Legal Studies Research Paper*, 2010-002. https://ssrn.com/abstract=1526734.

Manganga, K. (2012) 'The internet as public sphere: A Zimbabwean case study (1999-2008)', *Africa Development / Afrique et Développement*, 37(1), Special Issue on 'The African Public Sphere: Concepts, Histories, Voices and Processes', pp. 103–18.

Murrey, A. and Jackson, N. A. (2020) 'A decolonial critique of the racialized "localwashing" of extraction in Central Africa', *Annals of the American Association of Geographers*, 110(3), pp. 917–94.

Mutsvairo, B. (2016) (ed.) *Digital activism in the social media era: Critical reflections on emerging trends in Sub-Saharan Africa*. London: Palgrave Macmillan.

Njoroge, N. (Sat, 3 Sep, 2022), 'Photos of ailing Kenyan lady in Saudi Arabia spark fury online', *K24 Digital*. Available: www.k24tv.co.ke/news/ailing-kenyan-lady-in-saudi-arabia-78076.

Nyabola, N. (2018) *Digital democracy, analogue politics: How the internet era is transforming politics in Kenya*. London: Bloomsbury.

Nzegwu, N. (2006) *Family matters: Concepts in African philosophy of culture*. New York: State University of New York Press.

Ogundipe-Leslie, M. (1994) *Re-creating ourselves: African women and critica transformations*. Lawrenceville, NJ: Africa World Press.

Omanga, D. (2019) 'WhatsApp as "digital publics": the Nakuru Analysts and the evolution of participation in county governance in Kenya', *Journal of Eastern African Studies*, 13(1), https://doi.org/10.1080/17531055.2018.1548211.

Orock, R. (2021) 'Cameroon's authoritarianism fuels its Anglophone separatist war', *Africa Portal*. www.africaportal.org/features/cameroons-authoritarianism-fuels-its-anglophone-separatist-war/.

Oyewumi, O. (2003) *African women and feminism: Reflecting on the politics of sisterhood*. Trenton, NJ: Africa World Press.

Pommerolle, M. and Heungoup, H. (2017) 'Briefing – The "Anglophone Crisis": A tale of the Cameroonian postcolony', *African Affairs*, 116(464), pp. 526–38.

Price, R. (ed.) (1973) *Maroon Societies: Rebel slave communities in the Americas*. Garden City, N.Y.: Anchor Books.

Rydzak, J. (2018) 'Disconnected: A human rights-based approach to network disruptions', *Global Network Initiative*, pp. 1–33. Available: https://globalnetworkinitiative.org/wp-content/uploads/2018/06/Disconnected-Report-Network-Disruptions.pdf.

Sankara, T. (2007) *Thomas Sankara Speaks: The Burkina Faso Revolution 1983-1987*. New York: Pathfinder. 2nd Edition.

Steady, F. C. (2006) *Women and collective action in Africa*. London: Palgrave Macmillan.

Sunseri, T. (2022) 'The Maji-Maji War, 1905–1907'. *Oxford Research Encyclopedia of African History*. oxfordre.com. https://doi.org/10.1093/acrefore/9780190277734.013.15.

Tamale, S. (2011) (ed.) *African Sexualities: A Reader*. Oxford: Pambazuka Books.

Tamale, S. (2020) *Decolonization and African-feminism*. Ottawa, Ontario: Daraja Press.

Tamar, H. D., Ersoy, M., et al. (2020) 'Nigeria's #EndSARS movement and its implication on online protests in Africa's most populous country', *Journal of Public Affairs*, 22(3), https://doi.org/10.1002/pa.2583.

Tapuka, G. (2017) 'The Anglophone press in Cameroon: Mediating the Anglophone problem', *African Conflict and Peacebuilding Review*, 7(2), pp. 99–114.

The Daily Monitor newspaper (Sunday, 9 June 2019) 'Donors freeze funding to NGOs over corruption'.

Thompson, A. O. (2006), *Flight to freedom: African runaways and maroons in the Americas*. Kingston: University of West Indies Press.

Walla, K. (2017) 'Cameroon Government breaks the law and violates basic human rights', *Kahwalla*, www.kahwalla.com/blog.

Wayessa, G. O. (2019) 'The master plan is a master killer: Land dispossession and powerful resistance in Oromia, Ethiopia', *Regions and Cohesion*, 9(2), pp. 31–56.

Wright, W. J. (2020) 'The Morphology of Marronage', *Annals of the American Association of Geographers*, 110(4), pp. 1134–49, DOI: 10.1080/24694452.2019.1664890.

6

Critiquing Heteronormativity and the Male Gaze: Queering Development and Beyond

In previous chapters we have considered the relations between coloniality, international development and the white gaze. Here we build on our previous insights on the various forms of violence associated with development, on the coloniality of power and the functions of racialization within international development. We now turn to a consideration of how colonial heteronormativity and the male gaze have shaped international development, thus constraining the imaginaries of intimate relations and fostering or reinforcing gendered and sexual violence.

Notions of moral respectability emerged within and were central to the making of sexuality in modern Europe. The regulation of sexual desire and relations, in particular by enforcing heteronormativity and devaluing the labour and knowledge of women, trans and non-binary peoples, were conditions of the 'progress' of modern capitalist and Judeo-Christian societies. These normative relations were transferred via legal and administrative practices to a variety of other political regimes through colonial-capitalist relations, including the development paradigms so often under writ with Judeo-Christian normativities. It is important to keep in mind that, globally, genders were not always (or usually) organized in binary terms and that intersexed people, homosexual practices, cross-dressing and co-gendered identities were recognized and not deemed criminal in many Indigenous communities.

The 'coloniality of gender' (e.g. systematic racialized gender violence; see Lugones 2008; Icaza and Vazquez 2016) was a primary heteronormative foundation of developmentalism. The coloniality of gender refers to the fundamental role of gender and sexual exploitation and inequality within the coloniality of power. The establishment of colonial social and political systems was reliant upon an (unnamed and naturalized) set of interwoven gender-sexual Eurocentric presumptions about what constituted family relations. These presumptions included: the prioritization of the male-headed household; the formal and informal deference to patriarchal authority and hegemonic masculinities; laws regarding sexual 'respectability' that tightly regulated women's sexuality and reproduction (frequently in the name of 'overpopulation') and outlawed same-sex sexual relations; the (non)value of women's labour; and more. International organizations and Western and non-Western intellectuals and experts played significant roles in shaping sexual subjectivities and regulating sexuality and gender relations in societies of the Global South (Wieringa and Sívori 2013). As the authors of *Decolonizing Sexualities* assert, heteronormative social classifications can transcend gender and racial differences. Amy Lind explains that through a heteronormative lens, 'reproductive heterosexuality [has a] central place in modernist conceptions of development, family life and the nation' (2010: 37). This hegemonic understanding of gender is heterosexist, sexually dimorphic and patriarchal – that is to say, hierarchical; with able-bodied men in positions of power relative to women, young, the elderly and differently-abled men.

A powerful body of work is fundamentally unsettling Eurocentric cis-heteropatriarchy, including the scholarship in queer decolonial studies, queering development and transfeminist thought from and in the Global South. This includes work in decolonial and anti-colonial frameworks that exposes hegemonic productions of gender, sexuality, being and il/legibility while seeking to foster meaningful political alliances across difference (Bakshi 2016). A critical component of this scholarship has been to think through the politics of visibility and invisibility (Lind 2010; Jolly 2000) and the roles of queer movements within the project of the nation-state and nationalist imaginaries (Puar 2013; Rao 2020). We here consider the intellectual imperatives of teaching queering development and queer decolonial feminisms (Alqaisiya 2018) within contemporary debates around sex, wellbeing, pleasure in development studies and LGBTQ+ activism in transnational contexts.

We look at the historical trajectory of arguments for the inclusion of women's needs and perspectives within international development, from the paradigm of *Women in Development,* to that of *Gender and Development.* Scholars have identified the disparate marginalization experienced by women and children within racial capitalism and termed this gendered economic violence the 'feminization of poverty'. Feminists working in international development have thus drawn attention to women's acute or double vulnerabilities within societies of the Global South, including the ways in which even discourses around women's marginalization have been channelled into imperial narratives, for example in the imperial narrative of the 'brown woman as victim' (Seppälä 2016) or the woman and girl as social hero. The latter, as we shall see, has been epitomized in twenty-first century development ideologies like 'girl rising' and 'the girl effect'.

ANTICOLONIAL AND DECOLONIAL SOUNDTRACK

The song 'Wo Fie' by Angel Maxine (featuring Wanlov the Kubolor & Sister Deborah) went viral in Ghana in 2022.[1] 'Wo Fie' means 'your home' and the lyrics demystify queer love by literally bringing it home. Maxine sings, 'lesbians are in your house . . . anal sex happens in your house'. In the intro to the music video, the viewer is starkly informed that they 'may be arrested for watching this video', demanding recognition of the outlaw-ing of same-sex sexual relations in many post-colonial societies. A legal practice which has its roots in colonial penal codes. Bridging racial and sexual colonial violence, meanwhile, the Kenyan group Art Attack's song 'Same Love' celebrates experiences of same-sex-loving people in Africa, mixing genres and pulling from a global tapestry of songs and styles.[2]

Another powerful song is Loyiso Gijana's 'Madoda Sabelani' or 'men must answer' in isiXhosa. The song documents and grieves the killing of women by male perpetrators in South Africa, including Kgothatso Molefe, Uyinene Mrwetyana and Tshegofatso Pule.[3] Finally, Sally Nyolo's 1996 serenade song 'Tam Tam' combines a deeply moving melody with her haunting voice to call for a lover and partner to join her against the 'solitude that we suffer' that characterizes modern life.[4] The song is an audacious invitation to love. In the Eton language of Central Cameroon, she sings: 'you are without land, I am without sky (*one tegue si, ma tegue yop*) . . . you are without a companion, I am without a brother (*one tegue madjang, ma tegue ndòm*)'.

---

1. www.youtube.com/watch?v=IJOnOfUakcA.
2. www.youtube.com/watch?v=8EataOQvPII.
3. www.youtube.com/watch?v=jAN6Dv3KSWw.
4. www.youtube.com/watch?v=USk3FBaYqgA&t=5s.

A NOTE ON TERMS

We would like to first make a quick note on our use of the term 'queering', which has been a source of deliberation and critical thinking in our classrooms. Queering is used in this literature as a *verb* for radical, life-affirming action and political praxis against heteronormativity and to foster intersubjective relations beyond its remit. Queer constitutes a rejection of the binary distinction between homo- and hetero-sexual and allows an understanding of sexualities as non-essential and transitional. That is to say, as horizontal, fluid and reciprocal – rather than the fixed, masculinized tropes associated with Northern development donors (Mawdsley 2020).

In radical literature and solidarity action, 'queer' is never as a slur or pejorative for a person or community. Queer instead emerged as a political concept with the capacity to accommodate a multiplicity of intersectional (sex, class, race, gender) experiences and subjectivities. Sandeep Bakshi (2020: 1), in *Decolonizing Sexualities*, writes that:

> Decolonial queerness entails querying the workings of neo-colonial epistemic categories, systems of classification and taxonomies that classify people. Queering coloniality and the epistemic categories that classify people according to their body configuration – skin colour and biological molecular composition for the regeneration of the species – means to disobey and delink from the coloniality of knowledge and of being . . . decolonial queerness is necessary not only to resist coloniality but, above all, to re-exist and re-emerge decolonially.

When used as a radical term, 'queering' seeks to foster non-hierarchical relations of being and raise occasions for emancipatory political futures. Terminology and language are central to work on sexuality within international development. There have been a great many debates around the utility or otherwise of the expanding acronym LGBTQI+, for example, which is an acronym that can flatten, remarginalize or even Westernize in its uniformity (Nyanzi 2015). In English, many non-Western and Indigenous forms of relations and subjectivities cannot adequately be named or described. English language speakers have long only had two words to indicate closed circuits (man or woman; masculine or feminine), for example, with the third gender fluid pronoun of 'they' emerging more recently into popular useage. Whenever possible in the classroom and in the pages of this book, we use the terms and identifiers preferred by activists and people in their own contexts and communities. We ask that we and our students and readers be thoughtful and critical of any use of terms; we are humble in our usage and, as with each of our chapters, intend to open (rather than close) avenues of thought and solidarity.

Decolonial feminists, including Maria Lugones (2010) and Rosalba Icaza (2017), have articulated the need for thinking from a place of vulnerability and humility that refuses mastery. This includes decentring and unlearning the dominant training within the academy to think from the nowhere. Learning disobedience means thinking against generalizations and focusing on concrete embodied experiences. Rozalba Icaza and Rolando Vázquez (2016) argue that decolonial feminism is an invitation to think, be, do and sense that exceeds the dominant discourse about women, gender, sexuality and the body. Place-based knowledge and community needs are at the forefront. Chandra Talpade Mohanty (2003: 230) has also been an important voice in the decolonization of feminist theory and the necessity of an anti-capitalist critique. She argues that feminist theorizations need to be attentive to the material complexity, the reality and agency of women's bodies and lives in the Global South. A notion of social justice, of liberation, needs to be constructed from these perspectives in order to be inclusive and make visible the actual operations of discrimination, exploitation, oppression, exclusion and subordination. At the centre of such discussions are recognitions of the importance of power configurations in representations of intimacy, desire and sexuality. What are the assumptions embedded within scholarly and practitioner representations and imaginaries? What is the role of scholar activists in solidarity and LGBTQI+ advocacy (as we will see)?

EUROCENTRIC HETERONORMATIVITY

The idea that 'gender' is a social construction has been widely accepted by feminist and queer theorists as well as those working within the philosophical tradition of 'social constructionism'. This means that gender is not something that actually or intrinsically exists in the world or in nature, nor is it something we can grasp and clearly identify or quantify (much like race, as we saw in Chapter 1). Rather, gender is an analytical category constructed in order to be able to explain and organize the world in certain ways, usually in order to explain inequalities between men, women and non-binary people in different societies and historical contexts. For our consideration here, we need to understand that gender refers to the result of socially constructed ideas about the behaviour, actions and roles a particular sex performs. Gender is the term used to exemplify the attributes that a society or culture constitutes as masculine, feminine, androgynous, gender fluid or non-binary, etc. Sex, meanwhile, refers to physical or physiological differences between males and females, including both primary sex characteristics (the reproductive system) and secondary characteristics such as height and muscularity. Feminists and queer scholars have also argued that sex is not intrinsic either, as feminist philosopher Judith Butler (1990) argues, that sex is 'cleaned up' by society so that sex-based divisions can be taken as firm and established. By 'cleaning up', Butler means society simplifies and essentializes what are in fact complex and varied experiences into binaries ('male' and 'female'). This 'cleaning up' is inherently limiting. It enforces a gender restrictive worldview and polices the boundaries of male/female to prohibit messy frictions of identity and subjectivity in the margins.

Heteronormativity refers to the process by which dominant development institutions and structures have come to naturalize and therefore privilege heterosexual relations (Berland and Warner 1998). The heterosexual cisgender nuclear family was the principal unit through which the Euro-American drives to modernity and capitalist empire were realized, with each member within the household ascribed specific roles, functions and identities. Within Eurocentric purviews, these types of kin relations were viewed as the most 'productive', even as they entailed the ostracization, expulsion or assassination of elderly women, unwed women and LGBTQI. In *Caliban and the Witch: Women, The Body and Primitive Accumulation,* Silvia Federici (2014) powerfully exposes the simultaneous hunting and large-scale killing of women as 'witches' with the displacement of people from their land (and means of production) during the founding of the European modern capitalist nation-state. The life-giving work of women was rendered dangerous and disposable and, for Federici and other Marxist feminists, this violent process paved the way for subsequent capitalist dispossession.

Gender divisions emerged within the prism of Cartesian rationality (during the Enlightenment period), through which a hierarchization of man being maintained as dominant over woman; human as dominant over nature; the white race as dominant over Black and brown people, and so forth. As you will recall from our discussions on colonialism and the coloniality of power in Chapter 1, Eurocentric knowledges are centred upon the construction of multiple and recurring oppositions and hierarchical dualisms. These include reason/body; subject/object; culture/ nature; masculine/feminine. In this way, not only is masculine placed above feminine, but subjectivities and relations beyond and outside of the masculine/feminine binary are effaced. These preconceptions were subsequently extrapolated onto a global scale through European colonialism and neo-colonialism. Intimate and romantic relations, kinship networks and ways of being which do not conform to this rigid and hegemonized type have accordingly been invisibilized, demonized and marginalized. Within the coloniality of knowledge, Western epistemic knowledge propagates the myth of universality and global relevance/predominance.

Eurocentric knowledge assumes that their *local* knowledge production serves as a model for every other history being understood as universal (Chakrabarty 2000). This has often had profound implications for changes in gender and sex relations within colonial and post-colonial societies. In the wake of formal decolonization, 'development policies work as instruments of governance and as methods of constructing and legitimizing subjectivities' (Lind 2010). Heteronormative household models have also been influential and foundational to many development interventions (Jolly 2011), which often presume a male head-of-household who works outside of the home and a female partner who fulfils forms of labour gendered as feminine, often in the private domain. Commentators have noted that international financial institutions (IFIs) like the World Bank, for example, tend to assume in their policies that households are nuclear families comprising a male, his wife and their children (Jolly 2011). Such models exemplify the embeddedness of heteronormativity and, for a long time, the 'male gaze' within development policy and practice. These practices are inherently excluding.

THE MODERN/COLONIAL GENDER SYSTEM

As we can recall from the discussion in Chapter 1, Quijano's model of the coloniality of power is configured as a system, imposed on the entire planet, wherein Europe is promoted and reproduced as the most developed and sophisticated stage of humanity. Rationality and modernity are imagined as European products and experiences. This system operates across four spheres: the control of labour, authority, sex and knowledge. The decolonial feminist María Lugones offers a rethinking of the coloniality of power, asserting that the original formulation is in itself paradoxically patriarchal. 'Paradoxically' because the theorization of the 'coloniality of power' is intended to expose the will-to-power, yet the model itself reaffirms masculine power. In particular, she (2008: 1) identifies and calls out a theoretical 'indifference' to the 'systematic violences inflicted upon women of color' even by men who have been racialized as inferior and who are compatriots in struggle. The 'modern/colonial gender system', as Lugones frames it, impacts upon all genders, but differentially according to their intersection with other identity and material markers (like class, race, sexuality, and so forth). She pushes for the need to rearticulate the enforcement of sex/gender within the coloniality of power, including beyond systemic struggles for access to sex and control over resources and reproduction (as originally theorized). She reasons that 'Quijano accepts the global, Eurocentered, capitalist understanding of what gender is about' (Lugones 2008: 2). The sex/gender differentials built into and fostered by Eurocentric heteronormativity and patriarchy unfold along racial lines. As she writes, 'The elements that constitute the global, Eurocentered, capitalist model of power do not stand in separation from each other and none of them is prior to the processes that constitute the patterns' (2008: 3).

Lugones takes up Quijano's understanding of race as an historical invention, one constituted by the interaction of Europeans and those who were colonized and racialized as inferior, and which uses the same logic to understand the constitution of genders. This means recognizing that a new gender system was created from the interaction between the colonized and the colonizers. Lugones argues that there is a need for greater consideration of the relation between race and gender, writing:

> Colonialism did not impose precolonial, European gender arrangements on the colonized. It imposed a new gender system that created very different arrangements for colonized males and females than for white bourgeois colonizers . . . it introduced many genders and gender itself as a colonial concept and mode of organization of relations of production, property relations, of cosmologies and ways of knowing. (2010: 186)

This new gender system was put into effect through and because of the position of power and domination of the colonizers' culture and the predominance of their values, cosmologies and forms of knowledge. This is an understanding that goes beyond the dichotomous opposition of two cultures and towards a more serious consideration of the interaction of cultures in different positions of power. She argues that,

> The reason to historicize gender formation is that without this history, we keep on centring our analysis on the patriarchy; that is, on a binary, hierarchical, oppressive gender formation that rests on male supremacy without any clear understanding of the mechanisms by which heterosexuality, capitalism, and racial classification are impossible to understand apart from each other . . . To understand the relation of the birth of the colonial/modern gender system to the birth of global colonial capitalism – with the centrality of the coloniality of power to that system of global power – is to understand our present organization of life anew. (2010: 186–87)

Colonial laws established penal codes, commonly known as sodomy laws, that criminalized so-called 'unnatural sexual acts', which have often been upheld in post-colonial times (Tamale 2011; Rao 2020). Rama Salla Dieng (2023: 5–6) writes, 'Feminist protests in Senegal demonstrate how gender inequality intersects with class inequality and generation [in these places,] women's and youth bodies are political battlefields for patriarchal power and state violence'. From a coloniality of gender perspective we come to understand the ways in which Eurocentric understandings were imposed and implemented in ways that erased or altered those gendered and sex relations that pre-existed (Amadiume 1987). Prior to colonialism in much of the world, 'Certain practices, regimes, ways of being and feeling were not gendered at all, but [existed as] otherwise' (Icaza and Vasquez 2016: 4). Precolonial, colonial and postcolonial institutions and ideologies are emergent and colonial power is not totalizing.

The Nigerian anthropologist Ife Amadiume's (1987) book *Male Daughters, Female Husbands* tracks the decline of precolonial women's power because of the establishment of colonial power relations among the Nnobi of Nigeria. Oyeronke Oyewumi (1998) similarly criticizes Western notions of gender, claiming that not all human cultures organize social worlds in biologically deterministic ways. In her 1991 book *The*

Invention of Women: Making an African Sense of Western Gender Discourses, she criticizes Western feminism for insisting that all cultures do and must construct gender. She bases her analysis on Nigerian Yoruba culture, who according to her, did not maintain a hierarchized gender system prior to colonization. Oyewumi argues that researchers only 'find' gender when their research questions lead them to it. For this reason, Oyewumi argues that Western feminists see gender hierarchies everywhere. She writes, 'The notion that all cultures across time and space do and must construct gender introduces an incorrigible proposition in feminist thought. In spite of contrary evidence from other cultures, scholars continue to seek gender and male dominance in other cultures without first establishing whether gender as a social category is transcultural. This question has been bracketed off' (Oyewumi 1998: 1054). Another Nigerian feminist, Bibi Bakare-Yusuf (2003), criticizes some of Oyewumi's approach when analysing Yoruba culture, asserting that the gender neutrality in Yoruba language does not automatically indicate an absence of sex-based inequalities.

A more nuanced understanding of how genders are constituted within coloniality means considering both what pre-colonial gender arrangements were and how these were altered in the interaction with colonial ones, creating what Lugones calls the 'new' gender system.

WOMEN'S EARLY EXCLUSION: THE EMERGENCE OF WOMEN IN DEVELOPMENT AND GENDER & DEVELOPMENT APPROACHES

The Danish economist Ester Boserup developed a critique from the recognition of the role of patriarchy in development and the exclusion of women. Drawing on field observations from India as well as her work in Senegal, Boserup challenged development research and practice yet again with the release, in 1970, of her book *Woman's Role in Economic Development*. In this work, Boserup considered the ways in which women were discriminated against and marginalized within dominant development paradigms of the 1960s and 1970s. Boserup challenged the long omissions of women by Western-led international development practitioners and contributed to the emergence of a new ideational paradigm: *Women in Development* (WID). Some years later, the paradigm is mainstreamed via the UN's Decade for Women (from 1976 to 1985).

Importantly, however, Boserup and proponents of WID did not fundamentally critique the premise of international development and its capitalist and colonial roots. Rather, they maintained that there was a need for women to be included within existing programmes and, in particular, for a focus on women's education. This is what we refer to as a 'revisionist change' or an additive paradigm, one in which the structure of the system – which we know as patriarchal, heterosexual and colonial – is neither fundamentally challenged nor transformed. Critics of WID expose the ways in which it fails to trouble the premise of economic development and its unidimensional focus on women's production (at the expense of women's reproductive work). In the 1980s, from these criticisms, scholars and practitioners devised the responsive paradigms known as Women and Development (WAD) and Gender and Development (GAD). Within the latter, scholars recognized the need to attend to patriarchal power inequalities as well as the social marginalization and disenfranchisements that resulted from gendered socializations.

Drawing on Black feminist and critical legal studies scholar Kimberlé Crenshaw's (1989) concept of 'intersectionality', WAD and GAD approaches respond to the particular and disparate position of women of colour within patriarchal developmentalist societies. Crenshaw (1989: 149) explains that 'intersectionality is a metaphor for understanding the ways that multiple forms of inequality or disadvantage sometimes compound themselves and create obstacles that often are not understood among conventional ways of thinking'. Through intersectionality Crenshaw was able to emphasize the ways in which multiple identities interact concurrently, creating unique experiences of oppression (and privilege).

Working within the new insights provided by feminist intersectionality, WAD feminists specifically look at the role of capitalist production in gender hierarchies, in order to identify the structures of inequality, this includes the sexual division of labour and the hierarchical interactions between the productive and reproductive spheres (in which the reproductive spheres, controlled by women, are systematically under- and de-valued). Gender and Development considers many of these same factors.

However, GAD also emphasizes the importance of efforts towards understanding how multifaceted these issues are in the entangled context of culture, government and globalization and how 'gender' entails considerations of gender beyond women. The approaches of such projects are multiple, disparate and not easily summarized. In the classroom, we have drawn from concrete examples, for example the inclusion of women in microfinancing projects like Grameen Bank in Bangladesh in order to think through the ways in which such development programming impacts communities. Our students have engaged at length with the work of Lamina Karim (2014) to consider how the Grameen Bank Model plays upon gendered stereotypes of women as being 'more frugal' and therefore more 'lendable' – yet very often this has fostered new forms of entrenched communal indebtedness that all members struggle to repay. Should we demystify Grameen Bank's feminization of microcredit? Is women-specific microcredit celebrated and heralded in your communities? Karim's scholarship is important in contextualizing the often highly-celebrated pro-capitalist programming of the Bank, and opens up conversations about strategic hegemonic interventions said to be on or behalf of women – a subject to which we now turn.

HYPERVISIBILITY AND INVISIBILITY

Amy Lind (2010: 35) argues that 'both invisibility and hypervisibility serve as mechanisms of control and governance particularly in the realm of intimacy'. The term hypervisibilization refers to the over-exposure or heightened public awareness of certain social groups within the context of a certain global issue. An example of this is global media coverage of and development responses to the 'HIV crisis' in Sub-Saharan Africa. In particular, for example, Black queer men have been widely subject to development interventions through the lens of public health and disease control, racialized constructions and the HIV/AIDS epidemic. Within this remit, women and girls have also become increasingly visible – we might even say hyper-visible within international development during the neoliberal period (see Chapter 3).

The 2008 'girl effect' campaign – with backing from powerful corporate partners including TikTok, Nike and Vodafone – is a good example of an instance in which women's bodies have become hypervisibilized within international development. The campaign sought to leverage the unique potential of adolescent girls to end poverty for themselves. In a promotional video outlining the project, direct help and aid for girls is extrapolated to reach their families, their communities, their countries and the world.[5] We invite our readers to watch the promotional video (in the classroom) and to discuss the ways in which arguments about girls' and women's bodies are mobilized via colonial tropes of saviourhood. Over the last decade and a half, women's bodies have been highly spectated within international development – however, we have yet to see a real transformation of development power. Indeed, often women's bodies are spectacularized in debilitating and disempowering ways. The spectre of overpopulation, for example, is racialized and gendered. Women's bodies have long been spaces for strategic intervention, as contraception becomes a key feature of neo-colonial relations within international development.

On the other hand, invisibilization refers to the obscuring of certain societal groups in relation to a certain metric, again often in relation to a development project. An example of this is lesbians within mainstream development projects, which may explicitly target women with children or households. An aspect of the heteronormative international development agenda has been that, Lind (2010) argues, that LGBTQI+ people are frequently deemed 'unproductive' within hegemonic development paradigms. For example, within patriarchal nationalist contexts, LGBTQI+ communities can also, as Lind shows, be considered to be 'destructive' to the hegemonic aspirations of imagined nationalist communities (see also Puar 2013), as evidenced through the oppressive language of pathology and criminality.

QUEERING DEVELOPMENT

Having critiqued the heteronormative lens through which much international development work unfolds and materializes heterogeneous sexual and gender identities and practices – what is to be done? In their work in Palestine, Walaa Alqaisiya (2018: 39) asserts, 'in [the] quest to imagine an otherwise that troubles normative regimens, queering paves the way to think and practice decolonization in new ways'. Here we turn to work emerging in the last ten or so years, which asserts and affirms the need for and various routes toward queering development (Lind 2000; Jolly 2010; Rao 2020) and draw from a wider intellectual movement toward queer postcolonial studies (or what Rao calls the 'queer politics of postcoloniality').

---

5. www.youtube.com/watch?v=WIvmE4_KMNw.

In their piece 'queering development', Susie Jolly (2010) proposes several agenda items for wide-scale social change, including pushing for more inclusive development programming, uncovering and historicizing stories of gender non-conformity and non-heterosexual sexual relations and ensuring that the employees of development agencies have equal access to resources irrespective of sexual orientation. Part of the project of queering development is emphasizing how sex has always been part of the agenda of international development, albeit not one addressed as such. However, international development policy, practitioners and scholars have nevertheless tended to engage with the adverse aspects of sexuality, as Cornwall, Corrêa and Jolly (2008) remind us, such as disease, risk and violence. Queering development pushes us to take seriously the positive dimensions of sex, like bliss, desire, exploration, temptation and fulfilment. Most development agencies are uncomfortable with 'the plasticity of people's sexualities' and with sex as 'a good thing, a source of well-being and joy, not just of violence, disease, discrimination and poverty' (Corrêa and Jolly 2008: 39, 40). Listening to queer activists organizing on the ground, mental health, wellbeing, fostering joy, de-silencing are all areas for solidarity.

TRANSNATIONAL QUEER SOLIDARITIES

Well-meaning neoliberal development interventions aimed at supporting those with same-sex sexualities, such as aid conditionality, risk reifying such power imbalances and causing more harm than good. According to Bergenfield and Miller (2014), while over the past decade LGBT rights have increasingly been integrated into the mainstream development agenda, the focus has largely been on aid conditionality interventions, often in response to homophobic policies by governments in the Global South such as Uganda's homosexuality bill (ibid.). For example, in 2011, President Barack Obama instructed all American agencies whose work relates to international development and foreign policy to make sure their activities protect LGBT human rights.[6] The UK's Prime Minister, David Cameron, announced a similar policy of restricting aid based on human

---

6. See https://obamawhitehouse.archives.gov/the-press-office/2011/12/06/presiden
tial-memorandum-international-initiatives-advance-human-rights-l.

rights in recipient countries.[7] Rahul Rao (2020) argues that LGBT activists from the Global South, faced with hostility at home, have become attracted by what he calls 'homocapitalism'. He writes:

> Denied belonging within the nation, some activists have turned to making a case for inclusion, not in a language of justice or human rights, but through a refiguration of the queer as model capitalist subject whose inclusion promises a future growth and economic dynamism (25).

However, while Rao's critique may be relevant for bourgeois activists in particular spaces, other scholars have highlighted how such interventions fail to consult or listen to the concerns of the more marginalized activists and individuals who will be affected by such policies. Consequently, common ways of integrating same-sexualities into GAD policy and practice have ended up re-affirming longstanding North-South power dynamics. Euro-American institutions, academics and activists too often control and impose the terms of interventions, in turn implicitly reifying historical assumptions that the 'West knows best'. A letter written by over 50 social justice groups in Africa in response to David Cameron's announcement asserted that such policies were harmful to their objectives, potentially causing further violence and stigmatization against individuals of same-sex sexualities. In April 2010, activists in Nairobi launched their *African LGBTI Manifesto /Declaration* with a focus on holistic liberation. They write,

> As Africans, we stand for the celebration of our complexities and we are committed to ways of being which allow for self-determination at all levels of our sexual, social, political and economic lives. The possibilities are endless.[8]

Sandeep Bakshi explains how:

> Cultural racism within queer circuits functions in tandem with the cultural imaginary of the Global South as a necessary homophobic

---

7. See www.theguardian.com/politics/2011/oct/30/ban-homosexuality-lose-aid-cameron.
8. www.fahamu.org/mbbc/wp-content/uploads/2011/09/African-LGBTI-Manifesto-2010.pdf.

site and produces hegemonic codes of coloniality that garner support for neo-colonial and neo-imperial ventures by positioning the Global North as the sole guarantor of human rights for all people including women and queer subjects. (2016: 1–2)

The Ugandan feminist scholar Stella Nyanzi (2015) asks us to consider how 'queer can be queered in Africa'. How might transformative action be sought and pursued through the critical spaces opened by queering – the verb – which pushes the boundaries of what is thought to be normative? Nyanzi does this as she challenges the idea that queering is normatively situated in the West or the Global North. Against this tradition within queer studies, Nyanzi calls upon scholars to attend to specific and place-based histories of sexuality across the African continent, while defiantly refusing the tendency to reproduce a 'taxonomic approach that labels people in terms of intrinsic psychic traits [that] they are believed to possess' (Spronk and Nyeck 2021: 389). We have not begun to do justice to the rich, emergent scholarship on 'sexualities *from* Africa' (ibid.: 391) and the (in)stabilities of gender.

CONCLUSION

Our readers can engage with material (in the media, and in activist and academic literature) on transnational solidarities and the rise in attention to homophobic policies in international geopolitics. Given these dynamics, can same-sex sexualities be a focus for gender and development policy and practice without reaffirming longstanding North–South power dynamics which impose Western/Northern influences (Jolly 2000)? There are no easy answers to these urgent questions. Scholars have exposed the practice of 'pinkwashing' by which the relatively hegemonic expressions of LGBTQI+ rights – for example in Israel's military – are held up as global examples, even as they do not challenge settler colonial power structures and arrangements. In discussion with our students, they have forcefully and thoughtfully grappled with the forms of solidarity which challenge assertions that LGBTQI+ and QPOC concerns are 'Western' and 'Northern' and move towards postcolonial and decolonial queer solidarities. We have found Kothari's (2022: n. p.) articulation of solidarity within development as something forged within and maintained through 'the rhythms of everyday life rather than the mission statement of a global charity' (see also Dieng 2023). Our students have challenged us to think collectively about how to study and teach desire, intimacy and queer thought in more generative ways.

QUESTIONS FOR FURTHER THOUGHT

Consider Susie Jolly's argument that the '[f]reedom to determine one's sexual behaviour is closely connected to economic and political freedoms'. What does it mean that 'the personal is political' *and* why is this important for scholars or practitioners of development?

What do development and reproduction have to do with one another? In your response, consider *how* development operates 'as a desiring machine' (Fletcher et al. 2014) and how reproduction and ideas of population fit within this framework.

What is the significance of understanding and pursuing development as embodied, or development 'with a body' (Cornwall et al. 2012)?

Longer activity: Describe the ways in which girlhood is presented and valorized in Nike's 'Girl Effect' video and the campaign (www.youtube.com/watch?v=WlvmE4_KMNw). How does this reading of girlhood reflect neoliberal capitalist priorities and values?

FILMS ON GENDER

The girl effect: The clock is ticking. Launch of Nike 'Girl Effect' Programme. Available: www.youtube.com/watch?v=1e8xgFoJtVg.
Super Special. Available: https://screeningshorts.org.uk/?q=node/465 (.).
"HerStory" Video Challenge. Ethiopian film "Alem". Available: www.youtube.com/watch?v=usRO7MJ6YU8&feature=youtu.be.

FILMS ON SEXUALITY AND SEXUAL VIOLENCE

Please note some videos and materials address issues of physical, sexual and homophobic violence.

Call me Kuchu. Documentary film.
Global Gay: The Next Frontier in Human Rights. Documentary. Available: www.youtube.com/watch?v=e91BUAyr_Ho.

WEBSITES AND GREY MATERIALS

'Girl Rising'. https://girlrising.org/.

'"Orgies while people are dying": How charity Oxfam allowed sex abuse in ailing countries like Haiti'. *Democracy Now*. Available: www.youtube.com/watch?v=yU5nPLhv5Zc.

'Mapping Sexual Harassment in Egypt' by HarassMap Team, edited by Noora Flinkman, in *This is not an Atlas*. Bielefeld: transcript verglag.

Graphic Book, 'The Path of Peasant and Popular Feminism in La Via Campesina' (2021) https://viacampesina.org/en/graphic-book-the-path-of-peasant-and-popular-feminism-in-la-via-campesina/?utm_sq=gyps97kq3e.

'Period poverty and pedagogy of care', Maja Zonjić, Caitlin Baker-Wanhalla, Serena Cooper, Olivia Dobbs, Romy Gellen and Charlotte Hawkins, February 22, 2022: www.ppesydney.net/period-poverty-and-pedagogy-of-care/.

REFERENCES

Alqaisiya, W. (2018) 'Decolonial queering: The politics of being queer in Palestine', *Journal of Palestine Studies*, 47(3), pp. 29–44.

Alvarez, S. E. (2016) 'Beyond NGOization? Reflections from Latin America' in Bernal, V. and Inderpal G. (eds.) *Theorizing NGOs: States, Feminisms, and Neoliberalism*. Durham, NC: Duke University Press.

Amadiume, I. (1987) *Male Daughters, female husbands: Gender and sex in an African society*, London: Zed Books.

Bacchetta, P., Jivraj, S. and Bakshi, S. (2020) 'Decolonial sexualities: Paola Bacchetta in conversation with Suhraiya Jivraj and Sandeep Bakshi', *Interventions*, 22(4), pp. 574–85.

Bakare-Yusuf, B. (2003) 'Beyond determinism: The phenomenology of African female existence', *Feminist Africa*, 2, pp. 8–24.

Bakshi, S. and Jivraj, S., Posocco, S., eds. (2016) 'Introduction' in *Decolonizing Sexualities*. Oxford: Counterpress, pp. 1–16.

Bedford, K. (2010) 'Promoting exports, restructuring love: The World Bank and the Ecuadorian Flower Industry' in *Development, Sexual Rights and Global Governance*. London: Routledge, pp. 99–112.

Bergeron, S. (2010) '"Querying feminist economics" straight path to development: Household models reconsidered' in *Development, sexual rights and global governance*. London: Routledge, pp. 54–64.

Berlant, L. and Warner, M. (1998) 'Sex in public', *Critical Inquiry*, 24(2), 547–66.

Butler, J. (1990) *Gender trouble: Feminism and the subversion of identity*. London: Routledge.

Chakrabarty, D. (2000) *Provincializing Europe: Postcolonial thought and historical difference*. Princeton, NJ: Princeton University Press.

Chant, S. (2008) 'The "feminisation of poverty" and the "feminisation" of anti-poverty programmes: Room for revision?', *Journal of Development Studies*, 44(2), pp. 165–97.

Cornwall, A., Corrêa, A., and Jolly, S. (eds.) (2008) *Development with a body: Sexuality, human rights and development*. London and New York: Zed Books.

Cornwall, A. and Rivas, A. (2015) 'From "gender and equality" and "women's empowerment" to global justice: Reclaiming a transformative agenda for gender and development', *Third World Quarterly*, 36(2), pp. 396–415.

Currier, A. (2010) 'Behind the mask: Developing LGBTI visibility in Africa' in *Development, sexual rights and global governance*. London: Routledge, pp. 155–68.

Crenshaw, K. (1989) 'Demarginalizing the intersection of race and sex: A Black feminist critique of antidiscrimination doctrine, feminist theory and antiracist politics', *University of Chicago Legal Forum*, 1989(1), pp. 139–67.

Daley, P. (2008) *Gender and Genocide in Burundi: The Search for Spaces of Peace in the Great Lakes Region*. Oxford: James Currey.

Dieng, R. S. (2023) 'From Yewwu Yewwi to #FreeSenegal: Class, gender and generational dynamics of radical feminist activism in Sengegal', *Politics & Gender*, pp. 1–7.

Doan, P. (2010) 'Disrupting gender normativity in the middle east: Supporting gender transgression as a development strategy' in Lind, A (ed), *Development, Sexual Rights and Global Governance*. London Routledge, pp. 145–54.

Dosekun, S. (2015) 'For Western girls only? Post-feminism as transnational culture', *Feminist Media Studies*, 15(6), pp. 960–75.

Driskill, Q-L., Finley, C., Giley, B. J., and Morgensen, S. L. (2011) 'The revolution is for everyone: Imagining an emancipatory future through queer indigenous critial theories' in Driskill, Q-L. (ed.), *Queer indigenous studies: Critical interventions in theory, politics*. Tucson: Unviersity of Alabama Press, pp. 211–22.

Dutta, A. (2016) 'Afterword: Interrogating QTPOC critique, imagining north-south solidarities' in Bakshi, S., Jivraj, S., and Posocco, S., *Decolonizing Sexuality*. Oxford: Counterpress, pp. 282–7.

Ekine, S. and Abbas, H. (eds.) (2013) *Queer African Reader*. Nairobi and Oxford: Pambazuka Press.

Epprecht, M. (2013) *Sexuality and social justice in Africa: Rethinking homophobia and forging resistance*. London: Zed Books.

Fletcher, R. and Breitling, J., Puleo, V. (2014) 'Barbarian hordes: The overpopulation scapegoat in international development discourse'. *Third World Quarterly*, 35(7), pp. 1195–215.

Garland-Thomson, R. (2005) 'Feminist disability studies', *Signs*, 30(2), pp. 1557–87.

Hickel, J. (2014) 'The "girl effect": Liberalism, empowerment and the contradictions of development', *Third World Quarterly*, 35(8), pp. 1355–75.

Icaza, R. and Vazquez, R. (2016) 'The coloniality of gender as a radical critique to developmentalism' in Harcourt, W. (ed), *The Palgrave handbook on gender and development: Critical engagements in feminist theory and practice*. London: Palgrave Macmillan.

Impey, A. (2013) 'Songs of mobility and belonging: gender, spatiality and the local in Southern Africa's transfrontier conservation development', *Interventions: International Journal of Postcolonial Studies*, 15(2), pp. 255–71.

Jolly, S. (2000) '"Queering" development: Exploring the links between same-sex sexualities, gender, and development', *Gender and Development*, 8(1), pp. 78–88.

Kabeer, N. (2015) 'Gender, poverty, and inequality: A brief history of feminist contributions in the field of international development', *Third World Quarterly*, 23(2), pp. 189–205.

Karim, L. (2014) 'Demystifying MicroCredit: The Grameen Bank, ngos, and neo-liberalism in Bangladesh' in Bernal, V. and Grewal, I. (eds.), *Theorizing NGOs: States, feminisms, and neoliberalism*. Durham, NC: Duke University Press.

Keisha-Khan Y. Perry. (2009) '"If we didn't have water": Black women's struggle for urban land rights in Brazil', *Environmental Justice*, 2(1), pp. 9–14.

Khoja-Moolji, S. (2019) 'Death by benevolence: Third world girls and the contemporary politics of humanitarianism', *Feminist Theory* 0(1), pp. 1–26.

King, H. (2014) 'Queers of war: Normalizing gays and lesbians in the US war machine', in Forte, M. (ed.), *Good intentions: Norms and practices of imperial humanitarianism*. Montreal: Alert Press.

Koffman, O. and Gill, R. (2013) 'The revolution will be led by a 12-year-old-girl": Girl power and global biopolitics', *Feminsit review*, 105(1). DOI: https://doi.org/10.1057/fr.2013.16.

Kothari, U. (2022) 'Decolonizing research: The power of stories'. Keynote speech. The DevNet Annual Conference 2022.

Leve, L. (2014) 'Failed development and rural revolution in Nepal: Rethinking subaltern consciousness and women's empowerment' in Bernal, V. and Grewal, I. (eds.). *Theorizing NGOs: States, feminisms, and neoliberalism*. Durham, NC: Duke University Press.

Lewis, D. (2005) 'African gender research and postcoloniality: Legacies and challenges', in Oyewumi, O. (ed.), *African gender studies: A reader*. New York: Palgrave, pp. 381–95.

Lind, A. (2010) 'Introduction: Development, global governance, and sexual subjectivities' in *Development, Sexual Rights and Global Governance*. London: Routledge, pp. 1–20.

Lugones, M.(2007) 'Heterosexualism and the colonial/modern gender system', *Hypatia*, 22(1), pp. 186–209.

Lugones, M. (2008) 'The coloniality of gender', *Otherwise*, 2(2), pp. 1–17.

Lugones, M. (2010) 'Toward a decolonial feminism', *Hypatia*, 25(4), pp. 742–59.

Mawdsley, E. (2019) 'Queering development? The unsettling of geographies of South-South cooperation', *Antipode*, 52(1), pp. 227–45.

McFadden, P. (2000) 'Globalizing resistance: Crafting and strengthening African feminist solidarities', *The Black Scholar*, 38(2–3), pp. 19–20.

McFadden, P. (2016) 'Becoming contemporary African feminists: Her-stories, legacies and the new imperatives', *Feminist Dialogues series*, 1, pp. 1–7.

Mekgwe, P. (2008) 'Theorizing African feminism(s): The "colonial question".' *QUEST: An African Journal of Philosophy/Revue Africaine de Philosophie*, 20, pp. 11–22.

Mugambi, H. (2007.) 'The post-gender question in African Studies', in Cole, C. M, T. Manuh and S.F. Meischer (eds.), *Africa after Gender?*. Indiana: Indiana University Press. pp. 285–302.

Nagar, R. and Collective (2006) 'Introduction. Playing with Fire: A collective journey', 'The beginnings of a collective journey', 'Challenges of NGOization and dreams of Sangtin' and 'Postscript: NGOs, global feminisms, and collaborative border crossings' in Nagar, R. and Sangtin Writers Collective (eds), *Playing with fire: Feminist thought and activism*. Minneapolis: University of Minnesota Press.

Nnaemeka, N. 'Mapping African feminism', in A. Cornwall (ed) (2005) *Readings on Gender in Africa*. Oxford: James Currey, pp. 31–40. And in *Africana Research Bulletin*.

Oyewumi, O. (1997) *The invention of women: Making an African sense of Western gender discourses*. Minneapolis: Minnesota University Press.

Oyewumi, O. (2022) '(Re)Centring African epistemologies: An intellectual journey'. Speech for 2021 Distinguished Africanist Award, CODESRIA. https://journals.codesria.org/index.php/codesriabulletin/article/view/1973.

Oyewumi, O. 2003. 'The white woman's burden: African women in Western feminist discourse', in Oyewumi, O. (ed.) *African women and feminism: Reflecting on the politics of sisterhood*. Lawrenceville, NJ: Africa World Press, pp. 25–44.

Puar, J. (2013) *Rethinking homonationalism*. Cambridge: Cambridge University Press.

Rachel, B. and Miller, A. A., 'Queering international development?: An examination of new "lgbt rights" rhetoric, policy, and programming among international development agencies', *LGBTQ Policy Journal*. http://ssrn.com/abstract=2514066.

Rao, R. (2020) *Out of Time: The queer politics of postcoloniality*. Oxford: Oxford University Press.

Seppälä, T. (2016) 'Feminizing resistance, decolonizing solidarity: Contesting neoliberal development in the Global South', *Journal of Resistance Studies*, 1(2), pp. 12–47.

Tamale, S. (2008) 'The right to culture and the culture of rights: A critical perspective on women's sexual rights in Africa', *Feminist Legal Studies*, 16, pp. 47–69.

Tamale, S. (2011) (ed.) *African sexualities: A reader*. Oxford: Pambazuka Books.

Wieringa, S. and Sívori, H. (2013) 'Sexual politics in the Global South: Framing the Discourse' in Wieringa, S. and Sívori, H. (eds), *The sexual history of the Global South: Sexual politics in Africa, Asia and Latin America*. London: Zed Books.

Win, E. (2004) 'Not very poor, powerless or pregnant: The African woman forgotten by development', *IDS Bulletin*, 35(4), pp. 61–5.

Wilson, K. (2015) 'Towards a radical re-Appropriation: Gender, development and neoliberal feminism', *Development and Change*, 46(4), pp. 803–32.

7

Decolonizing the State and Reworlding: Global Imaginaries of Liberated Futures

Can social transformation that is beneficial to the peoples of the Global South take place within the Eurocentric nation-states they inherited from colonialism? Here, we consider the constraints placed on anti-colonial movements by their adoption of the European nation-state model as the normative and desirable political unit in which their dreams of development can be achieved. We also explore alternative geographical imaginaries seeking to transcend the bounded legacies of colonial empires by articulating new geopolitical communities with social worlds that emphasize peace, unity, equity and an end to the destruction of the natural world. In so doing, they aim to re-humanize post-colonial subjects by using emancipatory frameworks that point to a borderless world. In theorizing these spatial imaginations, Adom Getachew (2019: 2) uses the term 'anticolonial worldmaking' and Sabelo Ndlovu-Gatsheni (2023) 'reworlding' (drawing from postcolonial feminist thought; e.g. Spivak 1985).

While states and stateless societies have existed for thousands of years, the nation-state is a relatively recent phenomenon associated with the development of capitalist modernity in Europe. It expanded globally through European colonization and the construction of the capitalist world system (Amin 1976 and 1990; Hall 1993; Mamdani 2020). We here define the nation-state as a territorially 'imagined community' (Anderson 1991) devised by elites to counter the potentially destabilizing effects of the inequalities generated by capitalist social relations. Unity is maintained by promoting amongst its citizenry a homogenous national identity based on common cultural characteristics. The nation-state manages its national economy, regulates trade with other states and deploys its military to protect the interests of its national capitalists in competition with others. From the nineteenth century onward, nation-states have dominated the institutions of global governance, and since the 1940s they have been the main agents and geographical entities for development policymaking, management and implementation. Indeed, fears that the nation-state was being undermined by globalization and neoliberal market fundamentalism have proved premature given the rise of popular nationalisms and intense competition between capitalists following the 2008 financial crisis. Under neoliberalism, country branding has been used as a marketing strategy to attract foreign direct investment, giving countries an internationally recognized identity in the era of competitive globalization (Pike 2011).

National economic indicators such as Gross National Product and Gross Domestic Product are presented as objective measurements to compare levels of growth and progress both between and within nation-states. Yet, these national level statistics obscure spatial and social differences, unofficial cross border trade and global extractive relationships and looting (Bond 2006) (See Chapter 2); and, according to Jerven (2013), might just be poor data. Timothy Mitchell (2006: 1120) purports that the national economy emerged as a concept in the 1930s as a 'metrological project' to understand the relationship between the different social and technical elements of production and consumption within a society, using new technologies of organization, measurement, calculation and representation. Liberal economists were grappling with the social consequences of the capitalist crisis and promoted the idea that the economy was a distinct abstract sphere that could be separated from the realities of politics and culture, and work in a rational manner irrespective of the national context.

Ulrich Beck (2005: 287) questions this fixation with the national state as the primary unit of analysis, which he terms a 'methodological nationalism', whereby academic researchers take certain premises for granted. He contends:

Methodological nationalism equates society with nation-state societies. It sees states and their governments as the cornerstones of a social sciences analysis. It assumes that humanity is naturally divided into a limited number of nations, which on the inside organize themselves as nation-states, and on the outside set boundaries to distinguish themselves from other nation-states. It sees this outer delimitation, as well as the competition between nation-states, representing the most fundamental category of political organization.

Critics of methodological nationalism have highlighted its failure to address the social transformations generated by globalization, including cosmopolitanism, diasporas, and transmigrants (Beck 2005; Anderson 2019; Bhambra 2013), and the assumption, as Daniel Chernilo (2006: 12) writes, that the nation-state is 'the final and necessary form of social and political organization in modernity'; thus, disregarding the effects of racism and coloniality. Ndlovu-Gatsheni (2013) goes further, arguing that social science remains trapped in a nineteenth century imperial understanding of the social world, one which prevents radical thinking of new social worlds. We concur with Mamdani (2020: 34) that 'the political is twinned with the epistemological' and we need to decolonize the political as a necessary part of the global quest for freedom.

Europeans had the military power to reconfigure space and impose their ontological and epistemological conception of modernity. Because the nation-state model emerged out of a particular historical context in Europe and, in the Global South, was the progeny of the racially and ethnically stratified colonial state, its foundations are territorially unstable and full of internal contradictions. Despite this, political elites, as well as scholars, have accepted the nation-state model as the normative socio-political organization and its international borders, institutional structures and identities – constructed or legitimated by colonial powers – as inviolable, static and enduring.

Colonial states were necropolitical spaces comprising 'communities of separation and fear' inimical to universal social justice (Mbembe 2019: 129). Their very existence was predicated on a hierarchy of rights (along racial, gender, ethnic and spatial lines) and the use of violence to dominate and secure the state against uprisings from the colonized peoples. Indeed, if we take Claude Ake's (1996: 42) claim that 'because of circumstances that reach back to the colonial experience, most African states are in hostile relations with the bulk of their population'; then, using the nation-state as the agent and scale for transformation is inherently flawed and the pursuit of state-sponsored development in many countries perfunctory, contradictory and ineffectual.

We critique the nation-state model for two primary reasons. First, because of its internally structured inequality based on colonially constructed ethnic, racial and gendered hierarchies (see Chapters 1 and 3), which the post-colonial states have failed to transform – a problem addressed by Mamdani (1996, 2001 and 2020) and Mustapha (1999). Following Walter Rodney (1980), we historicize the anachronistic and journalistic terms 'tribes and tribalism', which are used to label and castigate Africans for failing to embrace European political modernity. We concur with Ake (1996: 42) that, for effective social transformation, we need to understand 'the nature of the state and the dynamics of the social forces in which it's embedded'. These include the commitment of the political leaders and the 'rival political communities of elites' in power. We challenge the coloniality of the continued balkanization of Africa, into Francophone, Lusophone and Anglophone states, and the racialized cartographic divisions of sub-Saharan/black Africa and North Africa, as well as the academic construction of the region of MENA (Middle East and North Africa) that has created an ontological and epistemic divide and which pan-Africanist leaders have sought to address politically in the African Union.

Second, because of the interrelatedness of the nation-state with capitalism both historically and contemporarily, we emphasize the spatial imaginaries of new social formations that anti-colonial and anti-capitalist scholars and activists envisaged as necessary to escape colonial and neo-colonial extractivism and to deliver social justice for Africans and the Global Majority. Our examples are of those seeking alternatives, such as Pan-Africanism, The Non-Aligned Movement, Third Worldism and The Tri-continental Conference of the Peoples of Africa, Asia and Latin America, as well as those attempting change within global institutional frameworks, such as The Lagos Plan of Action, the New International Economic Order (NIEo), regional economic unions and, more recently, South–South cooperation. We acknowledge the setbacks faced by these collective actions and urge our readers to investigate how they have either been undermined by global hegemonic powers or by internal rivalries based on ideological differences or elite competition.

In thinking about the potentialities for decolonial state-building, we draw inspiration from Patricia McFadden's (2008: 145) use of African feminist epistemologies to inform a critical analytic frame in order to move beyond an understanding of the state that uses 'narrowly defined heteronormative notions of masculinity and power'. Equally, we draw on Suren Pillay's (2018) discussion on how to think about the state from Africa and ask what can be learnt from histories of the nation-state in Africa, and from the anti-colonial geopolitical imaginations and non-Eurocentric conceptualizations of political communities to articulate the state *otherwise*.

DECOLONIAL AND ANTICOLONIAL PLAYLIST

Kareyce Fotso's song 'Poa'lag' (children of the village) captures a person's longing for her community and homeland during travel or rupture.[1] In the music video, Kareyce is pictured in a solitary hotel room with her acoustic guitar, calling to her homeland in the Bandjoun language of West Cameroon – *to the children of the village, how are you*? The song mixes the joy of belonging to a place and a people with the unique longing and pain of separation experienced by many rural and marginalized communities in post-colonial African societies, whose children migrate to urban areas and, very often, seek to travel abroad in the search for education, work and economic empowerment. 'Poa'lag' is a response to and a celebration of the struggles of the Bamileke people in post-colonial Cameroon.

EUROPEANIZATION OF THE WORLD

Anti-colonial and decolonial scholars have documented the Europeanization of the world, and with it the imposition of global capitalism, using diverse forms of labour that relied on the institutionalization of racial and epistemic hierarchies, and military dominance (Rodney 1972, Amin 1979 1980; Blaut 1993; Ndlovu-Gatsheni 2013; Ndlovu-Gatsheni and Tafira 2019). European territorial enclosures, border-making, ethnic constructivism and racialized internationalisms have shaped contemporary political identities and relationships within and between states. The concept of the nation-state, globally universalized as the normative political unit, has its origins in Europe's violent history and social political organizations. It is thought to be a product of the Treaty of Westphalia (1648), which settled conflict between Europe's two main religious traditions (Catholicism and Protestantism) and established the principle of

---

1. www.youtube.com/watch?v=FSd9hwCiMEo.

state territorial sovereignty as well as the ideal of cultural/religious homogeneity within states (Anderson 1991).

Thus, the nation-state embodied a European form of cultural nationalism, which was unsuited to the complex realities the colonizers found in the Global South and in the multi-ethnic states they left behind after decolonization. Mamdani (2020: 2) argues that it was the tolerance of minorities within the European nation-state as the key to 'securing peace' that defines 'the liberal character of political modernity'. However, Europeans failed to take 'tolerance abroad . . . instead liberal conquest inflamed the colonies', when force was used to impose the civilizing mission and thus the colonial state. As with other decolonial scholars, we insert racial and ethnic ideologies as central to the establishment of a violent colonial political modernity (see Chapter 5). Liberal scholars have paid little attention to the racial element in global capitalism, as well as the variety of social formations that existed prior to European colonization (see Chapter 3). We seek to provoke thinking about societal wellbeing beyond tolerance.

The colonial (plunderer) state

Abdoulaye Bathily's (1994) characterization of the colonial state as 'the plunderer state' reflects its raison d'etre. The political boundaries of the colonial territories in Africa were agreed in Europe at the Berlin Africa conference of 1884–85. A conference called by the German Chancellor Bismarck and King Leopold of Belgium for Europeans to partition the continent peacefully amongst themselves. European powers demarcated their spheres of influence on the map and then scrambled to make territorial claims effective on the ground. Colonial borders that have since been deemed artificial were drawn in an arbitrary manner and lacked respect for kinship groups, cultural groups and previous social political formations, dividing families and political communities alike (Asiwaju 1985; Falola and Usman 2009). Colonial borders bundled together culturally and linguistically diverse groups of people into zones of extraction and abandonment enforced by structured spatial inequalities. Colonial infrastructure was largely confined to areas of European settlement or resource extraction.

European empire-building required destroying the cultural foundations of non-Western modes of thought. People on either side of the border were subjected to different legal regimes, and elites took on aspects of European cultural identities, such as language, religion and education systems. Indigenous ontologies and epistemologies that relate to other ways of governing were labelled as 'primitive' and became neo-customary (e.g. seen as informal or lacking in official legitimacy) in colonial legal regimes. For effective administration, communities that were diverse and plural were homogenized through their classification into 'tribes' (ethnic) and racialized groups. 'Tribes' were bounded territorially to colonially designated homelands (Mafege 1971; Ranger 1983; Vail 1989). Mamdani (2001: 20) names these new social groupings 'political identities', as they were distinct from cultural and market-based identities, used to differentiate a 'bounded political community', and were legally enforced through law.

The colonial state legalized racism by institutionalizing administratively and economically – thus making it systemic (Mamdani 2001). Europeans were positioned at the top of the administration; the intermediary level was dominated by other foreigners: Asians and Arabs in Eastern Africa, and Lebanese and Europeans in West Africa. Indirect rule as a governance strategy (ruling through colonially approved local elites) was introduced by the British and the French in parts of their colonial empires, particularly in Africa and Asia, using pre-existing, or newly created administrative structures. The colonizers thought local rulers were more acceptable to the people and compensated for the lack of European manpower. Local chiefs could implement coercive colonial directives such as forced labour, forced cropping and taxation. African collaborators, often educated in Christian missionary schools, became intermediaries between the people ('tribes') and the colonial authorities. Some of these modernized Africans became nationalists and campaigned for independence; others formed a middle class with a vested interest in maintaining neo-colonial relations. As observed by Bathily (1994) with reference to West African states, the interest of the social forces that formed the colonial state was diametrically opposed to those of the bulk of the colonized people.

The colonial legacy of the nation-state

Ndlovu-Gatsheni (2013b: 157) refers to the 'nationality of power' occurring where the post-colonial state sought to replace the colonial state with the nationalist state. Unlike the colonial state that projected its power through various forms of violence, the nationalist state imposed its power through persuasion and consent and the production of a national imaginary that included new national symbols (e.g. flags, mottos, anthems and plants), name changing (e.g. Gold Coast became Ghana), new memorials and commemorations, new portraits of the head of state replacing the European ones, and national armies. Indigenization policies replaced white and brown people with Africans, which, as Mamdani (1996; 20–21) observes, 'deracialized the state' without 'de-tribalizing' it, as colonial ethnic classifications were maintained and became salient. Tanzania, under its first post-independence President, Julius Nyerere, was the exception. When national unity projects failed, as they had by the 1970s, the political elite reverted to what Mamdani (2020: 4) calls a 'postcolonial modernity' that encompasses the violence of European modernity and colonial rule.

Why did African nationalist leaders adopt the nation-state model? Basil Davidson (1992) argues that the nationalism that was promoted after independence was nation-statism that initially 'looked like liberation'. In practice, he continues, 'it was not a restoration of Africa to its own history, but the onset of a period of indirect subjection to the history of Europe' (10). Davidson claims that the nationalists knew that by accepting colonial partition they would be accepting the moral and political practices of colonial rule in its institutional dimensions and that it was a handicap. They realized, as Kwame Nkrumah states, that it would make them 'half free, half slaves' (163). Nevertheless, they saw gaining sovereignty as the primary task. The nation-state model was presented as essential to the political modernization needed for development and acceptance into global institutions. A more critical Amilcar Cabral (1973: 75) accused nationalist leaders of being ignorant of the historical reality they wanted to transform. Frantz Fanon, in his essay on 'The Pitfalls of National Consciousness', indicts the national bourgeoisie for replicating the colonials and promoting nationalism without humanism, thus 'imprison[ing] national consciousness in sterile formalism (1990: 165).

Through the United Nations (UN), established in 1945, former colonial and imperial powers could maintain epistemic hegemony over independent states under the guise of development. The UN signified a neutral institution ensuring global governance of a new international order that would transcend fascism and colonialism. The USA's President Truman, in his inaugural address of 1949 (see Chapter 2) which is often seen as marking the beginning of formal development, encouraged newly independent states to work through the UN to deliver development (Prashad 2007). He claimed 'this should be a cooperative enterprise in which all nations work together through the UN and its specialized agencies wherever practicable. It must be a worldwide effort for the achievement of peace, plenty, and freedom' (Truman 1949, n.p.). Optimistically, African anti-colonialists thought that a United Nations consisting of majority Global South states could provide the best opportunity for addressing inequalities and the global hegemony of colonial powers (Nkrumah 1963). Despite the UN's advocacy of the sovereign equality of all states, it was clear, in the negotiations of its charters, that states from the Global South were incorporated into a racially hierarchical international order as subordinates in which their interests could be marginalized if they failed to challenge collectively (Klose 2013; Jensen 2017).

Anti-colonialists' struggles for liberation were about social struggles aimed at correcting the social injustices of colonialism so that all people could benefit. Nation-building projects were expected to be inclusive and to redress the spatial and social inequalities of the colonial period. Nationalism was mobilized to promote development whilst development was seen as the engine for national cohesion. Social improvement programmes that were to unify the countries generally failed because, as Ake (1996: 17) writes, 'the political context . . . rendered [them] improbable' whilst making 'the adoption of an ideology of development inevitable'.

The post-colonial political reality has been that multi-ethnic and multicultural states struggle to exist with plurality. Ethnic identity became the main axis of difference that could be mobilized by political leaders in competition for power (Ake 1996), leading to low-intensity conflict and, in some cases such as Rwanda and Burundi, genocidal violence (Mamdani 2001; Daley 2008; see Chapter 5). We concur with Mustapha (1999) that African states have had few internal discussions of how to live with multiethnicity. Debate has instead focused largely on what administrative divisions would enable a more equitable distribution of national economic resources to satisfy regional elites. In effect, the national project failed due to the retention of the institutional structures and economic and social relations of the colonial period. Its weaknesses became apparent under the structural adjustment policies of the 1980s and 1990s, when social and regional inequalities deepened. To understand how Africans live with multiplicity or imagine diverse futures, further work needs to be conducted at scales below and above the state.

BEYOND THE NATION-STATE: NEW GEOPOLITICAL IMAGINARIES

While strategically adopting the nation-state model, some anti-colonial activists conceptualized new forms of internationalisms beyond the boundaries of the nation-state. These were regional and global in scope, embracing communities subjected to colonial domination and exploitation. Liberation theorists recognized the close connection between capitalism and the nation-state in the Global North and that positive social transformation could only be achieved through the unity of the oppressed. Getachew (2019), Ndlovu-Gatsheni (2023), Younis (2022) and Tamale (2022) are amongst the scholars to have revisited the histories of these anticolonial spatial imaginaries as the socio-political and ecological crises of capitalism have deepened in the twenty-first century.

Anti-colonial liberation struggles articulated inclusive forms of citizenship within and beyond the boundaries of the nation-state. Gemma Bird (2016) argues that these African perspectives on citizenship and belonging have been marginalized in citizenship studies. Bird refers to Léopold Sédar Senghor's conception of 'négritude', which heavily emphasized an understanding of identity divorced from national boundaries and borders but is closely attached to a conception of race and a desire to overcome colonial oppression. In effect, proponents of négritude did not challenge European modernity, but instead sought inclusion by asserting black humanity, unlike Pan-Africanism.

Pan-Africanism recognizes the existence of a global community made up of Africans and descendants of enslaved African peoples (Biney 2019; Ackah 1999; Ndlovu-Gatsheni 2013). Biney (2019: 177) defines it as simultaneously 'a movement, idea and ideology that seeks to restore the dignity, freedom and right to self-determination for all peoples of African descent around the global against historical conditions of enslavement, colonization, and new forms of domination'. Founded in the late nineteenth century by disaporic Africans (in Europe, the US and the Caribbean) to mobilize against the European scramble for Africa, it included the African American W. E. B. DuBois, the Virgin Islander Hubert Harrison, the Jamaicans Marcus Garvey, Amy Ashwood Garvey and Amy Jacques

Garvey. After World War II, Africans from the continent joined the movement, including Kwame Nkrumah, Julius Nyerere, Amilcar Cabral, Bibi Titi Mohamed, Funmilayo Ransome Kuti, Abdul-Rahman Babu and Fatima Babiker Mahmoud. The movement's first congress was held in 1900, from which the Pan-African association was formed with branches in Trinidad, Jamaica and the US. By the time of its 1945 Congress, the Pan-Africanist vision was clear: to create a collective movement that was neither pro-Western, pro-communist or pro-nationalist, but instead 'pro-African' and non-racialist.

African leaders, such as Nnamdi Azikiwe of Nigeria, Kwame Nkrumah of Ghana, Julius Nyerere of Tanzania, and Gamal Abdel Nasser of Egypt, thought the political and economic union of independent African states would provide the total liberation from colonial rule that they deemed critical for social development. They were aware of the constraints inflicted by the colonially inherited resource export-oriented national economies and that they could not resolve the structural inequalities unless they united. Nkrumah saw African political union as the only alternative to colonially inherited structural inequalities and cartographic divisions. He affirmed that: 'I am equally convinced that African union will come and provide that united, integrated base upon which our fullest development can be secured' (Nkrumah 1963). In doing so Africans could have larger markets, collective development plans and regional redistribution mechanisms. Nkrumah advocated for a United States of Africa. This form of continental union found its opposition amongst African leaders – specifically a conservative bloc aligned with the West and opposed to socialism and communism. The result was a compromise in the formation of the Organization of African Unity (OAU) in 1963, comprising the then-independent states of Africa. Some scholars argue that the OAU's most effective action was its stance against apartheid and continued colonial domination. It supported politically and financially liberation movements in Angola and Mozambique and those fighting white-dominated regimes in South Africa, Rhodesia and Namibia. This included the acceptance and integration of refugees from those states (Brankamp and Daley 2020). Such a progressive approach to refugees did not extend to those fleeing persecution in independent states. Instead, they became increasingly governed by either extant colonial laws on mobility and/or the international human rights regime of the UN.

Pan-Africanism has continued as part of a black radical tradition and is still a potent force uniting black people in their fight against oppression both in the Global North and in Africa, challenging the division between North Africa and sub-Saharan Africa. Spurred on by the Pan-African movement on the ground, following the ending of apartheid in South Africa and Namibia, African leaders reconstituted the OAU as the African Union in 2002. The constitutive agreement of the African Union (AU) included proposals for a Pan-African Parliament, Central Bank and Court. Other proposed unifying actions include the introduction of a Pan-African passport, the recognition of the African diaspora as its sixth region, and the role for civil society organizations in the development of economic, social and cultural programmes.

Guided by the nation-state model, African states have promoted a narrow national identity in their respective countries to legitimize their sovereignty. Consequently, the African Union remains remote from the people. Not all states have ratified or implemented nationally the charters they signed at the OAU/AU, especially those that would enhance the rights of their people, such as the 1981 *African People's Charter on Civil and Human Rights*. African scholars have not shied away from criticizing the African Union's version of Pan-Africanism. In 2005, the then-secretary general of the Pan-African Congress, Tajudeen Abdul-Raheem (2010: 233), in discussing the difficulties of cross border mobility in Africa, wrote 'the heads of states want a union of states, while what we need is a union of people . . . a broad alliance owned and led by our peoples to bring the frontier down and release our energies for a creative union that serves all the people'. African peoples' struggle for freedom of movement is also a struggle against those national and international capitalists who benefit from the immobility of Africans and the divisions of working people across borders.

African women, especially, have been marginalized, both in terms of their contributions to the Pan-African movement and 'their defiance of imperialist patriarchal culture' (Abbas and Mama 2014: 4). It was not until the seventh Pan-African Congress in Kampala, Uganda in 1994, that women were able to hold a pre-congress meeting and establish a women's wing – the Pan-African Women's Liberation Organization (Roy-Campbell 1996). The recommendations of the pre-Congress meeting (including surviving and resisting structural adjustment, and environmental concerns), indicate that African feminists envision their liberation as transnational and deeply intertwined with anti-imperialist and decolonial struggles (PAWLO 1994). While progress on women's issues was made at the eighth Pan-African Congress in Accra, Tamale (2020) contends that the patriarchal and state-led dominance of Pan-Africanism means that for the movement to fully advance women's interests its agenda needs to intersect with that of African feminists and non-state actors. The various iterations of Pan-Africanism since its inception provide confidence that while national leaders have failed, the movement can decolonize political consciousness beyond the local and national. The concept of 'Global Africa' has been popularized in recent years (Biney 2019), emphasizing inclusivity, and standing against the territorial nationalism, ethnic nationalism, militarism, Eurocentrism, racism, misogyny, homophobia and colourism that seek to divide African peoples in Africa and across the world.

ECONOMIC RESTRUCTURING AND JUST FUTURES

To escape Euro-American economic dominance, Samir Amin (1990: 170) has advocated the necessity of 'delinking from the logic of market-primacy'. Such a radical break would require exceptional levels of unity amongst formally colonized peoples. In the 1960s, postcolonial African states established regional economic unions to address their inherited economic weaknesses, initially drawing on the regional spheres and linguistic heritage of their former colonial powers before adopting a more inclusive geographical and African identity. By the twenty-first century, eight regional economic communities had been established with most states belonging to more than one. Regionalism as a mechanism for social transformation has had varying success. Most regional unions have failed to deliver economic benefits or to transform the lives of their citizens in meaningful ways. As with the nation-states, the effectiveness of these communities has been linked to military interventions in their regions, sometimes on behalf of the Global North.

The Lagos Plan of Action was a continental plan accepted by African heads of states at their summit in 1980 in Lagos, Nigeria. According to Ake (1996), the plan arose from the disappointment of African leaders with the failure of successive exogenous development strategies to result in economic progress in Africa. The plan emphasized economic restructuring, focusing on self-reliance and self-sustaining development. This plan was the opposite of the World Bank's (1981) *Accelerated Development in sub-Saharan Africa* report, which outlined the prescriptions for the introduction of neoliberalism in Africa. Ake (1996: 21) refers to these as 'competing agendas', and the eventual submission of African leaders to the West. The most recent plan, the African Continental Free Trade Area (AfCFTA), was established in 2022. It is claimed to be the largest free trade area in the world, connecting 1.3 billion people across 55 countries with a combined gross domestic product (GDP) valued at US$3.4 trillion (World Bank 2020).

The economic failure of regionalism has often been attributed to national elites, who have struggled with regionalization, as competition can limit their access to resources. This has been compounded by the methodological nationalism that informed development policy making. International development agencies and Western governments are often reluctant to negotiate with regional economic unions or to support regional development projects, except for China's historic support for the Tanzania-Zambia Railway in the 1970s. The US has tended to negotiate with individual countries, even in the revived East African Community (2000–present). Even with free-market globalization, capitalists in the Global North prefer to use their nation-states to leverage trade agreements in their favour, enabling them to have exclusive access to territorially defined markets. Due to the size of its potential free-market area, AfCFTA is presented by the World Bank as a very attractive entity for global corporations (World Bank 2020). The centring of Northern priorities undermines the capacity for regional collective decision making and for African states to have effective leverage in trade negotiations.

BUILDING POLITICAL COMMUNITIES IN THE GLOBAL SOUTH

Anti-colonial movements had a global conception of liberation and sought to build transcontinental alliances between oppressed people who were subjected to European colonial domination. Getachew (2020) calls these visions 'anti-colonial worldmaking'. She shows how anti-colonial nationalists in Africa were aware of how colonial racial domination reverberated throughout the international sphere and that the problem of empire was not just about the transformation of domestic politics but also international politics. Black internationalists who spent time in Europe were disillusioned with the forms of citizenship offered at the centre of empire and the racism that informed and justified the extractive colonial projects. By looking at 'the ways that the experience of colonial domination and international hierarchy gave distinctive shape to debates about sovereignty and state formation', Getachew (2020: 9) 'recenters the enduring legacies of European imperialism in our present'. Using evidence from the rise and fall of attempts at gaining self-determination in Africa and the Caribbean, she argues that anti-colonial nationalists were not tied to the Westphalian nation-state model and looked to build federations; they had their visions of a 'new egalitarian order' squashed by the exploitative economic relations and political pressure from powerful states, economic institutions, and private actors (11). What is instructive here is the ability to transcend racial and national boundaries – to build a global political consciousness.

Vijay Prashad (2007: xv) states that 'The Third World was not a place. It was a project' that originated at the 1955 conference in Bandung, Indonesia (Ndlovu-Gatsheni and Tafira 2019; Aneja 2019; Prashad 2007) attended by independent states, mainly Asian and African, to promote unity in the face of the USA and colonial powers, and to demonstrate clear differences of interest and alliances between the Global South's formerly colonial territories and the Cold War divisions of the world into the first and second worlds. Their platform was 'political independence, nonviolent international relations, and the cultivation of the United Nations as the principal institution for planetary justice' (Prashad 2007: 11). They formed the Non-Aligned Movement in 1961, which continued to exist until the fall of communism, even though the USA refused to accept Global South states' non-alignment during the Cold War.

According to Prashad (2007: 84), Third World states rejected 'the idea of nationalism that emerged from Europe's history' – and instead adopted a multinational (pluralist) perspective in acknowledgement of the cultural diversity of their countries, with the assumption that a new form of political modernity could be created. As a counter to the racial hierarchy and the lack of citizenship rights under colonialism, they absorbed the democratic goal of giving every citizen the vote, regardless of their literacy or social status. Epistemically, 'the regimes in the new nations adopted the Enlightenment's scientific heritage without any discussion of its cultural implications' (Prashad 2007: 90). With these internal contradictions, compounded by the nature of integration of states into the global economy and Cold War geopolitics, the alliances formed could not be sustained and achieve their full potential.

Isaac Saney (2019) writes of another Global South movement, the Tricontinental, which he described as the first concerted effort to forge a unified force capable of overthrowing the established international order and 'a radical example to Global South self-determination' (165). Initiated by Medhi Ben Barka, a Moroccan socialist, the Tricontinental was an attempt to reimagine the world order, a process that required the solidarity and determination of Global South leaders. Ben Barka, who was kidnapped and killed in 1965 supposedly with the backing of Moroccan and imperialist forces, had envisaged a more revolutionary anti-colonial transformation that was allied with socialism, and sought to rally worldwide anti-imperialist forces. Supported by Cuba, the Tricontinental's first meeting was held in Havana on 16 January 1966, after which it sought to organize regionally. At the conference, Amilcar Cabral (1973), in a speech entitled 'The Weapon of Theory', focused on the struggles to overcome the internal weaknesses of liberation movements as major constraints on attaining freedom. Weaknesses, such as the lack of ideology and an understanding of their societies' realities, needed to be overcome for liberation movements to identify 'with the deepest aspirations of the people to which they belong' (89). Saney claims that the Tricontinental impacted liberation movements around the world and may have facilitated Cuba's military intervention in Angola. The effectiveness of Tricontinentalism waned in the early 1980s, following the 1970s debt crisis, the rise of authoritarianism in many Global South countries, and the fact that some Global South leaders were aligned with the West, despite being a part of the Non-Aligned Movement. Though limited in its influence, the Tricontinental remains one of the most progressive expressions of transcontinental solidarity (Mahler 2018).

BUILDING TRANSFORMATIVE SPACES WITHIN EXISTING GLOBAL STRUCTURES

The challenges faced by those seeking to use revolutionary methods to reorder the world led others to seek to change the system from within. The New International Economic Order (NIEO) was an attempt to address global inequalities, especially unfair terms of trade, through the United Nations system. The group of 77 newly independent states that founded the United Nations Conference on Trade and Development

(UNCTAD) in 1974 declared the need for a structural change in global relations (Ake 1996; Ndlovu-Gatsheni & Tafira 2019). It made economic and political stipulations regarding equity and addressing the basic needs of people in the Global South. Twenty-three prescriptions for economic change were stipulated, including better terms of trade to enable Global South countries to gain effective control over their economies. NIEO's goal of empowering the Global South failed, and it ended in 1983 with the rise of neoliberalism.

South–South Cooperation was a UN project in response to its Global South members' demand for change. Established in 1978, it involved the setting up of the South Commission based in Geneva, aimed at strengthening South–South cooperation in international affairs and to promote South–South trade and collaboration within its entities (Aneja 2019; Prashad 2012). Prashad (2012: 9), in an analysis of the 'South project' from the 1970s–2000s, contends that the North, faced by the threat from the South, 'shunned the South Commission', and 'fought back aggressively' to impose the neoliberal order in the 1980s.

The ideological battles during the Cold War coupled with indebtedness after the oil price shocks of 1973 destroyed Southern aspirations for restructuring their links with the Global North. Samir Amin, writing in the 1990s, realized that Global South countries couldn't hope to raise living standards if they continued to adjust their development strategies in line with the trends set by a fundamentally unequal global capitalist system over which they have no control. He argued for 'delinking' from the logic of the global system or 'autocentric development', with each country 'submitting its external economic relations to the logic of domestic development priorities, which in turn requires a broad coalition of popular forces in control of the state'. Delinking, he continues, is not about 'absolute autarchy, but a neutralizing of the effects of external economic interactions on internal choices' (1990b: 157–8). Amin advocated a polycentric (regionalized) world involving progressive states in the Global North that includes an acceptance of a plurality of productive systems, political visions, and cultures.

SOUTHERN SOLIDARITIES IN A NEOLIBERAL WORLD

Neoliberal economic globalization in the late twentieth and twenty-first century benefited some economies in the Global South that possessed cheap sources of abundant labour and the productive capacity for industrial production sought by transnational corporations. This global shift transformed China, Malaysia, Brazil and, increasingly, India, into emerging economic powers challenging the hegemony of the Global North by investing in other Southern countries, drawing on early forms of cooperation as part of liberation struggles (Mawdsley 2019a). Russia, a post-communist power, embraced the free market, but still evoked earlier solidarities to be part of this group. The Southern discourse about this newest form of South–South cooperation focused on historical connections, respect for sovereignty, non-interference in political affairs, anti-imperialism and mutually beneficial or win-win economics (Cheru and Obi 2010; Fiddian-Qasmiyeh and Daley 2019).

Popular perspectives on the 1990s suggest that the bipolar division of the Cold War was then dissipating, and the world was becoming multipolar, with multiple trajectories for development and alternative modernities. A group of emerging powers consisting of Brazil, Russia, India and China became known by their acronym as the BRIC countries (Carmody 2013; Bond 2016). Their goal was to promote investment and trade between themselves and Global South countries. Following the 2008 financial crisis, Global South economies that were less impacted by the financial fallout were seen as posing a challenge to the North, as they took the lead in enabling the economic transformation of the Global South and the promotion of Southern solidarity. BRIC states represented themselves as pragmatic partners rather than 'aid donors' (Lumumba-Kasongo 2015). Their impact shifted the study of South–South relations, which was no longer just a concern of Global South progressives but became mainstreamed within the Western academy (Mawdsley 2019a and b; Fiddian-Qasmiyeh and Daley 2019). Liberal critics and popular discourse in the Global North emphasized what they regarded as colonizing practices by China, with Global South peoples having more nuanced perspectives. Western narratives attacking China's involvement in Africa represent the emergence of a new geopolitics of development.

Does the latest iteration of South–South cooperation represent a new approach to international development (Mawdsley 2012)? Global South countries are encouraged to mimic the Chinese developmental path which focused on investments in infrastructure as its route to modernity. Western complaints about China's actions in Africa tend to address the indebtedness caused by these infrastructural projects. But the need for infrastructure and its popularity has led the European Union, the USA (under President Donald Trump), and the UK to create specific funds for infrastructural projects in the Global South to counter Chinese influence.

To Prashad (2012: 11) 'BRICS formation has not endorsed an *ideological* alternative to neoliberalism'. Instead, BRICS have served to only further entrench Global South countries into the neoliberal global economy (Mawdsley, 2017, 2019b; Morvaridi and Hughes, 2019). Mawdsley (2017: 113) contends that Southern 'donors' use 'development finance as a vehicle to promote their own economic growth . . . [thereby providing] subsidized support for private sector growth (and state-owned enterprises) in the name of "development"'. For Morvaridi and Hughes (2018: 886–7):

> the outsourcing of traditional forms of technical development assistance from [Northern] countries to emerging economies assists in the drive to depoliticization inherent in neoliberal development strategies since it obscures the rich–poor, North–South, centre–periphery categories of dependency theory which remained problematic for the legitimacy of the aid enterprise throughout the post-colonial era.

Furthermore, Mawdsley (2019b: 4) points to attempts by Northern 'donors' to 'socialize' Southern 'donors' into development praxis. This involves Northern 'donors' overseeing, for example, India's relationship with African countries, as part of a geopolitical struggle to maintain their hegemony (Abdenur & Marques da Froncesca 2013). In addition, populist nationalism and increasing economic precarity in Global South countries might lead to a retreat from collective South-South cooperation as illustrated by the decline of BRICs by the 2020s.

The logics of neoliberalism are such that the era of Global South solidarity between states may have gone, but that does not foreclose the continued solidarity between Global South peoples through social movements against development. For Prashad (2012: 11) 'the Global South is a place of great struggle, of various tactics and strategies experimented with on the streets and in the halls of government. It is an unfinished story-one that has to have a good ending'.

CONCLUSION

Methodological nationalism in development thought has limited the capacity of social scientists to conceptualize how social transformation can be achieved through wider political frameworks. With nation-states seen as sacrosanct, the visions of transnational and transcontinental social formations that anti-colonial nationalists produced were dismissed as overly idealistic, even when Global North countries embarked on establishing regional economic unions. In this chapter, we have challenged our readers to think critically and creatively about the forms of political community that can deliver positive social change. We have introduced the problematic role of the state in the development project. Using the African continent as our empirical example, we have historically charted the origins and the coloniality of the nation-state that predominates in the contemporary period. We then introduced a selection of new geopolitical imaginaries, both regional and global, that anti-colonial leaders sought to realize outside the world market-oriented system. All these initiatives were undermined by Western governments' Cold War geopolitics and counter-revolutionary strategies, and their efforts to maintain economic hegemony. In the post-Cold war era, South–South cooperation, especially China's role as a major investor, forced Western governments and development institutions to mimic Global South investors or co-opt them to ensure global compliance to neoliberal free-market orthodoxy.

Twenty-first century nation branding and the global rise of populism suggests that the nation-state model still has political capital. These new postcolonial manifestations of populist nationalism in countries of the Global South, such as India and South Africa, conform to the nation-state model, rather than to decolonized alternative political communities. While we recognize the significant role that a people-centred state can play as a vehicle for socially just transformation, we encourage disobedient thought about how this might be done otherwise. What is clear from a consideration of history is that the peoples of the Global South remain persistent in their struggles for emancipation. An emancipatory framework that gets rid of the nation-state and its national capitalists will lead to collaboration beyond borders and, in turn, the abolition of the coercive institutions of the state. While highlighting the non-emancipatory aspects of the latest iterations of geographical imaginaries relating to the Global

South, we encourage our readers to consider radically the contours of how we might realize these just futures.

QUESTIONS FOR FURTHER THOUGHT

How does methodological nationalism condition how we think about development?

How can scholars or political actors draw upon conceptualizations of political communities in the Global South to articulate the state *otherwise*?

Do South–South relations represent new forms of colonialism or an opportunity to change the power dynamics with the Global North?

Are the 'emerging powers' a reflection of a reorientation of the global economic system? Please consider Lisa Tilley's (2020) 'extractive investibility in historical colonial perspective' in Indonesia.

Are there non-state or alternative state examples of South–South relations that have the potential to shift away from neoliberal regimes and correct development injustices, and what forms of spatial organization would facilitate them?

FILMS

Pan-Africanism. Available: www.youtube.com/watch?v=KSEeqWM2RhY&has_ verified=1/.

1955 Asian-African Bandung Conference (Pathé news extract). Available: www. youtube.com/watch?v=zg4OGtlxu3Y.

President Sukarno Opening Speech at the Bandung Conference, Indonesia, 1955. Available: www.youtube.com/watch?v=DRIch247vb8.

The Tricontinental Conference of 1966 in Havana, Cuba. Available: www.youtube. com/watch?v=dxCj_03MRvc.

REFERENCES

Abbas, H. and Mama, A. (2014) 'Editorial: Feminism and pan-Africanism', *Feminist Africa* 19: 1–7.

Amin, S. (1979) *Unequal development: An essay on the social formations of peripheral capitalism.* Translated by Brian Pearce. Brighton: The Harvester Press.

Amin, S. (1988) *Eurocentrism.* New York/ London: Monthly Review Press.

Amin, S. (1990a) *Delinking: Towards a polycentric world.* London: Zed Books.

Amin, S. (1990b) *Maldevelopment: Anatomy of global failure.* London: Zed Books.

Ake, C. (1996) *Democracy and development in Africa*. Washington, D.C: The Brookings Institution.

Abdul-Raheem, T. (1996) (ed.) *Pan-Africanism: Politics, economy and social change in the twenty-first century*. London: Pluto Press.

Abdul-Raheem, T. (2010) 'Taking Pan-Africanism to the People', Postcard dated 24 November 2005, in Biney, A. and Olukoshi, A. (eds), *Speaking truth to power: Selected pan-African postcards*. Oxford: Pambazuka Press.

Ackah, W. B. (1999) *Pan-Africanism: Exploring the contradictions: Politics, identity and development in Africa and the African diaspora*. Milton Park, Abingdon: Routledge.

Aneja, U. (2019) 'South-South Cooperation and competition: A critical history of the principles and their practice', in Fiddian-Qasmiyeh, E. and Daley, P. (eds.), *Routledge handbook on South-South relations*. London: Routledge, pp.141–52.

Aucoin, M. J. (2022) 'You can make it here!": Producing Europe's mobile borders in the New Gambia', *Political Geography*, 97, https://doi.org/10.1016/j.polgeo.2022.102641.

Anderson, B. (1991) *Imagined communities: Reflections on the origin and spread of Nationalism*. London: Verso Books.

Anderson, B. (2019) 'New Directions in migration studies: towards methodological denationalism', *Comparative Migration Review* 7(1), https://doi.org/10.1186/s40878-019-0140-8.

Asiwaju, A. I. (1983) 'The concept of frontier in the setting of states in pre-colonial Africa', *Presence Africaine*. DOI : 10.3917/presa.127.0043.

Asiwaju, A. I. (ed.) (1985) *Partitioned Africans: Ethnic relations across Africa's international boundaries, 1884-1984*. London: Palgrave Macmillan.

Asiwaju, A. I. and P.O. Adenyi (1989) (eds.) *Borderlands in Africa: A multidisciplinary and comparative focus on Nigeria and West Africa*. Lagos: University of Lagos Press.

Bathily, A. (1994) 'The West African State in Historical Perspective', in Osaghae, E. E. (ed.) *Between state and civil society in Africa*. Dakar, Senegal, pp. 41–74.

Bhambra, G. K. (2013) 'The possibilities of, and for, global sociology: A postcolonial perspective', *Postcolonial Sociology* 24, pp. 295–314.

Biney, A. (2011) *The political and social thought of Kwame Nkrumah*. London: Palgrave Macmillan.

Biney, A. (2019) 'Pan-Africanism', in Fiddian-Qasmiyeh, E. and Daley, P. (eds.) *Routledge Handbook on South-South Relations*. London: Routledge, pp. 177–88.

Bird, G. (2016) 'Beyond the nation state: The role of local and pan-national identities in defining post-colonial African citizenship', *Citizenship Studies*, 20(2), pp. 260–75.

Blaut, J. M. (1993) *The colonizer's model of the world: Geographical diffusionism and Eurocentric history*. Guilford: The Guilford Press.

Bond, P. (2006) *Looting Africa: The economics of exploitation*. London: Zed Press.

Bond, P. (2016) 'BRICS banking and the debate over sub-imperialism', *Third World Quarterly*, 37(4), pp. 611–29.

Boyce Davies, C. (2014) 'Pan-Africanism, transnational black feminism and the limits of culturalist analyses in African gender discourses', *Feminist Africa*, 19, pp. 78–93.

Brachet, J. (2016) 'Policing the desert: The IOM in Libya beyond war and peace', *Antipode* 48(2), pp. 272–92. https://doi.org/10.1111/anti.12176.

Brankamp, H. and Daley, P. (2020) 'Laborers, migrants, refugees: Managing belonging, bodies, and mobility in (post)colonial Kenya and Tanzania', *Migration and Society: Advances in Research*, 3, pp. 113–29.

Brankamp H. and Glück, Z. (2022) 'Camps and counterterrorism: Security and the remaking of refuge in Kenya', *EPC: Society and Space* 40(3), pp. 528–48.

Cabral, A. (1973) *Revolution in Guinea: African peoples struggle*. London Stage 1. First published in 1965; in the UK in 1969 & reprinted 1971 & 1973.

Carmody, P. (2013) *The Rise of the BRICS in Africa: The Geopolitics of South-South relations*. London: Zed Books.

Cheru, Fantu & Cyril Obi (eds.) (2010) *The rise of China and India in Africa: Challenges, opportunities & critical interventions*. London: Nordic African Institute & Zed Books.

Cheru, Fantu (2016) 'Emerging Southern powers and new forms of South–South cooperation: Ethiopia's strategic engagement with China and India', *Third World Quarterly*, 37(4), pp. 592–610.

Chernilo, D. (2006) 'Social theory's methodological nationalism: Myth and reality', *European Journal of Social Theory*, 9(1), pp. 5–22.

Chernilo, D. (2007) *A social theory of the nation-state: The political forms of modernity beyond methodological nationalism*. London: Routledge.

Cormack, Z. (2016) 'Borders are galaxies: Interpreting contestations over local administrative boundaries in South Sudan', *Africa* 86(3), pp. 504–27.

Davidson, B. (1992) *Black man's Burden: Africa and the curse of the nation-state*. Melton: James Currey.

Diop, C. A. (1987) *Precolonial Black Africa*. New York: Lawrence Hill Books.

Doevenspeck, M. (2011) 'Constructing the border from below: Narratives from the Congolese Rwandan state boundary', *Political Geography*, 30, pp. 129–42.

Dutta, M. J. (2020) 'Whiteness, internationalization and erasure: Decolonising futures from the Global South', *Communication and Critical/Cultural Studies*, 17(2), pp. 228–35.

Emiljanowicz, P. (2019) 'Tensions, ambiguities, and onnectivity in Kwame Nkrumah: Rethinking the "national" in postcolonial nationalism', *Interventions*, 21(5), pp. 615–34.

Emiljanowicz, P. (2022) 'Translocality and the future: Postcolonial connectivities in 1960s Ghana', *Postcolonial Studies*, 26(1), pp. 112–30. DOI: 10.1080/13688790.2023.2127664.

Erthal Abdenur, A. and Da Fonseca, J. (2013) 'The North's growing role in South–South cooperation: Leeping the foothold', *Third World Quarterly*, 34(8), pp. 1475–91.

Falola, T. and A. Usman (eds.) (2009) *Movements, borders and identities in Africa.* Rochester: Rochester University Press.

Ferretti, F. (2020) 'Subaltern connections: Brazilian critical geographers, development and African decolonisation', *Third World Quarterly*, 41(5), pp. 822–41.

Fiddian-Qasmiyeh, E. and Daley, P. (eds.) (2019) *Routledge handbook on South-South relations.* London: Routledge.

Frank, A. G. (1978) *World accumulation, 1492-1789.* London: Palgrave Macmillan.

Frank, A. G. (2007) *Reorient: The global economy in the Asian age.* Berkeley and Los Angeles: University of California Press.

Getachew, A. (2019) *Worldmaking after Empire: The rise and fall of self-determination.* Princeton: Princeton University Press.

Hall, S. (1993) 'Culture, community, nation', *Cultural Studies*, 7(3), pp. 349–63.

Herbst, J. (2000) *State and power in Africa: Comparative lessons in authority and control.* Princeton: Princeton University Press.

Hollstegge, J. and Doevenspeck, M. (2017) '"Sovereignty entrepreneurs" and the production of state power in two Central African Borderlands', *Geopolitics*, 22(4), pp. 815–36.

Jensen, S. L. B. (2017) *The making of international human rights: The 1960s, decolonization, and the reconstruction of global values.* Cambridge: Cambridge University Press.

Jerven, M. (2013) *Poor numbers: How we are misled by African Development Statistics and what to do about It.* New York: Cornell University Press.

Jones, H. (2019) 'Property, territory, and colonialism: an international legal history of enclosure', *Legal Studies*, 39, pp. 187–203.

Klose, F. (2013) *Human rights in the shadow of colonial violence: The wars of independence in Kenya and Algeria.* Philadelphia: University of Pennsylvania Press.

Kopytoff, I. (ed.) (1987) *The African frontier: The reproduction of traditional African societies.* Bloomington: Indiana University Press.

Lumumba-Kasongo, T. (2015) 'Brazil, Russia, India, China, and South Africa (BRICS) and Africa: New Projected Developmental Paradigms', *Africa Development*, 40(3), pp. 77–95.

Lund, C. and Boone, C. (2013) 'Introduction: Land politics in Africa: Constituting authority over territory, property and persons', *Africa*, 83(1), pp. 1–13.

Mafege, A. (1971) 'The ideology of tribalism', *Journal of Modern African Studies*, 9(2), pp. 253–61.

Mafege, A. (1991) *The theory and ethnography of african social formations: The case of the interlacustrine kingdoms.* Dakar: CODESRIA Book Series.

Mahler, A. G. (2018) *From the Tricontinental to the Global South: Race, radicalism, and transnational solidarity.* Durham, NC: Duke University Press.

Mamdani, M. (1996) *Citizens and subjects: Contemporary Africa and the legacy of late colonialism.* Oxford: James Currey.

Mamdani, M. (2001) *When victims become killers: Colonialism, nativism, and the genocide in Rwanda.* Oxford: James Currey.

Mamdani, M. (2020) *Neither settler nor native: The making and unmaking of permanent minorities*. Cambridge: The Belknap Press of Harvard University Press.

Mawdsley, E. (2012) 'The changing geographies of foreign aid and development cooperation: Contributions from gift theory', *Transactions of the Institute of British Geographer*, 37(2), pp. 256–72.

Mawdsley, E. (2017) 'Development geography 1: Cooperation, competition and convergence between 'North' & 'South', *Progress in Human Geography*, 41(1), pp. 108–17.

Mawdsley, E. (2019a) 'South-South Cooperation 3:0? Managing the consequences of success in the decade ahead', *Oxford Development Studies*, 47(3), pp. 259–74.

Mawdsley, E. (2019b) 'Southern leaders: Northern Followers? Who has 'socialized whom in international development', in Fiddian-Qasmiyeh, E. and P. Daley (eds.), *Routledge Handbook on South-South Relations*. London: Routledge. pp.191–204.

Mbembe, A., and F. Sarr(eds). (2023) *The politics of time: Imagining African becomings*. Cambridge: Polity Press.

McFadden, P. (2008) 'Plunder as statecraft: Militarism and resistance in neocolonial Africa', in Sutton, B; Morgen, S. and J. Novkov (eds.), *Security disarmed: Critical perspectives on gender, race, and militarization*. New Brunswick, NJ: Rutgers University Press, pp. 136–56.

Moyo, I. (2016) 'The Beitbridge–Mussina interface: Towards flexible citizenship, sovereignty and territoriality at the border', *Journal of Borderlands Studies*, 31(4), pp. 427–40, DOI: 10.1080/08865655.2016.1188666.

Moyo, I. (2020a) 'On decolonising borders and regional integration in the Southern African development community (SADC) region', *Social Sciences*, 9(32). DOI:10.3390/socsci9040032.

Moyo, I. (2020b) 'On borders and the liminality of undocumented Zimbabwean migrants in South Africa', *Journal of Immigrant & Refugee Studies*, 18(1), pp. 60–74, DOI: 10.1080/15562948.2019.1570416.

Moyo, I. and Nshimbi, C. C. (2020) 'Of borders and fortresses: Attitudes towards immigrants from the SADC region in South Africa as a critical factor in the integration of Southern Africa', *Journal of Borderlands Studies*, 35(1), pp. 131–46, DOI: 10.1080/08865655.2017.1402198.

Mitchell, T. (2008) 'Rethinking economy', *Geoforum*, 39, pp. 1116–21.

Morvaridi, B. and Hughes, C. (2019) 'South-South cooperation and neoliberal hegemony in a post-aid world', *Development and Change*, 49(3), pp. 867–92.

Ndlovu-Gatsheni, S. J. (2013a) 'Revisiting the national question and rethinking the political trajectory of Africa in the 21st century', *International Journal of African Renaissance Studies – Multi-, Inter- and Transdisciplinarity*, 8(2): pp. 32–57.

Ndlovu-Gatsheni, S. (2013b) *Empire, global coloniality and African subjectivity*. New York: Berghahn Books.

Ndlovu-Gatsheni, S. J. and Tafira, K. (2019) 'The invention of the Global South-and the Politics of South-South Solidarity', in Fiddian-Qasmiyeh, E. and Daley, P. (eds.) *Routledge Handbook on South-South Relations*. London: Routledge.

Ndlovu-Gatsheni, S. J. (2023) 'Beyond the coloniser's model of the world: Towards reworlding from the Global South', *Third World Quarterly*. DOI: 10.1080/01436597.2023.2171389

Nkrumah, K. (1963). *Africa must unite*. London: Oanaf.

Nyamnjoh, F. B. (2013) 'Fiction and reality of mobility in Africa', *Citizenship Studies*, 17(6–7). https://doi.org/10.1080/13621025.2013.834121.

Nyamnjoh, F. B. (2018) 'Incompleteness: Frontier Africa and the currency of conviviality', *Journal of Asian and African Studies*, 52(3), pp. 1–18.

O'Reilly, P. and Heron, T. (2022) 'Institutions, ideas and regional policy (un-) coordination: The East African Community and the politics of second-hand clothing', *Review of International Political Economy*, 2, https://doi.org/10.1080/09692290.2022.2062614.

Pan African Women's Liberation Organization (PAWLO) (1994) 'African Women: Organizing for their Future', *Bulletin of the Pan African Women's Liberation Organization*, May. Kampala: Pan-African Secretariat.

Ranger, T. (1983) 'The invention of tradition in colonial Africa' in Hobsbawm, Eric and Terence Ranger (eds.) *The invention of tradition*. Cambridge: Cambridge University Press.

Rodney, W. (1980) *A history of the Upper Guinea Coast 1545-1800*. London: Monthly Review Press. First published in 1970 by Oxford University Press.

Pike, A. (ed.) (2011) *Brands and branding geographies*. Warwrick: Open Monograph Press.

Pillay, S. (2018) 'Thinking the state from Africa: Political theory, eurocentrism and concrete politics', *Politikon*, 45(1), pp. 32–47, DOI: 10.1080/02589346.2018.1418203.

Prashad, V. (2007) *The darker nations: A people history of the Third World*. New York: Verso: The New Press.

Prashad, Vijay (2012) *The Poorer Nations: A Possible History of the Global South*. London: Verso Books.

Roy-Campbell, Z. (June 1996) 'Pan-African women organizing for the future: The formation of the Pan-African women's liberation organization and beyond', *The African e-Journals Project*. http://digital.lib.msu.edu/projects/africanjournals.

Saney, I. (2019) 'Dreaming revolution: Tricontinentalism, imperialism and Third World Rebellion', in Fiddian-Qasmiyeh, E. and Daley, P. (eds.) *Routledge handbook on South-South relations*. London: Routledge, pp.153–67.

Tamale, S. (2020) *Decolonization and African-feminism*. Ottawa, Ontario: Daraja Press.

Tilley, L. (2020) 'Extractive investibility in historical colonial perspective: The emerging market and its antecedents in Indonesia'. *Review of International Political Economy* 28(5), pp. 1099–1118.

Vail, L. (1989) (ed.) *The creation of tribalism in Southern Africa*. Berkeley: University of California Press.

Vives, L. (2017) 'Unwanted sea migrants across the EU border: The Canary Islands', *Political Geography*, 61, pp. 181–92.

Wolff, E. A. (2021) 'The global politics of African industrial policy: the case of the used clothing ban in Kenya, Uganda and Rwanda', *Review of International Political Economy*, 28(5), pp. 1308–31.

World Bank (1981) *Accelerated development in sub-Saharan Africa: An Agenda for Action*. Washington: World Bank.

World Bank (2020) 'The African Continental Free Trade Area'. Available: www.worldbank.org/en/topic/trade/publication/the-african-continental-free-trade-area.

Younis, M. (2022) *On the scale of the word: The Formation of Black anticolonial thought*. Berkeley: University of California Press.

FILMS

Pan-Africanism: PAN-AFRICANISM: Testing Ideas on Reality (2017) Directed by Obehi Ewanfoh. Available: www.youtube.com/watch?v=KSEeqWM2RhY.

Asian-African Bandung Conference (Pathe news extract) (1955). Available: www.youtube.com/watch?v=zg4OGtlxu3Y.

President Sukarno Opening Speech at the Bandung Conference, Indonesia (1955). Available: www.youtube.com/watch?v=DRIch247vb8.

The Tricontinental Conference of 1966 in Havana, Cuba (1966). Available: www.youtube.com/watch?v=dxCj_03MRvc.

8

Beyond Tokenism: Pluriversals and Decolonizing Solidarity for Thriving and Dignified Futures

We have made a case for the imperative of development abolition. Now we will turn to look at some of the collective and pluriversal projects for meaningful, flourishing, liveable futures that emphasize wellbeing and ecological balance beyond the paradigm of development. We invite you to imagine radical alternatives along with us. If the coloniality of knowledge and Western capital-centric hegemony has 'created a space in which only certain things could be said or even imagined' (Escobar 1995: 39), and if we, ourselves, are taught within and shaped by these frames of knowing, how can we travel beyond the horizon and into dignified/decolonial futures? What are some of the ways of thinking and being in the world that move beyond or exist outside of international development paradigms? What are some of the accompanying considerations when embarking into new ways of thinking?

Up to this point, we have considered a range of challenging readings of international development and, by extension, Eurocentrism and the coloniality of power. Of course, this is not an exhaustive account: our book and the courses upon which it is built could never be – nor has it sought to be – a catalogue, nor an almanac. We do not make prescriptions for how decolonization or abolition occurs; we have rather gestured towards possibilities and opened up questions for thought. Our aim is that our conversations will foster the kind of necessary critical thinking and inquiry which informs praxis – that is to say, action and action-oriented possibilities in the world and vice versa. Working within the activist tradition of abolitionist geographies, the project of abolishing international development entails working towards reparative and transformative justice. Transformative justice involves fundamental change of the systemic conditions that foster harm, exploitation, extraction and violence. Decolonizing solidarity demands deep listening, radical love across difference (hooks 2002) and an explicit attention to repairing the harms propagated by the Global North upon the South. The first stage of transformative justice is recognition and taking responsibility. Repair means intentionally creating space and time for wounds to heal and for harms to be mediated and compensated.

Our considerations of anti-racist, abolitionist and queering approaches have led us here, to this final consideration of breaking with the forms of hegemonic thinking deeply embedded within international development practice, ideology and scholarship; beyond the cisheteropatriarchy, growthism and extractivism that are at the heart of coloniality in the present. Our final teaching and learning materials are about highlighting the ways in which seemingly impossible changes or futures are not inconceivable. Life-affirming ways of knowing, being and practice exist: delinking, degrowth, reparations and repair, debt justice, networks of direct action, redistribution, mutual aid, buen vivir, ubuntu and more.

ANTICOLONIAL AND DECOLONIAL SOUNDTRACK

The Zimbabwean singer and songwriter, Vusa Mkhaya's 2006 song 'Ubuntu' sets the tone and rhythm for our tentative consideration in this chapter.[1] Mkhaya is known for creating impressive songs within the *imbube* genre in South Africa, which uses a cappella voices to move and educate listeners on topics of socio-economic importance.

PLURIVERSALITY BEYOND TOKENISM

Pluriversality is a vision that allows us to engage simultaneously with a wide range of alternatives (alternately referred to as pluriversals/ otherwises/other horizons). The move towards different (and many) futures, is founded upon the possibility of such a move in the first place. Pluriversality is the name for this possibility. Emerging as a concept in struggle from the Zapatista aspiration for 'a world where many worlds fit' in Chiapas, Mexico, the notion of the pluriverse challenges the premise of universality, a cornerstone of Eurocentric modernity. It is a way of

---

1. https://open.spotify.com/track/2MyJexWyT2dyaZGu4foEcS.

understanding the world as multiplicitous, recognizing the diversity and complexity of human experiences, cultures and knowledge systems. It affirms that there is not one single and universal way of knowing/being (or developing), but rather multiple and co-existing realities continuously in conversation with one another. These perspectives are united by a shift in focus towards respecting and valuing nature, rather than exploiting it. Indeed, calls for the revival of indigenous knowledges and ways of being have importantly focused on reframing the relationship between humanity in nature from one in which nature is demeaned and exploited to one where it is respected, valued and cared for (Kothari 2014; Kothari 2018; Singh 2019; Gudynas 2011).

In the 1980s (Ziai 2007), the 'post-development' school of thought expressed dissatisfaction with Western-dominated models of 'modernity', with some envisioning an era where development would no longer be a central organizing principle (Escobar, 2007). The argument went that by disengaging from capitalist constructions of growth, we could allow for possibility and for worlds informed by other political ideas. In response to this, the last four decades have witnessed diverse efforts to engage grassroots, popular and Indigenous knowledge(s) to unsettle and radically transform development practice and thought. However, despite the desire to alter development's deeply-rooted Eurocentrism, these attempts have frequently been challenged as superficial forms of 'tokenism', these being nothing more than symbolic displays of inclusion that do not challenge political or economic structures nor the power imbalances that inform them and that they (re)produce. For example, Gudynas (2011: 442) argues that there is a cycle in academic discussions of development, wherein 'Western development is . . . declared deceased and then at the same time being resuscitated . . . dead and alive at the same time!' The challenge here is to unlearn international development in ways that do not unconsciously and carelessly re-establish its very prominence. As we explored in our Introduction, pedagogical disobedience empowers students and activists with a powerful toolkit to navigate and transcend the duelling threats of material violence and discursive misappropriation within the realm of development practice and studies.

Alternatives to Western development have always been around. Their recent relatively prominent public profile is the result of decades of struggle, social movements and critical development scholarship, centring ontologies and knowledge(s) that were previously marginalized under colonialism and which have been continuously disregarded within neo-colonial conditions (Kothari et al. 2015). Kothari et al.'s (2019) *Pluriverse: A Post Development Dictionary* shows and celebrates the existence of alternatives to Western development, many of which originate within communities in the Global South. The Nigerian environmental activist and scholar Nnimmo Bassey opens the collection with the urgent project of collectively 'break[ing] the chains of development'. Within the project to pursue, retrieve and actualize pluriversals, in 2019 Kothari, launched the 'Global Tapestry of Alternatives' (GTA), a framework that allows for a mutual sharing, collaboration, dialogue and support amongst radical paradigms in the pursuit of decolonizing approaches to development. The GTA is an open platform that links together various radical, social, and epistemological movements to support transformative development while explicitly seeking to avoid the institutionalization of such movements. A bottom-up approach within this tapestry of alternatives can decolonize development on local and global scales, challenging the colonial matrix of power therein.

DECOLONIZING SOLIDARITY

The conversation surrounding the relationship between the Global North and South has taken a new turn, as discussions increasingly centre on the need for decolonizing solidarity. In our classrooms in Oxford, decolonizing solidarity is one of many avenues through which we enter into conversation about creating dignified futures (as we discussed in our Introduction and Chapter 1). Now, situating ourselves and our (un) learning within considerations of responsibility and action is a crucial component of focusing on transformative relations of solidarity. Our students recognize that decolonizing solidarity is imperative because the Global North has historically exploited and dominated the Global South, resulting in gross inequality and resource depletion. As a first step towards fostering more just futures, it is crucial that solidarity between the North and South is founded upon mutual respect, understanding and struggle. This requires acknowledging and challenging the power imbalances perpetrated through colonialism and imperialism.

Solidarity directed towards decolonization means 'constructing the conditions for a different kind of encounter that both opposes ongoing colonization and seeks to heal the social, cultural, and spiritual ravages of colonial history' (Gaztambide-Fernández 2012: 42). It exceeds traditional forms of solidarity within coloniality, like networks of solidarity that presume similarity, self-interest, the pre-eminence of economic growth/ profit, and the fairy-tales of 'mutual benefits' and 'win-win' paradigms. This goes beyond the mere recognition of power imbalances while simultaneously refusing simplistic easy solutions as it entails both the rejection of harmful and essentializing narratives of identity and culture and an end to the practices that harm and undermine the dignity of people and communities.

In their work on decolonizing solidarity, Gisela Carrasco Miró (2018: 164) powerfully reminds us to oppose 'development's expressions of solidarity that largely work to exculpate, exonerate, or ignore complicity in ongoing colonization and racism, thus deepening inequalities and reinforcing injustice'. We intentionally identify ways in which each of the radical ways of being explored below – buen vivir, ubuntu and degrowth – have been mobilized by elites to reinforce ecological, racial and gendered injustices. It is imperative that the work of decolonizing international development does not fall into these hegemonic patterns, and we have done our best in the writing of this work to show our humility as well as our gratitude for the scholars and activists motivating our disobedient teaching praxis and pushing us to do better and continue our own journeys of unlearning.

For example, working in the tradition of Thomas Sankara, the Senegalese political economist Samba Sylla (2022: 14) writes, 'the real first test for international cooperation and solidarity is to demonstrate whether it helps increase African self-reliance'. Solidarities work towards decolonization when communities forge their own trajectories, through their own paradigms of existence, including through forms of 'delinking' (Amin 1990) that nurture flourishing and thriving worlds. Some of the most powerful templates for coalition building and solidarity emerge from intergenerational anti-racist and anti-fascist struggles, in which differently positioned people alternately take space, create space, defend space or foster room to breathe differently. Our differences (whether racial, sexual, abled, gender or class-based) are not uniquely hindering, but in generative solidarity we need to be vigilant to our differences, especially the discomfort or inequalities (privileges and injustices) that arise from them.

BUEN VIVIR

Against the dominant international development fantasy of crafting and honing travelling models for development practice, we encourage our students to engage with the promises of alternative pathways that do not seek universal status. We now turn in greater detail to some of these alternative paradigms, each of which do not presume to 'fix' development, but to provide different frameworks, sets of relations and processes (Gudynas 2011). One such approach is that of buen vivir (in Ecuador) or the similar vivir bien (in Bolivia), otherwise known as sumak kawsay in Kichwa by Andean people in Ecuador. Buen vivir is a relational, holistic and community-centred approach to life based on indigenous ontologies and values within South America. These dual life-affirming orientations can be conceptualized as a philosophy that encompasses 'knowledge, codes of ethics and spiritual conduct in relation to the environment, human values and the vision of the future' (Kothari et al., 2015: 367). Buen vivir refuses the human–nature binary (taking nature as a static canvas to be acted upon and extracted)) and emphasizes the interconnectedness of all life and beings in ensuring survival and flourishing. It refuses the model of a linear trajectory of development, taking it as a dynamic and evolving concept that 'is continually being created' (Gudynas, 2011: 443) and being shaped by the cultural, historical and geographical contexts in which it is practiced (Kothari et al. 2015). These distinct features make buen vivir a valuable contribution to the decolonization of development.

The recognition of buen vivir and vivir bien as constitutional rights in Ecuador and Bolivia, respectively, demonstrates the significance of these approaches to life and their potential to shape development policies and practices (Gudynas 2011). The 2008 Constitution of Ecuador requires that the state promote and protect buen vivir through social, economic, and environmental policy and mandates. The constitution includes specific provisions aimed at promoting buen vivir, including the protection of the rights of nature, the recognition of indigenous knowledge, and the promotion of alternative economic models that prioritize social welfare over profit. The Tunghurahua case exemplifies how buen vivir can challenge dominant development norms and negotiate alternative strategies that reflect the needs and rights of both humans and nature: Indigenous communities in the Tungurahua region in Ecuador filed a lawsuit against the state-owned oil company, Petroecuador, for environmental destruction caused by its oil operations. In 2005, the Constitutional Court ruled in favour of the community and ordered Petroecuador to compensate affected people and to take measures to mitigate the interrelated health and environmental harms caused by its operations. The Tungurahua case is significant because it represents one of the first instances in which a court has recognized the rights of nature and has imposed obligations on corporations to respect those rights. Mobilizing the principles of sumak kawsay, the Tunghurahua people successfully negotiated a redesigned watershed project that reflected their needs and rights. Kauffman and Martin (2014) argue that this approach of living with nature can challenge dominant development paradigms at a larger scale.

According to Gudynas (2011), the recognition of indigenous ontologies and the strengthening of cultural identities thorough their inclusion in the buen vivir framework has led to the production of more holistic and less anthropocentric development practices. Rather than solely focusing on economic growth and progress, buen vivir prioritizes well-being and sustainability for both people and the environment and seeks to integrate indigenous knowledge and practices into initiatives. While this is a powerful example of how buen vivir can challenge dominant development paradigms, buen vivir is first and foremost a relational ontology rooted in place-based relations in the Andes. It is very instructive for students and activists to consider how the buen vivir framework can or should be mimicked or transplanted. Gudynas (2011) argues that for buen vivir to be effective in other contexts, it must be recognized as important by both the state and development institutions, and new relationships between humans and nature will need to be fostered in contexts beyond Bolivia and Ecuador.

More damningly, in Bolivia, Pablo Solón (2018) critiques the argument that the codification of buen vivir within legislation mounts an effective challenge to dominant development paradigms. Solón contends that the adoption of buen vivir in Bolivia has been primarily cosmetic and has not reflected the foundational commitment to rethinking human–nature relations. This is laid bare in the ongoing or even intensifying natural resource extraction, which activists and scholars have termed 'neo-extractivism' (Petras and Veltmeyer 2014). Solón's critique highlights the importance of not just codifying buen vivir in legislation, but also providing substantial structural support to ensure the principles are put into practice. This example shows that while buen vivir (sumak kawsay) can be a valuable approach for decolonizing development, its success depends on more than just the codification of its principles.

Through an in-depth consideration of buen vivir as a praxis, students and activists alike can become familiar with it as a potential pathway towards the subversion of dominant neo-colonial elements of development. The scaling-up of buen vivir presents certain challenges, particularly given its place-specific dimensions. As Solón (2018:8) notes, 'The future of Vivir Bien . . . depends on the recovery, reconstruction, and empowerment of other visions worldwide that point towards the same broad objectives'. Buen vivir can be a valuable component of a broader movement towards decolonizing development, but it is not the only way.

UBUNTU

How do relational ontologies foster alternative forms of development and fundamentally shift ways of knowing, being and acting? A powerfully relevant relational ontology is that of ubuntu which recasts what it means to be human. A guiding ubuntu maxim is that 'a person is a person through other people'. The Kenyan philosopher John Samuel Mbiti defined the significance of what he called African theologies in 1969 within the ubuntu tradition: 'I am because we are; and since we are, therefore I am' (*Ego sum quia sumus; et quia sumus, ergo sum*) (108). Against the cartesian individualism of European enlightenment thinking (e.g. René Descartes' 'I think, therefore I am' or *cogito ergo sum*), ubuntu holds that each member of a community is rendered meaningfully alive through already-existing and always-dynamic relations within that community (e.g. Mbiti 1969). Ubuntu emphasizes mutual support, authentic togetherness and solidarity as opposed to individualism, competition, capitalist growth and consumption, key components of coloniality (Shumba 2011). Ubuntu represents a praxis of being that emphasizes collective responsibility and the active and thoughtful cultivation of socio-political coherence and wellbeing. This shift in perspective has the potential to disrupt the power dynamics perpetrated by coloniality and to foster more just systems of knowledge and being.

Ubuntu is a Nguni Bantu term for a relational ontology that originated in Southern Africa, u-bu-ntu is comprised of three particles, with 'u being the article, 'ntu' the root of the word, referring to being, and 'bu' denoting an abstract or generalized state (Ntibagirirwa 2018). The concept is found throughout the continent and indeed many African societies have sister philosophies to the ubuntu guiding ontology. Johann Broodryk (2002), for example, argues that the concept of ubuntu is apparent within many African languages and regions, including the concepts of numunhu (in Shangan/Tsonga), vhuthu (in Venda/Tshivenda), bunhu (in Tsonga), umntu (in Xhosa, Transkei), nunhu (in Shona, Zimbabwe), utu (in Swahili, Kenya), abantu (in Uganda), bomotho (in Lingala, DRC), burkindi (in Mooré, Burkina Faso), botho (in SeTswana, Malawi), obuntu (in Luhya, Western Kenya) and mmandu (in Igbo, Nigeria). Importantly, ubuntu does not reproduce 'methodological nationalism' and is not restricted to a single nation state (Chernilo 2011; Ifejika 2006) – this is a colonial framework we have critiqued at length in Chapter 7.

As an African means of understanding be-ing in the world, ubuntu emphasizes togetherness and prioritizes the collective over the individual. Written this way, be-ing renders the word alive, dynamic and reminds us that our being is unfinished within this 'living philosophy' (Dladla 2017). Ubuntu subverts the notion of humans as 'atomised individual[s] of the Western tradition', offering instead an understanding of people as 'embedded in social and biophysical relations', including the more-than-human (Le Grange 2019). Zethu Cakata explains that the 'true essence' of ubuntu is found in the seTswana metaphor *'feta kgomo o tshware motho'* meaning 'it is African to prioritise human life over wealth' (Cakata and Hlabangange 2020: 3). In this, ubuntu 'views human flourishing as the propensity to pursue relations of fellowship with others, such that relationships have fundamental value' (Metz et al. 2017). In the spirit of ubuntu, a person's wellbeing and fulfilment are not in opposition to the wellbeing of the community, but are actually intertwined. The ubuntu ethic has significant potential to inform more socially and environmentally just forms of being and relationality. The emphasis on fellowship-based wellbeing and the interconnectedness of humans with non-human beings, can create potential for healing and redress. For the South African philosopher Mogobe B. Ramose (1999), movement is integral ubuntu – just as it is fundamentally an emancipatory and anti-colonial philosophy of being (similarly, see Dladla 2017 on ubuntu as a 'philo-praxis of liberation'). The reclamation of an African conception of reality via ubuntu, for Ramose (1999) and Dladla (2017), must occur alongside territorial and land decolonization, repair and racial justice.

Ubuntu has been an important tool for promoting social justice and addressing historical inequalities, particularly in the anti-apartheid struggle in South Africa. It highlights the significance of community, reciprocity and dignity in engendering conversations about recognition, redress and reconciliation (Hlabangane 2020). By emphasizing the inter-connectedness of all people and nature, ubuntu can help to promote a sense of shared responsibility for advancing holistic forms of justice and being. The Ivorian political philosopher Gnaka Lagoke (2018: n.p.) argues that ubuntu is at once a 'restorative pedagogy, a corrective epistemology, and a redemptive value system for . . . a world of justice'. In the Mooré concept of burkindi (Burkina Faso), for example, integrity, goodness and sharing (even self-sacrifice) are celebrated.

An ubuntu understanding of development is one based upon building self-reliant, self-sufficient communities that are united by solidarity, sharing and co-existence. As a practice, we look to examples of ubuntu within education for guidance. Nyamnjoh (2012: 129) describes how pedagogies informed by ubuntu oppose the exogenous influence of the West (via 'academic imperialism') and the pervasive colonization of the mind which, he argues, risks performing an 'annihilation of African creativity, agency and value systems'. In the context of decolonial education, students are co-creators of knowledge rather than passive recipients of information. Ubuntu-inspired pedagogies stress the cultural relevance and backgrounds of students in teaching and learning processes. Le Grange (2019) argues that ubuntu's relational understandings of self and (non)human relations fundamentally oppose the damaging, hierarchiz-ing, Othering processes so fundamental to the operations of coloniality embedded within education.

Still, the integration of ubuntu values and ethics into contemporary development structures has been met with scepticism and concerns regarding its dilution, co-optation and shallowness. The very premise of 'integration' or 'inclusion' presupposes that systems and structures remain, albeit in slightly altered form. As we have seen with buen vivir, the inclusion of indigenous knowledge(s) within development has been limited at best and strategic at worst. Briggs and Sharp (2004) echo this when they powerfully demonstrate how indigenous knowledge have long been 'integrated' into the functioning and stated priorities of the World Bank: rather than fundamentally shifting power relations and dynamics, this inclusion has resulted in limited and essentializing views of 'traditional' African knowledge that actively undermine potentials for decolonization.

Thus far, the application of ubuntu within Southern African contexts has mostly been restricted to the educational and academic spheres and has infrequently been taken up within broader political or governmental systems. Tambulasi and Kayuni (2005) have argued that in Malawi, ubuntu can be instrumentalized to maintain opaque systems of governance, as they argue was the case with the presidency of Bakili Muluzi (from 1994 to 2004). Muluzi practiced a kind of institutionalized generosity in the form of frequent public distributions of funds and materials (like maize) during political rallies. Yet, as Tambulasi and Kayuni (2005: 153) demonstrate, 'nobody, not even the relevant ministries . . . knew the sources of the financial and food items that he was distributing to the poor' and such public demonstrations of generosity were unequal (restrained to political supporters rather than opponents (154) and likely furthered a politics of passivity and dependency. They argue that a combination of democratic 'good' governance and ubuntu would be more suitable. As students and activist remarked upon reading Tambulasi and Kayuni's work, the insincere application and co-optation of supposedly indigenous ontologies by elites can be done in ways that further entrench impoverishment and undermine communal wellbeing. Similarly, Ndumiso Dladla's (2017) work calls out the misapplication of ubuntu during South Africa's post-apartheid transition by elite politicians. Dladla characterizes this as a 'perverse employment of [ubuntu that] has been largely supported with the aid of sophistic academic posturing by the largely white academic establishment in South Africa' (Dladla 2017).

The Zimbabwean womanist Molly Manyonganise's (2015) reflection on ubuntu reveals its propensity to enact both 'oppression and liberation' as well as its capacity to 'engender patriarchy'. Tracing the Shona definition of a human being alongside an awareness of the organization of African philosophy as a field of study dominated by men, she shows how scholars of ubuntu have handily overlooked the ways in which 'the girl child is not valued and is not accommodated in the Shona definition of what a human being is' (Manyonganise 2015: 2). Despite being largely based upon and promoted by masculinist values in Zimbabwe, she argues that there is a redemptive value in ubuntu (or *hunhu*) that necessarily 'position[s] women clearly' (2015: 7). Konik cites the feminist theorist Drucilla Cornell to give hope to mobilizing ubuntu's unrealized potential for transforming and decolonizing development: 'the widespread use of ubuntu, everywhere from beauty shops to television', 'at least signal[s] its political and ethical potency' (Cornell, cited in Konik 2018). These uncertainties and intricacies comprise difficulties for readers, educators and activists interested in decolonial and pluriversal futures. Understanding ubuntu as part of a 'global tapestry of alternatives' can help to address some of its limitations and unrealized potentials by enabling a situated approach to development within global agency, linking it to other radical alternatives like buen vivir.

DEGROWTH

Livingston (2019) depicts the growthism that underwrites much of development thinking as a 'cancerous model'. They hold up Botswana as a parable for countries guided by the 'telos of growth',[2] a development model which simultaneously stimulates growth and decay. The reconfiguration of 'cattle' into the techno-economic commodity of 'beef', as they illustrate through the example of Botswana, fosters forms of 'self-devouring growth'. Capitalism, as Jason W. Moore (2015: 2) explains, 'is not an economic system; it is not a social system; it is a *way of organizing nature*' (italics original). The obsessive objective of economic growth and the emphasis on economic growth as a primary indicator of 'progress', which is driven by the Western capitalist model of voracious consumption, has created a permanent metastasizing state, leading to forms of slow violence and slow demise across the board (see Chapter 3). The political ecologists Alexander Dunlap and Jostein Jakobsen (2019) describe this paradigm as a 'capitalist worldeater', as it extracts, devours and ultimately destroys natural life.

Environmental destruction and loss, gross income and health inequalities, land degradation, inflation and economic crisis are just some of the consequences of what the economist Ezra Mishan (1967) referred to as 'growthmania' (e.g. the hegemonic mania or energetic delusions prompted by a growth-driven economy). Currently, the global political economy is 'addicted to growth': debt continues to be a dominant mechanism of value-making, political systems in the Global North are 'locked

---

2. Degrowth scholars have shown that renewables cannot power the industrial economy at its current scale. See Dunlap et al. 2023.

into cycles of creating new jobs to respond to capitalism's creation of surplus populations or unemployed people as a result of technology, efficiency, automation, [etc. meanwhile there are] psychological imperatives to consume' (Kallis et al. 2020). Take for instance, the incessant advertisement and the cultural illusion through which consumer choice becomes the dominant form of citizenship action (ibid.).

In our pursuit of more 'growth', nearly half of the world's tropical forests have been felled, our soil is overexploited and depleted, and we are in the midst of a sixth mass species extinction (Kolbert 2014). Industrialized countries of the Global North use more than three times their share of the world's biocapacity, extracting massive amounts of land, labour, resources and energy from the Global South. The feminist political ecologist Farhana Sultana writes of the ways in which climate change reiterates colonial relations, reinscribing violence and loss in communities and upon bodies already vulnerable within the coloniality of power. She refers to the 'unbearable' unevenness of climate change as 'climate coloniality' (Sultana 2023) and reminds us that 'decolonizing climate' work must simultaneously redress and repair epistemic and material violences, deeply entwined as they are. Jason Hickel and colleagues (et al. 2022: n.p.) explain that this net appropriation is enabled through the leveraging of Northern 'economic dominance to depress the costs of labour and resources extracted from the south'. The capitalist solution to this, 'green growth', is an oxymoron and a dangerous distraction as sustainable growth is still growthism (Kothari et al. 2015) and, as Dunlap and Jakobsen (2019) explain, green projects remain embedded within economies of violence and generate displacements and conflict. In this way, the Sustainable Development Goals (SDGs), represent the public desire for more liveable forms of economic development, but they ultimately rebrand and exacerbate (capitalist) development and inequality.

Giorgos Kallis et al. (2020) adds that many of the seemingly progressive approaches to the problems and symptoms of growth-addiction, like aspirations for techno-fixing, greater efficiency, the use of renewables, and conservation efforts, actually only reinforce the system rather than changing it. The focus on conservation by individuals (e.g. campaigns to change lamps, retrofit houses, use less water, etc.), for example, are premised on the 'rebound effect'. In other words, the belief that reduced consumption in one aspect will result in increased consumption in other areas, such as opting for public transportation for a few months to compensate for the carbon emissions generated during your vacation.

Moreover, working alongside the passive narrative of 'poverty' (as discussed in Chapter 2), growthism is founded upon promises of a better life, one always deferred to a near and supposedly obtainable future. However, as Jason Hickel (2019: n.p.) explains,

Ending global poverty through economic growth alone will take more than 200 years (based on the World Bank's inhumanly low poverty line of \$1.90 a day) and up to 500 years (at a more generous poverty line of \$10 a day) . . . any more meaningful measure of poverty reveals that the vast majority of the world's labouring classes live in poverty and are likely to do so in the medium- to long-term future!

Impoverishment is actively generated and sustained by actually-existing capitalism (we use 'actually-existing' to distinguish this capitalism from ideas/mythologies about capitalism developed by capitalists; see Chapter 2). Overconsumption as the root of active processes of impoverishment and the current paradigm of development-consumerism perpetuate the very forms of impoverishment that it would claim to fight.

One workable alternative, as outlined in *The Limits to Growth* (Meadows et al. 1972), is a transition from growth to equilibrium. In keeping with this, the degrowth movement focuses on social changes and sufficiency, asserting that more radical and systemic transformation is needed to address the root causes of unsustainable consumption and production rather than simply trying to mitigate the symptoms through technological fixes and individual behaviour change. The degrowth movement draws from post-development and dependency theory, socialism, anarchism and communism, to propose reducing consumption and cutting production in industrialized countries as a means of realizing liveable futures. Degrowth reverberates with established conversations highlighting the 'overdevelopment' of Euro-America as constitutive of the 'underdevelopment' of Africa, Latin America and much of Asia (e.g. Rodney 1972). Degrowth was initially articulated within Francophone scholar-activist work in the 1970s in response to environmental and ecological crises. It has since evolved and shifted, gaining considerable prominence in the last five years in response to growing awareness regarding the violent nexus between capitalist development, coloniality and environmental change, or what Farhana Sultana has termed 'climate coloniality' (Sultana 2022).

The aim to downscale is centred in the Global North, where the current social metabolism (e.g. the economy's material and energy throughput) exceeds the Earth's biophysical boundaries (Demaria and Latouche 2017). Growth in the North is dependent on extraction and exploitation in the South: Dorninger et al. (2021) estimate that 10.1 million tons of raw materials and 379 billion labour hours are extracted from the Global South to the Global North each year. Hickel (2017) argues that rich countries have an ecological debt and must take steps to 'decolonize' the atmosphere. This means enabling countries of the Global South to have their fair share of the atmospheric commons, which has long been dominated and depleted by the actions of wealthy Global North countries. Hickel's argument highlights the unequal distribution of environmental resources and harms, and the need for rectification and repair from the Global North. Federico Demarias (2019: n.p.) explain that 'the degrowth project challenges the hegemony of economic growth and calls for a democratically led redistributive downscaling of production and consumption in industrialized countries as a means to achieve environmental sustainability, social justice and well-being'. An ethic of conviviality is central, whereby being and happiness are valued over 'having' and consuming (Mehta and Harcourt 2021). Conviviality refers to an action of living together in mutually supportive ways, emphasizing repair, redistribution and the interconnectivity of community, ecologies, and intimate relations.

For proponents of degrowth, the first step is a radical challenge to the mythologies of capitalism. This is an active radical political project, one in which we might challenge the very ideological coordinates of capitalist society and their embeddedness. It attacks the pseudo-religious totem of modern societies, the illusory telos of growth, which orients capitalist and communist societies alike. Kallis, Varvarousis and Petridis (2022) write that, 'unlike failed radical projects of the past, degrowth does not offer only a new way of realizing humanity's dreams: *it changes the dreams themselves*'. The 'changing of dreams' – or the radical break from seductive illusions of growthism – does not involve a monolithic or universalist paradigm as a replacement. Rather, as Serge Latouche (2010: 520) argues, degrowth is a 'matrix of alternatives which reopens a space for creativity by raising the heavy blanket of economic totalitarianism'.

Degrowth is a deliberate and strategy-driven movement that promotes slowing down, valuing time, local, self-sufficient economies, the cultivation of social connection and redistributing resources and wealth based upon convivial relations. There are multiple degrowth designs outlined in the readings we conduct with our students. One such concrete example is that outline by French ecological economist Serge Latouche, of the 8 Rs: re-evaluate, reconceptualize, restructure, relocate, redistribute, reduce, reuse and recycle. Students ask for and seek out concrete examples of the application of radical alternatives and our students have drawn upon the example of the Catalan Integral Cooperative (CIC) in Catalonia, Spain to explore the aptitudes and experiences of degrowth. CIC was founded in 2010 as a cooperative aiming to promote mutual support, social transformation, and self-sustainability in agriculture, energy and housing (Chiengkul 2018). Yet, as Chiengkul discusses, some participants within radical collectives likely benefit from 'enabling factors' which allow them access to the initiatives. What does it mean if the people living most precariously in global capitalism are structurally, geographically, politically and linguistically excluded from some on-the-ground projects? While CIC is a powerful example of radical anti-capitalist collective action, our students have discussed the ways in which capitalism is only one constitutive element of the coloniality of power (Grosfoguel 2008) and the need for degrowth movements to combat multiple axes of coloniality. Much as with buen vivir and ubuntu (above), there have been recent moves that might point to the mainstreaming of degrowth approaches. The IPCC referred to 'degrowth' for the first time in their report, *Impacts, Adaptation and Vulnerability* in 2022, highlighting the rising public awareness of and conviction in certain degrowth characteristics and the simultaneous appropriations and 'lip service' played by hegemonic institutions.

The decolonial feminist geographers Padini Nirmal and Dianne Rocheleau (2019) assert that degrowth existed in various forms before being formally defined as a concept in the European academy. This might involve, for example, pre-colonial subsistence socioecological relations and cultural traditions, such as harvest celebrations which have been suppressed or lost due to colonialism and Eurocentrism. Nirmal and Rocheleau (2019) argue that the degrowth movement's focus on European economic and political theory has resulted in irrelevant and potentially damaging outcomes to communities who lack essential necessities like education, health, nutrition and shelter. They call for a decolonial degrowth that addresses political struggles against capitalist economics, neoliberalism, imperialism, extractivism and environmental destruction. To do this, degrowth needs to 'shrink its sense of universality' (Nirmal and Rocheleau 2019) and engage with other radical paradigms as an equal player among multiple radical alternatives. As they write: 'A decolonized degrowth must be what the growth paradigm is not, and imagine what does not yet exist: our separate, networked, and *collective* socio-ecological futures of sufficiency and celebration in the multiple worlds of the pluriverse' (Nirmal and Rocheleau 2019: 18).

Otherwise sympathetic scholars and activists have mounted an internal critique of degrowth for failing to account for gendered and sexual difference (Dengler and Lang 2022; Wichterich 2015), in particular the ways in which care work (which is highly gendered) is the foundation for economic systems (Bauhardt 2014). To avoid reinforcing complex injustices and marginalization, it is important to consider how certain forms of labour and work reproduce these issues when advocating for their very reorganization within the degrowth movement. Dengler and Lang (2022), for example, assert the potentials of a gradual and emancipatory *commonization of care* – based upon a recognition that care-work is a form of commons upon which all people depend at one time or another in their lives. They demonstrate the potentials with the example of the activist-founded Regeneración Childcare Collective in New York City, which offers unpaid care for the children of people and organisers in social struggle. According to their website, they are 'a childcare collective that sees childcare as a form of intergenerational activism'. The focus on intergenerational work and memory is central, as the collective explains in their manifesto: 'Intergenerational movements sustain themselves through periods of intense repression and regenerate over time';[3] within neoliberal capitalist social relations, the commodification of childcare can function to alienate and isolate carers. The *commoning* of care work pushes against this. Their weaving together of degrowth and feminist perspectives can offer valuable insights into creating a more just and sustainable future as they highlight how care work is a crucial aspect of a sustainable (and just?) society. In 2016, the Feminism and Degrowth Alliance (FaDA) was founded to promote and cultivate deco-

---

3. The Regeneration Manifesto is available: https://thecommoner.org/wp-content/uploads/2019/10/20-regenerationmanifesto.pdf.

lonial feminist approaches to degrowth. The platform brings together feminist and degrowth perspectives, fostering spaces for collaboration, exchange and advocacy.

CONCLUSION

We are living in a moment of the proliferation of alternative approaches, anti-capitalist, indigenous and decolonized development(s). Building upon previous chapters which have considered queering, abolitionist and repairing approaches, we have explored ubuntu, buen vivir and degrowth as ways of thinking and be-ing beyond the (mal)development paradigm. Throughout this book, we have remained aware of how decolonization has become a 'buzzword' even among corporate and capitalist circles. In our examination here, we have exposed the ways in which each of these ways of being/knowing have been misappropriated into capitalist, extractive and colonial paradigms. We remain guarded against these forms of false consciousnesses. It is also for this reason that the relative 'metaphorization of decolonization' (Tuck and Yang 2012) is incredibly dangerous. It is important to remain alive to the ways in which ideas have material consequences *and* that substantive decolonization is a project to build transformative relations, collaborate in solidarity with movements to return land and, ultimately, repair the world so ravaged and damaged by the coloniality of being. There are no escapes from the colonial will-to-power. In our teaching, research and activism we work within the powerful tradition of anti-racist praxis (Esson and Last 2020) to address our lack of innocence as self-reflexive criticism is essential in actualizing commitments to decolonization.

QUESTIONS FOR FURTHER THOUGHT

We invite you to sit with the imperative to dismiss and break from even forms of 'sustainable development' or 'democratic development' or development with diverse representation. How do you respond to the argument that development should be eradicated? And why?

How do these various pluriversals work in tandem or, possibly, against one another?

What does it mean to advocate for the North to un-develop itself/ themselves and to centre climate justice in the decolonization of development? We invite you to think critically about the potentials for degrowth to support biodiversity preservation, epistemic justice, and the decolonization of international development.

Consider criticisms of degrowth as 'naïve', 'provincial' or 'rustic' – what effect do such criticisms have? Part of these conversations requires creating the space in which students come to recognize some of their own preconceived notions about the impossibilities of seeing, imagining, dreaming beyond the growthism of capitalism, for example.

What does it mean that degrowth is such a heterogeneous project? How might degrowth prevent its own standardization and measurement, as this paves the way for the creation of a single monolithic version?

How might scholars and activists based in the Global North engage in meaningful, respectful and reciprocal ways with Indigenous thought? How do we make sure that these forms of solidarity do not affect colonial appropriation and extraction?

VIDEOS

Decolonise development: Thoughts and theories. *Cambridge Society for Economic Pluralism*. Available: www.youtube.com/watch?v=Z6HEiFvZLDc.

Rutazibwa, O. (2017) *On babies and bathwater: Decolonizing development studies*. Institute of Development Studies. Available: www.youtube.com/watch?v=qdVUBYlYtF4.

Anna Berry and Dr. Jason Hickel Talk about Capitalism and Degrowth. Available: www.youtube.com/watch?v=-2KOsM8ZE_g.

Decolonising Development Seminar – looking Back and Looking Forward. Available: www.devstud.org.uk/2020/09/02/decolonising-development-looking-back-looking-forward/.

Exploring degrowth: www.youtube.com/watch?v=rXwPwgzqdWA.

WEBSITES

Pinet, M. and Leon-Himmelstine, C. (2020) How can COVID-19 be the catalyst to decolonise development research? *Debating Development Research*. Available: https://oxfamblogs.org/fp2p/how-can-covid-19-be-the-catalyst-to-decolonise-development-research/.

Can we electrify our way out of climate change – or do the rich also need to consume less? https://developingeconomics.org/2020/11/10/can-we-electrify-our-way-out-of-climate-change-or-do-the-rich-also-need-to-consume-less.

Citing Indigenous Knowledge. APA Publication Manual, 7th edition provides guidance on citing Indigenous Traditional Knowledge and Oral Traditions as well as rules for applying bias free language for Indigenous Peoples from around the world. www.camosun.libguides.com/apa7/IndigenousKnowledge.

PODCASTS

Radical alternatives in historical perspective – the August Revolution in Upper Volta/ Burkina Faso, with Thomas Sankara: https://brief.libsyn.com/024-sankaras-revolution.

REFERENCES

Aillon J. L. and D'Alisa G. (2020) 'Our affluence is killing us: What degrowth offers health and wellbeing', in K. Zywert and S. Quilley (eds), *Health in the Anthropocene: Living well on a finite planet.* Toronto: University of Toronto Press.

Akbulut B., Demaria F., Gerber J-F., and Martínez-Alier J. (2019) 'Who promotes sustainability? Five theses on the relationships between the degrowth and the environmental justice movements'. *Ecological Economics*, 165. DOI: https://doi.org/10.1016/j.ecolecon.2019.106418.

Bauhardt, C. (2014) 'Solutions to the crisis? The Green New Deal, degrowth, and the solidarity economy: Alternatives to the capitalist growth economy from an ecofeminist economics perspective', *Ecological Economics*, 102, pp. 60–68.

Boyd, C. E. (2009) '"You see your culture coming out of the ground like a power": Uncanny narratives in time and space on the northwest coast', *Ethnohistory* 54(4).

Briggs, J. and Sharp, J. (2004) 'Indigenous knowledges and development: A post-colonial caution', *Third World Quarterly* 25(4), pp. 661–76.

Broodryk, J. (2005) *Ubuntu management philosophy: Exporting ancient African wisdom into the global world.* Knowres Pub.

Cakata, Z. and Hlabangange, N. (2020) 'Editorial', *International Journal of African Renaissance Studies–Multi-, Inter-and Transdisciplinarity*, 15(2), pp. 2–8.

Chernilo, D. (2011) 'The critique of methodological nationalism: Theory and history', *Thesis Eleven*, 106(1), pp. 98–117.

Coates, T. (2014) 'The Case for Reparations', *The Atlantic*. Available:Available:www.theatlantic.com/magazine/archive/2014/06/the-case-forreparations/361631/.

Cornwall, A. (2020) 'Decolonizing development studies', *The Radical Teacher*, 116, pp. 37–46.

D'Alisa, G. (2019) 'Degrowth', in de Sousa Santos, B., et al (eds.), *Dicionário Alice.* Available: https://alice.ces.uc.pt/dictionary/?id=23838&pag=23918&id_lingua=2&entry=24248.

D'Alisa, G. (2019) 'The state of degrowth', in Chertkovskaya, E., Paulsson, A. and Barca, S. (eds.), *Towards a political economy of degrowth.* Lanham: Rowman & Littlefield.

D'Alisa, G. and Kallis, G., (2019) 'Degrowth and the state', *Ecological Economics*, 169 (106486). DOI:https://doi.org/10.1016/j.ecolecon.2019.106486.

Demaria, F. (2019) 'Degrowth: A call for radical socio-ecological transformation', *Global Dialogue*. Available: https://globaldialogue.isa-sociology.org/articles/degrowth-a-call-for-radical-socio-ecological-transformation.

Demaria, F., Kallis, G. and Bakker, K., (2019) 'Geographies of degrowth: Now-topias, resurgences and the decolonization of imaginaries and places', *Environment and Planning Economics: Nature and Space*, 2(3), pp. 431–50v. https://doi.org/10.1177/2514848619869689.

Dladla, N. (2017) 'Towards an African critical philosophy of race: Ubuntu as a philo-praxis of liberation', *Filosofia Theoretica: Journal of African Philosophy, Culture and Religions*. 6(1). DOI: DOI: 10.4314/ft.v6i1.3.

Dorninger, C. et al. (2021) 'Global patterns of ecologically unequal exchange: Implications for sustainability in the 21st century', *Ecological Economics*, 179(106824), pp. 1–14.

Dunlap, A. and Jakobsen, J. (2019) *The violent technologies of extraction: Political ecology, critical agrarian studies and the capitalist worldeater*. London: Palgrave Macmillan.

Escobar A. (2017) 'Other worlds are (already) possible: Self-organization, complexity and post capitalist cultures', in Savyasaachi and Kumar R. (eds), *Social movements: Transformative shifts and turning points*. New Delhi: Routledge.

Escobar A. (2018) *Designs for the pluriverse: Radical interdependence, autonomy, and the making of worlds*. Durham, NC: Duke University Press.

Escobar, A. (1995) *Encountering development: The making and unmaking of the Third World*. Princeton: Princeton University Press.

Esson, J. and Last, A. (2020) 'Anti-racist learning and teaching in British geography'. 52(4), 668–77.

Federici, S. and Linebaugh, P. (2018) *Re-enchanting the world: Feminism and the politics of the commons*. Oakland: PM Press.

Foramitti, J., Varvarousis, A., and Kallis, G. (2020) 'Transition within a transition: How cooperative platforms want to change the sharing economy', *Sustainability Science*, (2020).

Gaztambide-Fernández, R. A. (2012) 'Decolonization and the pedagogy of solidarity', *Decolonization: Indigeneity, Education & Society*, 1(1), pp. 41–67.

Gudynas, E. (2011) Buen vivir: Today's tomorrow, *Development*, 54(4), pp. 441–47.

Hanaček, K., Roy, B., and Kallis, G., (2020) 'Ecological economics and degrowth: Proposing a future research agenda from the margins', *Ecological Economics*, 169, p.106495. DOI: https://doi.org/10.1016/j.ecolecon.2019.106495.

Hickel J. (2020) *Less is more: How degrowth will save the world*. London: Random House.

Hickel, J. and Kallis, G. (2019) 'Is Green growth possible?', *New Political Economy*, April, pp. 1–18. https://doi.org/10.1080/13563467.2019.1598964.

Hlabangange, N. (2021) 'The underside of modern knowledge: An epistemic break from Western science' in *Decolonising the human: Reflections from Africa on difference and oppression*, Steyne, M. and Mpofu, W. (eds.). Johannesburg, South Africa: Wits University Press, pp. 164–85.

Hoffmann, N. (2017) 'What can the capabilities approach learn from an ubuntu ethic? A relational approach to development theory'. *World Development*, 97, pp. 153–64.

hooks, b. (2000) *All about love: New visions*. New York: William Morrow.

Ibhawho, B. and J. I. Dibua (2003) 'Deconstructing Ujamaa: The Legacy of Julius Nyerere in the quest for social and economic development in Africa', *Africa Journal Political Science* 8(1).

Icaza, R. and Vázquez, R. (2013) 'Social struggle as epistemic struggles', *Development and Change*, 44(3), pp. 683–704.

Ifejika, N. (2006) 'What does ubuntu really mean?' *The Guardian*, 29 September. Available: www.theguardian.com/theguardian/2006/sep/29/features11.g2.

Kallis, G. and Varvarousis, A., and Petridis, P. (2022) 'Southern thought, island-ness and real-existing degrowth in the Mediterranean', *World Development*, 157, pp. 1–11.

Kallis, G. et al. (2020) *The case for degrowth*. Cambridge: Polity Press.

Kauffman, C. M. and Martin, P. L. (2014) 'Scaling up buen vivir: Globalizing local environmental governance in Ecuador', *Global Environmental Politics*, 14(1), pp. 40–58.

Kolbert, E. (2014) *The sixth extinction: An unnatural history*. New York: Henry Holt and Company.

Konik, I. (2018) 'Ubuntu and ecofeminism: Value-building with African womanist voices', *Environmental Values*, 27(3), pp. 269–88.

Kothari, A. (2019) 'Earth Vikalp Sangam: Proposal for a global tapestry of alternatives', *Globalizations*, 17(2), https://doi.org/10.1080/14747731.2019.16 70955.

Kothari, A., Demaria, F. and Acosta, A. (2015) 'Buen vivir, degrowth and ecological swaraj: Alternatives to sustainable development and the growth economy', *Development*, 57, pp. 362–75.

Laduke, W. (1999) *All Our Relations: Native Struggles for Land and Life*. Cambridge: South End Press.

Lagoke, G. (2018) 'All African people's conference of 1958: The historic significance of a revolutionary gathering', Conference presentation at *All African People's Conference 2018*. Institute of African Studies, University of Ghana.

Latouche, S. (2009) *Farewell to Growth*. Malden: Polity Press.

Latouche, S. (2010) 'Editorial – degrowth', *Journal of Cleaner Production*, 18, pp. 519–22.

Le Grange, L. (2019) 'Ubuntu' in Kothari, A. et al. (eds.), *Pluriverse: A post-development dictionary*. New Delhi, India: Tulika Books.

Manyonganise, M. (2015) 'Oppressive and liberative: a Zimbabwean woman's reflections on ubuntu', *Verbum et Ecclesia* 36(2), pp. 1–7.

Maraca, B. (2012) 'Towards a fair degrowth-society: Justice and the right to a "good life" beyond growth', *Futures*, 44, pp. 535–45.

Marquina-Márquez, A., Virchez, J., Ruiz-Callado, R. (2016) 'Postcolonial healing landscapes and mental health in a remote Indigenous community in subarctic Ontario, Canada', *Polar Geography*, 39(1), pp. 20–39.

Martınez-Alier, J. (2012) 'Environmental justice and economic degrowth: An alliance between two movements', *Capitalism Nature Socialism*, 23, pp. 51–73.

Mbiti, J. S.1969. *African Religions and Philosophy*. Nairobi: E.A.E.P.

Mehleb, R. I., Kallis, G. and Zografos, C. (2021) 'A discourse analysis of yellow-vest resistance against carbon taxes', *Environmental Innovation and Societal Transitions*, 40, pp. 382–94. https://doi.org/10.1016/j.eist.2021.08.005.

Mehta, L. and Harcourt. W. (2021) 'Beyond limits and scarcity: Feminist and decolonial contributions to degrowth', *Political Geography*, https://genderandsecurity.org/sites/default/files/Mehta_Harcourt_-_Beyond_Limits_Scarcity_-_Feminist_Decolonial_Contributns_to_Degrowth.pdf.

Merino, R. (2016) 'An alternative to "alternative development"?: Buen vivir and human development in Andean countries', *Oxford Development Studies*, 44(3). DOI: https://doi.org/10.1080/13600818.2016.1144733.

Mignolo, W. (2011) *The darker side of Western modernity: Global futures, decolonial options*. Durham, NC: Duke University.

Miró, G. C. (2018) 'Trilateral South-South cooperation for development: towards a decolonisation of solidarity', *Revista CIDOB d'Afers Internacionals*, 120, pp. 147–70.

Mishan, E. (1967) *The cost of economic growth*. New York and Washington: Praeger.

Moore, J. W. (2015) *Capitalism in the web of life: Ecology and the accumulation of capital*. London: Verso.

Murrey, A. (2020) 'Thomas Sankara and the political economies of happiness' in Falola, T. and Oloruntoba, S. (eds.), *The Palgrave Handbook of African Political Economy*, London: Palgrave MacMillan, pp. 193–208.

Nelson, A. (2022) *Beyond money: A post-capitalist strategy*. London: Pluto Press.

Nirmal, P. and Rocheleau, D. (2019) 'Decolonizing degrowth in the post-development convergence: Questions, experiences, and proposals from two Indigenous territories', *ENE: Nature and Space*, 2(3), pp. 465–92.

Ntibagirirwa, S. (2018) 'Ubuntu as a metaphysical concept', *J Value Inquiry*, 52, pp. 113–33 https://doi.org/10.1007/s10790-017-9605-x.

Nyamnjoh, F. (2011) 'Relevant education for African development: Some epistemological considerations', in *Philosophy and African development: Theory and practice*, pp. 139–54.

Nyamnjoh, F. B. (2012) '"Potted plants in greenhouses": A critical reflection on the resilience of colonial education in Africa', *Journal of Asian and African Studies*, 47(2), pp. 129–54. https://doi.org/10.1177/0021909611417240.

Oppong, S. (2000) 'Indigenizing knowledge for development: Epistemological and pedagogical approaches', *Africanus*, 43(2), pp. 34–50.

Otero, I., et al. (2020) 'Biodiversity policy beyond economic growth', *Conservation Letters*, 13(e12713). https://doi.org/10.1111/conl.12713.

Patel, K. (2020) 'Race and a decolonial turn in development studies', *Third World Quarterly*, 41(9), pp. 1463–75.

Petras, J. and Veltmeyer, H. (2014) *The new extractivism: A post-neoliberal development model or imperialism of the 21st century?* London: Zed Books.

Power, M. (2006) 'Anti-racism, deconstruction and "overdevelopment"', *Progress in Development Studies*, 6(1), pp. 24–39.

Pueyo, S. (2020) 'Jevons' paradox and a tax on aviation to prevent the next pandemic', *SocArXiv*, 12 May. (Preprint) https://osf.io/preprints/socarxiv/vb5q3.

Ramose, M. B. (1999) *African philosophy through Ubuntu*. Zimbabwe: Mond Books.

Sankara, T. *Selected Speeches*. in *Thomas Sankara Speaks*. London: Pathfinder Press.

Sekulova, F. et al. (2021) 'The governance of nature-based solutions in the city at the intersection of justice and equity', *Cities*, 112(103136). https://doi.org/10.1016/j.cities.2021.103136.

Senier, S. (2013) '"Traditionally, disability was not seen as such": Writing and healing in the work of Mohegan medicine people', *Journal of Literary & Cultural Disability Studies*, 7(2), pp. 213–17.

Shumba, O. (2011) 'Commons thinking, ecological intelligence and the ethical and moral framework of Ubuntu: An imperative for sustainable development', *Journal of Media and Communication Studies*, 3(3), pp. 84–96.

Simpson, L. B. (2014) 'Land as pedagogy: Nishnaabeg intelligence and rebellious transformation', *Decolonization: Indigeneity, Education & Society*, 3, pp. 1–25.

Simpson, L. R. (2004) 'Anticolonial strategies for the recovery and maintenance of Indigenous knowledge', *The American Indian Quarterly*, 28, pp. 373–84.

Simpson, L. B. (2016) 'Indigenous resurgence and co-resistance', *Critical Ethnic Studies*, 2(2), pp. 19–34.

Smith, A. (2007) 'Introduction: The revolution will not be funded' in INCITE! Women of Color Against Violence, *The revolution will not be funded: Beyond the non-profit industrial complex*, Durham, NC: Duke University Press.

Solón, P. (2018) 'Vivir Bien: Old Cosmovisions and New Paradigms', *Great Transition Initiative*, https://greattransition.org/publication/vivir-bien.

Sultana, F. (2023) 'The unbearable heaviness of climate coloniality', *Political Geography*, 99, https://doi.org/10.1016/j.polgeo.2022.102638.

Sylla, N. S. (2022) 'Live as African: On the relevance of Thomas Sankara's agenda for economic liberation', *University of Bayreuth African Studies Working Papers*, 33, Africa Multiple Connects 5. Bayreuth: Institute of African Studies.

Tambulasi, R. and Kayuni, H. (2005) 'Can African feet divorce Western shoes? The case of 'ubuntu' and democratic good governance in Malawi', *Nordic Journal of African Studies* 14(2), pp. 147–61.

Tandon, Yash (2008) 'An exit strategy' in *Ending aid dependency*. Oxford: Pambazuka Books.

Tsagkari, M, Roca. J. and Kallis, G. (2021), 'From local island energy to degrowth? Exploring democracy, self-sufficiency, and renewable energy production in Greece and Spain', *Energy Research & Social Science*, 81(102288). https://doi. org/10.1016/j.erss.2021.102288.

Tuck, E. and K. Wayne Yang (2012) 'Decolonization is not a metaphor', *Decolonization, Indigeneity, Education & Society*, 1(1), pp. 1–40.

Varvarousis, A. (2020) 'The rhizomatic expansion of Commoning through social movements', *Ecological Economics: Special Issue: Commons and social movements-a vicious cycle?* DOI: https://doi.org/10.1016/j.ecolecon.2020.106596.

Varvarousis, A., Asara, V., and Akbulut, B., (2020) 'Commons: A social outcome of the movement of the squares', *Social Movement Studies: Special Issue name: Movements and Activism beyond Post-Politics*. https://doi.org/10.1080/147428 37.2020.1793753.

Wainwright, J. (2008) *Decolonizing development: Colonial power and the maya*. Malden, MA: Blackwell.

White, S. (2002) 'Thinking race, thinking development', *Third World Quarterly*, 23(3), pp. 407–19.

Wichterich, C. (2015) 'Contesting green growth, connecting care, commons and enough' in Harcourt, W. and Nelson, I. I. (eds.), *Practising feminist political ecologies: Moving beyond the 'green economy'*. London: Zed Books, pp. 67–100.

Ziai, A. (ed.) (2007) *Exploring post-development: Theory and practice, problems and perspectives*. London: Routledge.

Zografos, C. and Robbins, P., (2020) 'Green sacrifice zones, or why a green new deal cannot ignore the cost shifts of just transitions', *One Earth*, 3(5), pp. 543–6.

Conclusions

You have reached the end of this book, but your journey of unlearning and re-learning will continue. Our book provides a (re-)entry point. It is not, however, the definitive text on decolonizing development. In the process of writing this book, we were continuously motivated by the flourishing of materials in a variety of media, including academic books and articles, commentaries, films, poetry and novels, that have widened the scope of epistemic disobedience and are not just excavating and un-silencing non-hegemonic worldviews but actively and creatively thinking of alternative decolonizing concepts and methodologies. Building on earlier work, scholars and activists are pushing the conceptual boundaries to imagine another world. We hope that this book has assisted you in the process of unthinking a development education in the Global North and in sections of the Global South in which development has been presented as intrinsically 'good'.

We encourage our readers to continue with the journey of pedagogic disobedience, challenging and unlearning 'received wisdoms', norms, and 'facts' about development that are inculcated through the education system and in public discourse. Begin by questioning their origins, the context in which they have developed, and the positionality of the authors before moving to consider what people in the spaces that development is being enacted in actually think – avoid seeking their views from international NGOs' promotional literature and videos. Look for those produced by people on the ground or who have the lived experience of oppression.

Although we use the binary categorization of the world – that is into the Global North and Global South – we are aware of the critics who see these terms as euphemisms and the lack of relationality they invoke. However, we return to the meanings that earlier scholars and activists used to articulate global differences and to form transcontinental alliances between oppressed peoples – in the same way in which the term 'Third World' was conceptualized before it was mainstreamed, corrupted, depoliticized and used in a derogatory way to stigmatize and 'other' the people who once initiated it as an empowering concept. We referred in the Introduction to the importance of language in resistance and the tendency by dominant groups in society to belittle the language oppressed groups use to explain the nature of their condition.

For our white-identifying readers situated in the Global North (and the Global South), we hope the book will contribute to divesting you of 'white innocence', indignation and saviourism. Paraphrasing the writer Dionne Brand in *A Map to the Door of No Return*, you can no longer claim that you did not know because you have not been there. Nor will your donation to a charity compensate for your discomfort. You are relationally entangled in structures that perpetuate the violence of development (insightful materials on this include https://cultivatingalternatives.com/tag/settler-responsibility/ and *Decolonialidad Europa's* Charter of Decolonial Research Ethics). No palliative fairtrade schemes directed from the Global North will change the asymmetries of power that govern the relationship between Northern consumers and Global South producers. The South must acquire the power to determine the terms of the game.

For our readers in the Global South, who may have become intoxicated or enchanted with the ideology of development, we ask you to look critically around you, become well-versed in the history of your people, look beyond the boundaries of your nation-state, and reflect on whether Western modernity has given you greater security, materially as well as personally. Reflect on whether your home is encased in steel security bars, if you drive without stopping at night, your electricity is erratic, the people in your home country are dying from preventable diseases, you cannot be treated in your home country with medical equipment that is readily available in the Global North, you cannot travel freely within or outside your continent, and moreover, whether you are living in a condition of deliberate 'maldevelopment' (Amin 1990) that does not see you as fully 'human'. Then remember all those things, the spiritual, the respect for people and for non-human living beings, the sociality that you, your friends and family, may have dismissed as 'bush', backward, regressive, and think about how you might interpret them differently. Think how you might, as the Jamaican Rastafarian singer, Bob Marley, advises, 'emancipate yourself from mental slavery', as 'none but ourselves can free our minds' (Marley and the Wailers 1980).

Our primary goal in this book has been to show how the oppressed, the marginalized, the 'poor' of development have been actively, since the 1940s, seeking to change the dominant Eurocentric narrative of development and the violence they have encountered, epistemic and physical, as they dare to theorize, organize, and enact alternative visions that challenge global white supremacy. Theoretically, we position ourselves as being part of a tradition of radical scholarship that engages transcontinentally to learn, identify commonalities, and build solidarity. We have learned the most about these processes from examples across Africa – the continent where we do most of our scholarly and intellectual work. We encourage our readers to look for possibilities, potentials and communities elsewhere in the Global South. We have not begun to do justice to this vast scholarship within the limits of this book.

We began this book with an exploration of impoverishment because our experience and the data has shown that global inequalities have increased, especially since the start of neoliberalism in the 1980s; also, that government projects that address the welfare of the people have largely ceased, and in some cases been privatized altogether or devolved to NGOs. Across the world, the struggle for survival has become acute, even for those who were once considered middle class.

From our strategic vantage point in Oxford University, we have observed how policies and knowledge projects emanating from the Global North's institutions and governments continue to be implicated in active impoverishment whilst their proponents become richer, including academics. Following Uma Kothari, we can observe the hidden face of 'race' and racisms in the decision-making that results in the multiplicity of violence that this model of development continues to produce. We have situated the origins of global development thought and policy within the Global North, including in the post-war United States of America, where the full humanity of black people was deliberately not recognized in its Constitution and Jim Crow laws enforcing racial segregation were still in force until the1960s. In Europe, 'international development' was cultivated during a moment in which colonial powers were facing demands for independence, using brutal force to oppress opposition to their rule, as was the case of the French in Algeria and Cameroon, the British in Kenya, the Portuguese in Mozambique and more. Too few scholars of 'development' have asked *how can peoples with such histories of enslavement, displacement, dispossession, ecological degradation and deliberate dehumanization and impoverishment of their own fellow citizens become impassioned champions of positive social transformations amongst the racialized peoples of the Global South?* In Chapter 2, we build upon the pioneering work of Walter Rodney, Samir Amin, Leonce Ndikumana, Jason Hickel and others to explore precisely these persistent contradictions within a neo-imperial global political economy.

Similarly, the violence of development, with its own contradictions, has not always been dealt with centrally in the literature on development (although there are notable exceptions, particularly within the post-development turn, as we document). The violence produced in the implementation of development projects is seen as beneficial to the communities, at least in the long-term; these are regarded as 'necessary sacrifices' that discount people's immediate experiences. We have here pushed the discussion of the violence of development further by arguing that development *is* violence, by showing how different forms of violence are embedded in the development project as it inherits, and is infused with, colonial thought, logics and practices. We have centred African feminist voices addressing how patriarchal and gendered forms of violence are structured within the states that have emerged from colonialism. In addition, we have shown how ecological violence has made the reproduction of all forms of life uncertain, and even impossible, in extractive zones.

Throughout, we have drawn inspiration from Global South scholars who theorize coloniality and centralize decoloniality. While our theoretical readings have been centred on the work of scholars and scholar-activists, we have looked to how public intellectuals – songwriters, filmmakers and artists – have conceptualized the conditions of coloniality and impoverishment. We encourage our readers to think about how colonial discourse pervades the everyday, especially in 'white saviourness' and celebrity philanthropy, and the ways in which the term 'charity' has been misused to obscure paternalist and racist colonial relationships (these are practices demystified in Chapter 1).

We challenged the tendency to dehistoricize poverty and violence and to blame the Global South for the failures of development. In so doing, we consider how the peoples of the Global South have been marginalized in development policy and praxis. We return to Walter Rodney and Thomas Sankara, who could not contemplate how development could succeed without the people being full participants in shaping their own destiny. We identify those actors in the Global South who are complicit in ongoing economies of impoverishment. In Marxist dependency theories, these people were conceptualized as 'comprador bourgeoise'.

The term 'elites' is now widely used, especially for those in politics and those working for international development institutions whom the Tanzanian political scientist and politician Abdul-Rahman Babu described as 'aid-addicts' reliant on 'aid-dealers' and 'aid pushers'. We have questioned the use of the altruistic word 'donors' to label neo-colonial exploiters and refused to use the term 'victims' to describe those who refuse or survive development. Therefore, we urge our readers to be creative in thinking of alternative nomenclature to describe the participants in this exploitative relationship.

We have considered how the European model of the nation-state within colonially-constructed territories has resulted in the failure to build the form of political communities needed to overcome the colonial legacy of impoverishment and future exploitative relations. Inspired by new scholarship revisiting and bringing to prominence 'reworlding' perspectives from the South, we show how Global South leaders and people sought to work collectively to create different, pro-people and ecologically holistic global imaginaries. Global North powers, threatened by the collective mobilizations and emancipatory potentials of these socio-political communities, have too often utilized covert and overt means to shut them down. Nevertheless, they continue, and they persist. We have shown how academic complicity in nationalist thinking, described as methodological nationalism, has contributed to delegitimizing worldviews emanating from the Global South.

We have not engaged with the mainstream development literature that seeks a return to the 'developmental state' (Mkandawire 2001 and 2010). While we acknowledge that social welfare improvements are best accomplished collectively, we have noted the successive democratic charades which pass as elections in many states in the Global South and look forward to forms of a political community that can deliver social justice to its people. Authoritarian developmental states are unlikely to deliver equity for their populations. These state formations reinvigorate nation-building and nationalism, as Mkandawire (2010) argues, and fail to recognize the plurality amongst the people they claim to be serving, by enacting policies that hinder the free mobility of African people within the continent. Theoreticians of liberation such as Frantz Fanon and Amilcar Cabral have argued that unless there are practical, neither ethnic nor nepotistic, links between the political elite and the people, development is likely to end in tragedy. Drawing from Patricia McFadden (2000, 2008, 2016), we are optimistic that new conceptualizations of a state as one which works with its people for social change will emerge through active struggle and coalition. We remain attentive to the permanent restructurings of imperial power that influence, appropriate, hinder and sabotage radical grassroots political projects, particularly on the African continent.

We acknowledge the importance and saliency of Frantz Fanon's arguments in his essay critiquing nationalism and national consciousness (Fanon 1963). Nevertheless, we refrain from universalizing our critique of national consciousness. Where direct colonialism persists into the twenty-first century, where people are fighting for self-determination and self-rule in ongoing decolonialization movements, many seek to cultivate a national consciousness to mobilize locally and to gain international legitimacy. As such, we note the continued operations of the United Nations' Special Committee on Decolonization that was established in 1961 (see www.un.org/dppa/decolonization). In articulating decolonization, we have distinguished our praxis (see the Introduction) from the set definitions offered by hegemonic institutions, like the UN. The UN, for example, has replaced the word 'colonial' with the ahistorical euphemism 'non-self-governing' in referring to territories and people under continued colonial domination.

Remaining attentive to hegemonic and colonial cajolery, dismissals and 'moves to innocence' (Tuck and Yang 2012) is a steadfast feature of anti-colonial and anti-imperial disobedient practice. We remind ourselves and our readers that international development has persisted as long as it has now because it is deeply seductive. We must not contribute to the ongoing cultivation of empty 'development' promises, which all too often pave the way for further entrenchments of structural, racial and gendered violence. These forms of development propaganda (visible in development marketing campaigns, early childhood schooling in the Global North, mainstream 'international development' courses all over the world, the speeches of politicians, and more) enclose and divert the energies, time and labour of too many people who are moved by its ideologies of social change and betterment. As educators, we have taken a stance in our classroom: development must be abolished. Together with our students, we unpack why and how we have come to this conclusion. This starting point should be neither bleak nor distressing (the worst form of bad faith arguing maintains that interventions are 'still' (and always) necessary in the immediacy, otherwise 'people will die', as we have discussed in Chapter

1). Rather, the recognition that we must contribute to the break with international development becomes an entry point for engaging with centuries of radical projects and collectives that have long offered and gestured towards other socio-ecological and economic relations.

This book calls for a disobedient unlearning of development that centers the struggles of oppressed peoples for freedom. We have illustrated how their struggles have concrete as well as ideational and epistemic dimensions (through imagining other worlds or worlds otherwise) and have taken the form of riots, protests, as well as more revolutionary attempts to live outside-within (marronage) and with the minimum of engagement with the state, especially its security apparatuses. Resistance to development continues to be put down with brutal force by the state. We draw on the powerful body of literature on marronage to illustrate not only past attempts of living outside-within racial capitalist spaces, but to encourage our readers what they might offer in terms of lessons for those among them seeking alternative futures. We have scarcely touched on the scale of resistance against coloniality and racial domination and heteronormativity. Our intervention is to provoke the reader to look elsewhere and more deeply. The emergent literature on 'queering development' and queering decolonial sexualities is thoroughly challenging patriarchal and colonial intimate relations. Rather than engage with sexuality through the prism of population control, disease or medical intervention, this work pushes us to think seriously about happiness, pleasure and horizontal intimate relations.

Some of our readers might have started out by thinking that there is no alternative to capitalist development. In Chapter 8, we invited readers to imagine what it would mean to abolish development and to think and imagine otherwise. We continue the work of thinking through a range of life-affirming practices and epistemes. The exciting horizons of decolonial and pluriversal options are exploding taken-for-granted assumptions about political and economic relations. We are in a watershed moment of radical scholarship on indigenous, non-Western and anti-capitalist epistemes. Yet, as our consideration of buen vivir in Ecuador and Bolivia and ubuntu in Southern Africa shows, we must turn away from the colonial fantasy that there is a 'model' that can be made to travel. Instead, the collective project of eradicating 'international development' is founded on learning, unlearning and fostering long-term solidarities with the communities where we work.

While writing this book, we have recognized how active the process of learning disobedience is. We continuously check ourselves from centring Eurocentric modes of thought. Both of us have been trained in the (Anglophone) Western university and the process of breaking from these models of thought, being and practice is ongoing. Along the way of repairing the world, activists repeatedly remind us of the importance of maintaining substantive commitments to material and non-metaphorical decolonization: the returning of land, abolition of odious debt, the refusal of debt repayments, the reconfiguration of dominant economies towards degrowth and redistribution, the adoption of legal protections for queer and trans people and more.

How do we critique and unsettle coloniality without the European canon rearing its head, and without reproducing uneven, racialized, heteronormative colonial logics? Our work continues to be 'academic' and structured within capitalist knowledge-economies; this is a book for sale in a marketplace, it will not be evenly accessible throughout the world. Our grammars, logics and articulations are problematic and sometimes exclusionary – even as we remain passionate about and committed to system change. The project of decolonizing and abolishing development, for us, requires life-long (un)learning, recognition, self-analysis and solidarity. We enact our commitments to the practice of liberations from where we are. As educator-activists at Oxford, there are moments when we must be intentionally quiet, hesitant, humble and de-centred. For us, being humble or – (as the *Gesturing Towards Decolonial Futures* collective (https://decolonialfutures.net/) encourage us) – being 'cute' is an act of disobedience; it is a refusal of the institutional privileges/pretences of Oxford (themselves colonial vestiges). There are also occasions for us to take risks, to endanger ourselves, to act and speak in solidarity with activists, intellectuals and communities of struggle. We look for radical traditions amongst Western thought to build the solidarity that we need to enable us to thrive on this planet as conscious scholars seeking to transcend racialization through co-working, co-thinking and with mutual respect. We continue to seek out gestures otherwise.

REFERENCES

Amin, S. (1990) *Maldevelopment: Anatomy of global failure*. London: Zed Books.
Babu, A. R. M. (1996) 'Aid Dealers, Aid Pushers and Aid Addicts', *NGO Monitor*, 1(1), pp. 21–2.

Brand, D. (2001) *A Map to the Door of No Return: Notes to Belonging*. Toronto: Vintage Canada.

Fanon, F. (1963) *The wretched of the earth*. Reprinted Penguin Books 1990. See chapter entitled 'The Pitfalls of National Consciousness'.

Gesturing Towards Decolonial Futures (GTDF) Collective. Available: https://decolonialfutures.net/.

Journal of Economics, 25, pp. 289–313.

Marley, B. & The Wailers (1980) *Redemption Song*. Released June 1980.

McFadden, P. (2000) 'Globalizing resistance: Crafting and strengthening African feminist solidarities', *The Black Scholar*, 38(2–3), pp. 19–20.

McFadden, P. (2008) 'Plunder as statecraft: Militarism and resistance in neocolonial Africa', in Sutton, B; Morgen, S. & J. Novkov (eds.), *Security disarmed: Critical perspectives on gender, race, and militarization*. New Brunswick, NJ: Rutgers University Press, pp. 136–56.

McFadden, P. 2016. 'Becoming contemporary African feminists: Her-stories, legacies and the new imperatives' *Feminist Dialogues series*, November.

Mkandawire, T. (2001) Thinking about developmental states in Africa. *Cambridge Journal of Economics*, 25(3), pp. 289–313. http://www.jstor.org/stable/23600389.

Mkandawire, T. (2010) 'From maladjusted states to democratic developmental states in Africa', in Edigheji, O. (ed.) (2010) *Constructing a democratic developmental state in South Africa: Potentials and challenges*. Cape Town: Human Sciences Research Council Press.

Tuck, E. and K. Wayne Yang (2012) 'Decolonization is not a metaphor', *Decolonization, Indigeneity, Education & Society*, 1(1), pp. 1–40.

Index